Helping Young Children with Behaviour Difficulties

A HANDBOOK

M. Chazan, A.F. Laing, J. Jones, G.C. Harper
and J. Bolton

CROOM HELM London & Canberra
UNIVERSITY PARK PRESS Baltimore

© 1983 M. Chazan, A.F. Laing, J. Jones, G.C. Harper and J. Bolton
Croom Helm Ltd, Provident House, Burrell Row,
Beckenham, Kent BR3 1AT

British Library Cataloguing in Publication in Data

Helping young children with behaviour difficulties.
1. Child psychopathology
I. Chazan, M.
618.92'89   RJ499
ISBN 0–7099–0777–X

Published in North America by
UNIVERSITY PARK PRESS
300 North Charles Street,
Baltimore, Maryland 21201

ISBN 0–8391–1914–3

Library of Congress Card Number: 83–080750

Printed and bound in Great Britain

CONTENTS

B. Practical Steps

PART TWO

DECIDING WHAT TO DO

4. USING CREATIVE AND LANGUAGE ACTIVITIES

5. SPECIAL HELP IN THE CLASSROOM

APPENDICES

TABLES AND FIGURES

Tables

Figures

PREFACE

In our research work in a wide range of nursery
schools and classes, we have found that many of the
staff feel a need for help and advice in the
management of children presenting problems of
behaviour. This Handbook is intended as a response
to this need, and its preparation was made possible
through a grant from the Department of Education
and Science, which funded a two year project,
beginning on 1st January 1980 and located in the
Department of Education of the University College
of Swansea, on 'The Management of Behaviour Problems
in Young Children' (the Welsh Office gave a
supplementary grant to enable a Welsh version of
the Handbook to be produced).

In compiling the Handbook, our main aim has
been to provide nursery staff with material that will
be of practical use and will encourage them to
think positively and constructively about ways of
handling children with behaviour problems. We have
tried to avoid a 'cook-book' approach or suggesting
that there is one right way of solving any child's
difficulties. As far as possible, we have used
non-technical language. We hope that the Handbook will be useful to teachers and others in
nursery schools and classes, reception classes in
infant schools, and playgroups, as well as in
relevant training courses. As we emphasise in the
Handbook, the principles underlying the management
of behaviour problems are not very different from
those which should guide staff in dealing with
children in general. We would hope, therefore, that
the Handbook will not only be found of value in the
handling of individual children needing special
help, but will also provide guidelines for nursery
staff in their daily work, whether or not they have
a serious behaviour problem in their group.

Explanations have been provided in Appendix III
(Explanatory Notes) of terms specific to the British
scene.
     The preliminary draft of the Handbook was used
experimentally in a number of nursery groups, and
the final version owes a great deal to the percept-
ive feed-back given by the staff involved. We
should like to express our thanks to them for their
help and also to the Department of Education and
Science, the Welsh Office and the members of Liaison
Committee D for their support throughout the project.
The research team also gratefully acknowledges
the generous help given, in the areas concerned, by
the Chief Education Officers and members of their
staffs; the playgroup advisers and organisers in
the region; the children and parents involved;
and Mrs. Sheila Morgan and Mrs. Ann White, the
secretaries attached to the project.
     It should be noted that the names of the
children mentioned in the Handbook are fictitious
code-names and not their actual names, and that
all views expressed (other than those attributed
to specific sources) are those of the writers alone.

                              Maurice Chazan
                              Alice F. Laing

INTRODUCTION

Chapter 1

USING THIS HANDBOOK

(a) Aim of Handbook
The aim of this Handbook is to help nursery school
teachers and others responsible for looking after
groups of young children to deal constructively
with any behaviour problems they may meet in their
daily work. The Handbook provides guidance on (1)
picking out the children who are especially in need
of help; (2) finding out as much as possible about
the nature of the child's behaviour difficulties;
and (3) planning and carrying out measures which
are likely to lead to the better adjustment of the
child in the group or classroom.
    While we do not want to put undue emphasis on
the problems of young children, we believe that it
is very important to prevent, through early action,
the development of behaviour and attitudes which
may interfere with a child's adequate social functioning. Although in some cases outside assistance
may be needed, in all cases the adult in regular
contact with the child has a vital role to play
in fostering harmonious emotional and social
development. In preparing this book, we have tried
to put ourselves in the place of nursery staff who
are anxious to give special help to an individual
child while attending to the needs of all members of
a sizeable group. Throughout, we put a great deal
of stress on the desirability of maintaining a
positive attitude towards children who are difficult
or unresponsive, and we underline the value of a
systematic approach towards helping these children.

(b) Plan of Book
Incorporated in the handbook are several assessment
schedules (Appendix A) and a Record Book (Appendix B).
Their relationship with the various sections of the
Handbook and instructions for using the book are to

be found below.

Sufficient numbers of assessment schedules and record books for your class may be duplicated by any method you find convenient.

(c) How to use this Book

The handbook is designed to guide you through the steps of assessing a particular child's behaviour difficulties and planning and implementing an individual programme which you hope will lead to better adjustment in the future.

We suggest that you might begin by quickly skimming through the book, more to get an idea of its aims and basic layout than to grasp all the detail. Once you understand something of its nature and structure then it will be helpful for you to look at each section again more thoroughly. You may find it makes more sense if you have a particular child in mind while you are doing this preliminary reading.

Set out below are step-by-step instructions on how to use this book to tackle the behavioural difficulties of a child in your care.

1. (a) Read the section "Recognising Behaviour Difficulties" (pp. 8-15).

(b) Fill in Schedule 1 : Swansea Behaviour Checklist (Appendix A, pp. 257-261) for class or group and select child/ren needing further assessment.

Omit this identification stage if you already have a child in mind.

2. (a) Read the section "Understanding the Problem" (pp. 16-57).

(b) Complete Assessment Schedules 2-5 (Appendix A, pp. 262-289).

(c) Complete the appropriate section in the Record Book (Appendix B, pp. 290-302).

3. (a) Read the section "Deciding What To Do" (pp.58-254).

(b) Select most suitable approach/es from

Play Activities (pp. 92-128)
Behaviour Modification (pp. 128-177)
Problem-Solving Approaches (pp. 177-202).

You may also like to consider some of the ideas contained in Creative Activities (pp. 60-67) and Language Activities (pp. 67-80).

4. (a) Read section "<u>Making a Plan of Action</u>" (pp.203-254).

(b) Work out a programme of activities and write down details of your plan in the Record Book.

(c) Implement your plan of action.

5. (a) Monitor the child/ren's progress in appropriate pages of the Record Book.

(b) Review progress periodically and alter your programme if necessary.

PART ONE

LOOKING AT CHILDREN'S DIFFICULTIES

Chapter 2

RECOGNIZING BEHAVIOUR DIFFICULTIES

(a) <u>What behaviour should we expect of children of this age</u>?
Children of nursery school age have already come a
long way in their emotional and social development.
By the age of 3 or 4, most children will be able to
accept a limited amount of separation from their
parents without undue anxiety. They will be well
on the road to gaining some measure of independence
and self-control. They wll respond to friendly
adults other than those with whom they have close
and intimate bonds, and show great pleasure in
conversing with them. Most will be reasonably easy
to manage both at home and in a group outside. On
the whole they will enjoy opportunities for mixing
with other children, some being happy in any
gathering of young children, but many preferring a
small group of familiar companions. They will be
wide-awake and alert, seeking to engage in activities
and enjoying play of various kinds - individual
and social, constructive and messy, reality and make-
believe.   To some extent, they will share with
others and be prepared to take turns; many children
of this age group will show a surprising degree of
consideration for others. They will take some
pride in their personal possessions and show persistence at tasks that arouse their interest. The
'typical' nursery school child will be bright, happy
and cheerful, generally free from excessive anger
and fear.
       However, we would be unwise to expect too much
conformity, co-operation and tranquillity from three
to four-year-olds, who still have much to learn
about self-control and many social skills yet to
acquire. Children at this stage will often be
frustrated by their inability to do everything they
wish to do, or to get everything that they want, so

8

that they may now and then resort to temper tantrums or to the destruction of objects lying to hand. Sometimes, when they realise that their mother is not around, they will show some anxiety and want to cling to the nearest familiar adult. Unexpected events, strangers, loud noises or unfriendly animals may show that they are capable of 'unreasonable' fears. They will not always be as tolerant as they usually are, or be prepared to wait their turn as patiently as their elders. When tired or bored, their behaviour may be very troublesome, and when really upset, they may wet the bed or have a nightmare. In short, almost all young children present some behaviour problems, and tears are never far away even in the case of the happiest child.

You should bear in mind, too, that children's behaviour varies greatly according to the person they are with and the situation they are in. Everyone will have difficulty with some children at one time or another. A child's relationships tend to be very person-specific, that is, they will react positively to some adults but less so to others. It is quite normal for nursery staff to get on better with some children than others, and you should not feel a sense of failure if you are unable to deal with a child.

We should not, therefore, rush into calling children 'real problems' merely because they do not consistently maintain an adult-like standard of 'good' behaviour, or because they do not always conform. It is difficult to know precisely what patterns of behaviour we should consider to be of significance in a child's development. Some behaviour problems will disappear with time, others may eventually become serious. It would be useful to be able to distinguish between transitory and more permanent problems, but this is usually impossible in the age group with which we are concerned. However, it would seem that children who present <u>many</u> or <u>more extreme</u> behaviour problems at the pre-school stage are 'at risk' of having later difficulties if they do not receive appropriate help. It is all too easy, also, for any behaviour which interferes with effective functioning or normal social interaction to become fixed. So even if we are unable to <u>predict</u> the consequences of young children's behaviour, it is important to help children in their <u>current</u> functioning and adjustment. Such help must be given in the context of understanding the child's development as a whole, and in a manner which preserves the child's dignity.

9

The <u>first step</u> is to recognise those children who show more than the usual problems characteristic of their age group, not for the sake of picking them out but to gain better insight into the nature of their difficulties and to give them the attention they need.

(b) <u>Which children are likely to need special attention because of their behaviour?</u>

The number of children in any nursery class or play-group in need of special attention because of their behaviour will vary greatly from group to group. Some classes and groups give priority to children who have developmental difficulties of many kinds, including physical and mental handicap, and the adults in charge will, accordingly, be prepared to cope with a fairly high proportion of behaviour problems. Classes or playgroups serving areas where social disadvantage is common may well have a higher than usual proportion of children presenting problems of adjustment.

It is not possible, therefore, to give you any precise indication of how many children in your class or group are likely to require help because of their behaviour. All one can say is that, on the basis of surveys which have been carried out so far, about 1 child in 10 is likely to need some attention because of poor social or emotional adjustment at the nursery school stage. Not every class or group will contain children who show behaviour difficult-ies, but if you have a class of 16 to 20 children, you may well find that at least one or two of them come into this category, though their problems will mostly be moderate rather than severe.

Types of problem

It is not desirable, and rarely useful, to think of children's problems in terms of distinct types or categories. Most children show a wide range of behaviour, at times being quiet and inhibited, at others lively and outgoing. But the children likely to be in need of help will, in the main, be those who are:

   (i)   shy/withdrawn/timid
  (ii)   immature/dependent
 (iii)   restless/overactive
  (iv)   aggressive/anti-social/destructive

Recognizing Behaviour Difficulties

(i) Shy/withdrawn children

Richard (aged 4) tends to be passive, withdrawn
and dreamy, over-anxious and timid. Occasionally he is difficult to make contact with.
He watches others play but makes no attempt
to join in; he rarely talks to others. He
lacks confidence, and has difficulty in
coping with new situations. He will follow
his teacher around for a while, not saying a
word; often he is content to play on his
own for long periods. His teachers consider
that this is not an extreme problem, 'for
Richard does not actively shun other children's
company but seems not to need it'. He has
good hand-eye co-ordination and good self-
help skills, enjoying puzzles of various
kinds.

Shy, withdrawn children like Richard do not
cause any trouble to others in the group, and so
they may easily escape notice, or at least fail to
receive much attention. However, some of them are
already adopting ways of responding to their environment which are unhelpful to their general development and which will prevent them from making the most
of their school experiences. Such children tend to
keep very much to themselves and to say little or
nothing to others, either adults or peers; they
are unwilling to take part in the usual activities
of the group, and may not be making a relationship
with anyone. They may lack confidence, being timid
and fearful, especially in new situations, and they
frequently show anxiety and tension. Some, though
not by any means all, will appear unhappy and
miserable much of the time.
Many shy, withdrawn children will, however, come
out of their shells, perhaps only very gradually, if
they are not rushed and if they are encouraged
gently but systematically. Most, in fact, want to
join in with others and to be like them, but cannot
bring themselves to do so because of their lack of
self-confidence; all will need more than the usual
amount of adult attention.
A very small number of children (about 4 or 5
in 10,000) show extreme withdrawal and an almost
total unwillingness to communicate with others, as
well as exhibiting a variety of strange mannerisms.
These children, referred to as 'autistic', will
certainly need a full medical and psychological
assessment.

(ii) Immature/dependent children

Jonathan (aged 3) frequently clings to adults
for assurance and does not attempt to attend
to his own needs. He tries to join in group
activities but finds it very difficult because
of his inability to communicate adequately.
He is also prone to temper tantrums, and is
extremely restless, nearly always on the move.
He rarely perseveres long enough to make the most
of any activity.   He can be destructive and
disruptive.   He has been observed to crawl
around the classroom during 'Play School' making
babyish noises.   He enjoys water play with one
other child, and being alone in the home corner.

Children such as Jonathan tend not to be as
independent and self-reliant as most of their
contemporaries.   They look for adult support and reassurance far more than others of their age, particularly when faced by anything new or unfamiliar.
Often, they are not happy to let mother go when they
come into the group, and seem to be worrying all the
time about her absence.   They frequently cling to
the nearest adult, and require an excessive amount
of comforting physical contact.   You will certainly
be aware of any very immature children in your group.

(iii) Restless/overactive children

William (aged 4) is highly restless and overactive.   His concentration is fleeting, and he
disrupts group play continuously.   He is always
on the move, boisterous and wearing to others.
He is over-excitable and often disobedient.
He is very demanding in nearly all situations,
and is generally shunned and disliked by others.
He has no understanding of the need to be careful with delicate objects and tends to suck
and chew toys baby fashion.   He does respond
to adult attention and likes water and dough
play as well as riding a tricycle, but his
language is poor, he walks and runs awkwardly
and he is unable to cater for his basic self-
needs.

Recognizing Behaviour Difficulties

You will not have much difficulty, either, in identifying restless, overactive children like William in your group, though you will need to distinguish between those who are restless because they are bored and those who cannot settle to anything and move around a great deal most of the time. Most young children show a lot of restlessness and mobility, but those who are overactive in an aimless way are a particular cause for concern, because this kind of behaviour is likely to interfere with their learning. Such children will lack concentration, be very easily distracted and be unable to work towards a definite goal. In the more extreme cases, the child will not sit still for a moment, run about without purpose, and handle toys and other things in a random manner. Sometimes restlessness and overactivity are combined with anti-social and destructive behaviour, to which we now turn.

(iv) Aggressive/anti-social/destructive children

Eric (aged 4) is aggressive, anti-social, disobedient and generally demanding. He is frequently rude, and offers verbal aggression if thwarted or frustrated. He hits other children, and indulges in frequent temper tantrums. He is unable to share toys, and over-reacts if his demands are not met. He seeks to be the centre of attention, but tends to dislike physical contact. He functions well in a number of areas, including language and self-help skills, and has good mobility and co-ordination.

Most children of nursery school age have occasional temper tantrums, especially when they are tired or frustrated, though they tend to indulge in bad temper more at home than in the school or playgroup. Most young children, too, will at times be anti-social and even destructive, seeming to enjoy damaging their own or other people's things. Some of the children in your care, however, will behave like Eric, seeming to go out of their way to be aggressive or destructive. Their general way of behaving will be to grab toys from others, to seek to annoy them in a variety of ways, often hitting and banging them. They will readily scream and shout at the slightest provocation, or with none. No play materials will be safe with them for long.

They will be a very disturbing influence in a group, and be unpopular with the other children.

Look for Strengths

We have given a generalised picture of various types of behaviour problem you are likely to have to deal with in your group. Because this picture has been so negative, we would again stress that every child has strengths and good points and that you should always keep these in mind when you are seeking to identify children with behaviour problems in your group.

(c) Using the Swansea Behaviour Checklist

Provided that you feel that you have got to know the children in your class or group well enough (e.g. you have had them in your care for at least a month) we suggest that you should complete the Swansea Behaviour Checklist (Schedule 1) for each child (see Appendix A, pp.257-261).

The Behaviour Checklist is intended to help you to identify those children in your class/group who seem to need special attention. It is meant as a brief screening device, not to provide a detailed record of the child. However, the checklist does give you scope for recording the child's strengths as well as any problems which he may be presenting. This is because, as we have already pointed out, it is important that, from the outset, you should adopt and maintain a positive attitude towards the child - something which is not always easy to do. You will also find that the child's strengths will be a good starting point for any procedures you adopt to help the child towards better adjustment.

You should find that completing the checklist will help you in clarifying your thoughts about the children in your charge. But if you think that filling in the checklist would not add greatly to your recognition of any behaviour problems in your group, you may omit this step and proceed to the assessment and action stages without this formal preliminary screening.

If you decide to complete the Behaviour Checklist, this should not take up a great deal of your time. All you have to do at this stage is (1) to tick the ten descriptions which most closely approximate to the child's current behaviour, (2) to record your ratings to give a mini-profile of behaviour and (3) to answer two questions about the child. You may

find that the descriptions given do not fit a particular child exactly, but mark those which give the
best description. In order to keep the checklist
a reasonable length , we have used categories which
are narrower than would be possible in a longer
schedule.

Most children of nursery school age will score
a number of b's, and no scoring system will precisely identify those children who need help. But,
on the basis of our experience with the checklist
to date, we suggest that you should think carefully
about any children who record 2 or more 'c's or
6 or more 'b's. It is very likely that such
children would benefit from further assessment.
Consider also any children who score 4 'b's in the
aggressive or withdrawn categories.

Chapter 3

UNDERSTANDING THE PROBLEM

BACKGROUND

(a) <u>What Does Assessment Involve?</u>
The identification of children with emotional or
behaviour problems in your nursery group is the first
step in gaining insight into the needs of these
children. The next step is to make a careful
assessment of the problem. A comprehensive assessment involves (a) describing in precise terms both
the nature of the difficulties presented and the
context in which these occur; (b) getting to know
something of the child's home background; (c)
drawing up a profile of the many aspects of the
child's development; (d) highlighting those factors
which seem to be associated with the child's behaviour; and (e) trying, from what is known about
the child and the background, to make inferences
about the child's needs and to draw up a programme
of action which will lead to better adjustment.
The Warnock Report stresses that there are
four main requirements of effective assessment.
These are:

1. parents must be closely involved;
2. assessment should aim to discover how
   a child learns and responds over a
   period, and not merely record
   performance on one occasion;
3. assessment must include the investigation of any aspects of a child's
   performance that is causing concern;
4. the family circumstances as a whole
   must be taken into account in any
   assessment of a child's needs.

16

It can be added that all too often lengthy assessment procedures are carried out without any
further specific action following, but unless
identification, assessment and intervention are
regarded as closely linked in every case, much of
the effort put into the first two stages may be
wasted.

A full assessment of a child's special needs
is a complex matter, and in many cases requires the
expertise of professionals outside the nursery group,
for example, those working in the school psychological service. However, those in daily contact
with the child - parents and nursery staff - can
always contribute a great deal to assessment. Even
when outside help is called in, the professionals
involved will spend only a limited amount of time
with a child and his or her family and will rely on
parents and nursery staff for much of the information
on which they will base their assessment of a case.
They need to do this, since children behave very
differently in different situations. Many children
who are aggressive or destructive in the nursery
group are perfectly well-behaved and fully controlled
in the one-to-one situation, for example when
tested or observed at play by a psychologist in an
office or clinic. Some children, too, who are
happy and co-operative in the nursery group present
serious problems at home, and some who are no
trouble at home present difficulties outside. Who-
ever is involved, assessment is always a matter
for team-work, with each one concerned taking a
broad view of the situation while making a particular
contribution. It is necessary, too, to exercise
caution in reaching conclusions about the causes
of behaviour, as there are many factors associated
with behaviour problems in young children. These
will now be discussed.

(b) Factors Associated with Behaviour Problems in
Young Children
It is rarely possible to state with precision what
has caused a child to behave in a particular way
at any time. Even in cases which seem, on the
surface, to be straightforward, careful assessment
often shows a combination of factors to be at work
rather than one definite factor. The 'precipitat-
ing' factor which appears to have been directly
responsible for an outburst may be less important
than other 'predisposing' factors which have helped
to bring about an explosive situation. For example,

a mild reproof by an adult may provoke a violent temper tantrum in a child, but it may well be the case that the child is reacting to a prolonged experience of stress at home rather than to being told off in the nursery group. Further, it is often difficult to sort out cause and effect, whether, for instance, a speech difficulty is causing emotional disturbance, or is caused by it. Nor should we always look for extreme or 'abnormal' circumstances in the life of the child who is a problem. Children have to face 'normal' stresses of many kinds, e.g. when they have to start something new, such as going to a nursery group for the first time, or when there are changes in the structure of the family, perhaps as a result of illness or bereavement.

Temperamental differences. We tend to emphasise the environmental factors related to disturbance in childhood, probably because they are easier to pin-point than other factors. But we should not forget that children are temperamentally different, and that temperament or emotional disposition seems to be genetically determined to quite an extent, that is, it has a major 'innate' component. Individuals, even within the same family, vary widely in their susceptibility to emotional disturbance, and considerable differences in temperament have been found in very young children. Some are very placid and rarely cause any trouble, others are easily excited and over-react to quite ordinary occurrences; some are nearly always happy and cheerful, others are often miserable or moody; and while some are easily 'put off' and readily distracted from the activities in which they are engaged- others show much persistence, even in the face of difficulties. The interaction between adult and child is certainly affected by temperamental make-up on both sides: most adults find that they get on better with some children than with others. We now tend to think in terms of interaction - a two-way process - rather than of the child merely responding to his environment. Children help to shape their own environment in many ways - for example, a difficult child may cause a mother's attitude, which was positive to begin with, to become rejecting.
     At this stage, you may like to consider whether there are any kinds of behaviour in children which you find hard to tolerate, or any children with particular temperaments whom you cannot bring your-self to like. If this is the case, think about

possible reasons for your reactions. Understanding
one's own response to individual differences tends
to help in dealing effectively with children.

Physical factors. Physical factors, especially
handicap or ill-health, may also play a part in the
causation of behaviour disturbance. An association
is sometimes found between brain-damage and hyper-
activity, and although 'brain-damage' is perhaps
too readily used as an explanation for behaviour
problems, it is desirable that a medical opinion
should be sought in cases of extreme restlessness
and mobility (as it should be in any case where
physical factors are involved and the child is not
already under medical supervision). Physically
handicapped or delicate children will often be frustrated at not being able to do what others are capable
of doing, and while most of this frustruation is
unavoidable, adults can help greatly by making sure
that such children are given tasks at which they
can succeed.

Delayed general development. Frustration and
feelings of inadequacy are also the frequent experience of children who are mentally handicapped or
slow in their general development. These children
often have difficulty in controlling their impulses
and in assessing the demands of the external world;
and they take longer than others to achieve some
measure of independence. Slow learners are likely
to have more behavioural difficulties than normal
children, and these difficulties tend to persist
over a much longer period of time. They are also
likely to be retarded in speech and language, and
as a result their ability to communicate with and
relate to others will be impaired, and they will
have less idea of themselves as individuals. Indeed,
delayed language development is bound to have
generally adverse effects on the child's emotional
and social growth (pp.68-70). Often the key to
the management of behaviour problems in slow-learning
children is providing them with plenty of well-
graded activities, carefully planned to promote their
motor, sensory, linguistic and cognitive development.

Brian (aged 4 years) appears to be extremely immature in all aspects of development, more like a two-year-old than a four-year-old. He did not walk until he was 2+ and had no speech at all until 3+; his language development continues to be slow. At home he has many temper tantrums; in school, although being kept occupied reduces the occurrence of such tantrums, he becomes frustrated when he cannot communicate his wishes and needs. He is lethargic, frequently clings to adults for assurance, and rarely plays with other children.

Factors in the nursery group. As the Warnock Report points out, behaviour problems may be brought about or accentuated by factors relating to the school, such as its premises, organisation or staff. It is always worthwhile for nursery staff, without becoming over-introspective, to consider whether attitudes, classroom practices or other factors connected with the nature of the nursery group have anything to do with a child's behaviour problems. It is even possible that factors relating to the nursery group itself may be of major importance in the causation of disturbed behaviour. Children in nursery groups are, for the most part, handled with great sensitivity by the adults in whose care they are placed. Nevertheless, they may react badly to uncomfortable conditions in the nursery setting or to the way they are treated by adults or peers in the nursery group. To illustrate, children may be upset by

(a) over-criticism by adults when any mis-demeanour occurs, especially if the emphasis is put on blaming the child's intrinsic nature - 'I've never come across such a terrible child in all my life!' rather than specific actions, thus contributing to the building up of a negative self-image. It is all too easy for a whole staff to label a child as 'naughty' and a 'nuisance' to include only a catalogue of mis-demeanours in any records kept, and to have little time for such a child, who will soon feel rejected;

(b) carelessly expressed remarks or even covertly-held attitudes relating to children from particular social backgrounds or ethnic groups;

(c) receiving much less attention from adults than others in the group, which may well happen if a child does not demand attention in some way;

(d) adults making excessive fuss when a child is clumsy, is incontinent or has some other accident, causing embarrassment and undue guilt-feelings;

(e) listening to very frightening stories - while most three to five-year-olds take these in their stride, some children, particularly those from highly disturbed backgrounds, may find them anxiety-provoking;

(f) excessive demands made on them resulting in frustration at failure to perform a task;

(g) being in a highly authoritarian and inflexibly-organised group, which allows little freedom or choice of activity.

As the child matures, acceptance by other children in the group becomes increasingly important. Young children are not as conscious of individual differences, and in the nursery group, social rejection rarely results from being handicapped or a member of an ethnic minority group. However, some children may be the victims of aggression, or, being somewhat aggressive themselves, have retaliatory action directed at them. It is not always possible to prevent a child from being upset by other children or from becoming socially isolated or rejected, but timely and tactful intervention by an adult may help in potentially explosive situations.

Even without any of the upsetting experiences outlined above, some children find it difficult to accept the initial separation from the mother and may take a long time to adjust to the physical,

cognitive and social demands of the nursery group.
Putting pressure on these children may exacerbate or
prolong their difficulties in adjusting to being
with other children.

It is, of course, undesirable to overprotect
children within the nursery group or to encourage
them to avoid meeting normal challenges. It is
also important not to exaggerate the potential
sources of upset, but incidents that seem trivial
to the adult may cause considerable distress to a
child and even result in unwillingness to attend
a nursery group. In the main, however, disturbance
in young children is likely to be related to factors
in the home, where influences have the greatest
impact. The extent to which the young child's
basic needs are met depend a great deal on family
background, and some of the many situations at
home which may adversely affect the child's emotional
development will be outlined below.

Factors in the Home. Clearly, if children are not
given enough to eat, or if they are otherwise neglected or physically abused at home, their emotional growth will be affected, but there are many
other family situations which have a bearing on a
child's behaviour. Increasingly, children are
growing up in homes where the even tenor of family
life is disturbed by unemployment, or in homes upset
by divorce. All too often, one family problem
leads to another, so that a variety of adverse
factors is frequently found rather than a single one,
as the following cases illustrate:

> The family background of Jonathan (aged 3), an
> immature, over-dependent child with speech
> and language problems and frequent temper
> tantrums, has several adverse features. He
> was premature, and because of his very
> low birth weight (3 lbs.) was kept in
> hospital for several weeks. He was re-
> admitted to hospital at 10 months, for
> reasons not entirely clear, and suffered
> separation from his parents for over a
> month. His mother finds it difficult to
> cope, and Jonathan sometimes arrives at
> school unkempt and unwashed,although at
> other times he will be well clad and spot-
> less. His father recently had a heart
> attack, a cause of great worry to the
> family, as there is the possibility that

he may lose both his job and his home
(attached to his job) as a result of his
ill-health. Appointments at clinics
for speech therapy are rarely kept.

William (aged 4), who is disruptive, overactive and unsociable, is the middle child
of three, having a brother of 5½ and a
younger sister (18 months) with cystic
fibrosis. His father, a semi-invalid,
is considerably older than his mother,
both parents coming from poor backgrounds themselves. The house is
materially and hygienically of a very
low standard, and is kept under supervision by health visitors as well as
social workers. William has had little
intellectual stimulus, routine or discipline at home, and according to his
teacher, he over-reacts to the attention
given to him by adults in the nursery.
He is emotionally, linguistically, socially
and cognitively immature as a result of
his poor home background and lack of
training.

It is not possible here to discuss all the
factors in the home which may affect social and
emotional development, but most nursery groups will
contain some children feeling strain or pressure as
a result of one or more of the following:

1. Unsatisfactory housing conditions. In
addition to poverty, housing conditions can be
regarded as a major factor in the break-up of
families and the causation of ill-health, strain and
disharmony in the home, with consequent adverse
effects on children's emotional adjustment. The
social development of young children will be especially impaired by a lack of space and opportunity
for play and other activities both within and outside the home. Living in high-rise, and even low-
rise, flats is a particular disadvantage for under-
fives. Their activities are severly restricted;
they are often isolated, with few opportunities to
mix with other children; and their mothers tend to
suffer from frustration, loneliness and depression.
Where there is overcrowding, with children perhaps
having to share the same bed, fatigue and

irritability in the family circle may well be the
result. Children coming to the nursery group from
disadvantageous social conditions may well have
little idea of how to play; they will tend to be
destructive rather than constructive in their activities. Other possible effects of social disadvantage include inadequate language skills and
restless or anti-social behaviour, though it must
be emphasised that such adverse effects do not
inevitably result from adverse living conditions.

2. A lack of routine at home. Some children
are given plenty of warmth and affection at home,
but are brought up in an atmosphere of chaos, with
little routine or regularity in times of meals or
of going to bed. Young children need a coherent
framework of routine, if one tempered by occasional
flexibility, and those who frequently stay up late
at night may come to the nursery group over-tired,
irritable and restless (see William).

3. Prolonged separation from the mother. If
the normal bonds of attachment linking mother and
child are broken, perhaps because the mother has to
go into hospital or for other reasons, the child may
show signs of acute distress, sometimes followed
by a period of apathy. In some cases, developmental
progress, especially in language and social respons-
iveness, is slowed down. These effects are not
necessarily long-lasting, but are likely to be man-
ifest in the child's behaviour outside the home at
least for a time. Children suffering a fairly
lengthy separation from the mother will need understanding and sensitive handling in the nursery
group (see Jonathan).

4. Domestic crises. Even the very young child
can be disturbed by open rows or a general atmosphere
of tension at home. Parental disharmony has been
found to be highly associated with behaviour problems
presented by young children at home, and may also
result in a child showing considerable anxiety and
tension in the nursery group (see Jonathan).

Nicola, aged 4, is restless, lacks concentration
and deliberately destroys her own and other
children's property. She is the youngest
of a second family. Both families have
been closely-knit, although the eldest
daughter had left home to live with her
natural father because she could not get

on with her mother. Nicola very much
misses this sister. Although mother only
works part-time, Nicola reacts badly
to her going out to work. Nicola generally
seems happy and carefree, and comes to
school well-dressed. However, she often
shows signs of insecurity and immaturity.
That her insecurity was not unwarranted
was demonstrated by her parents splitting
up during the course of the project.

5. Parental illness. Parental ill-health,
physical or mental, may contribute to the causation
of behaviour problems in young children (see
Jonathan and William). It is easy to see how, for
example, the relationship between mother and child
can be damaged if ill-health prevents the mother
from giving the child adequate care, or makes her
irritable or moody. Mental illness in the parents,
in particular, has been found to be strongly linked
with the presence of behaviour problems in pre-school
children. As a consequence of mental ill-health,
parents may not only be erratic in their handling
of the child, but may present a model of anxiety,
tension, aggression or even bizarre behaviour which
the child will be ready to copy. Not infrequently,
a child's behaviour in the nursery group is a re-
flection of parental behaviour.

6. Unsatisfactory parental attitudes and
practices. It is not possible to state with certain-
ty what the association is between parental attitudes
and practices and the child's emotional development,
and it is important not to make over-simplified
interpretations of the relationship between parental
behaviour and children's behaviour. However, there
is no doubt that most children react sensitively
to the way in which they are treated by their parents.
Many parents show a wide range of feelings and
practices in relation even to a single child rather
than go to extremes, but certain attitudes and
practices are highly likely to result in problem
behaviour in the child. In particular, three main
patterns can be highlighted - (a) rejection;
(b) over-protection; and (c) inconsistency.

(a) Rejection

There are many possible reasons for parental rejection of a child. For instance, the child may
be unwanted, being seen as adding to financial
difficulties or preventing the pursuit of a career,
or because the child is mentally or physically
handicapped; the mother may be on her own, without
support; the parents may be very young and not
ready for the responsibility of bringing up children;
or the parents may not understand the child's fundamental need for acceptance and love. Parental
rejection, too, takes a variety of forms. In many
cases,rejecting parents tend to be unaffectionate,
disapproving and hostile to the child, harsh in
their methods of control and destructive of the
child's confidence and self-image; but in some
instances, parents may pamper and indulge a child
to conceal their rejecting attitude from others
and perhaps also from themselves. Or they may
vacillate between harshness and indulgence as the
mood takes them.

The effects of parental rejection on children
are likely to be devastating, although not always
immediate. Sooner or later, most children who
experience rejection will come to be antagonistic
to adults and perhaps also to other children; and
they will often be lacking in self-confidence, either
withdrawing from challenges or seeking to assert
themselves by means of aggression and anti-social
behaviour. Rejected children at the nursery group
stage will tend to demand a lot of attention and
affection which they will often try to obtain by
unacceptable means, from nursery staff, who have a
difficult task in meeting some of their needs while
not being in a position to take over the parental
role in these cases.

> Eric (aged 4) is aggressive, overactive and
> disobedient. He has an older brother (6 years)
> and a new baby sister. His mother, while
> not neglecting him materially, has given him
> little attention, and the new arrival has
> tended to make the situation worse in this
> respect. Eric lacks positive attention,
> particularly from his mother, and is bound
> to feel rejected to a considerable extent.

(b) Over-protection

Over-protective parents prolong infantile care and are reluctant gradually to diminish physical contact with the child. They encourage the child to turn to them immediately for help in the face of any difficulty, however mild. The child is discouraged from becoming less dependent on parental assistance with growing maturity. Over-protective parents may be permissive and indulgent, satisfying every whim the child has; or else they may be dominating, interfering and restrictive. Reasons for over-protective parental attitudes include the child being delicate or handicapped; the parents trying to compensate for affection missing from the marriage or in their own lives; psychological disturbance in the parents; or ignorance of children's needs.

Over-protected children tend to be slow to adapt to new situations, to cling to adults, and to be passive and submissive. They will need considerable time to adjust to school or playgroup, and will benefit from carefully graded social training, which encourages independence and greater participation in activity with others.

> Howard (aged 4) is an over-protected, dependent, timid and tearful child. He is the older son of young parents, his brother being nearly 2 years old. The husband's mother tries to exert a great deal of influence on the young parents, and Howard's mother resents this very much. She is a gentle person, rather shy and very protective towards her children. In the past, she has not allowed the boy to go out to play with other children - she considered them too rough and ill-mannered. Howard has spent his early years with a number of adults constantly at his beck and call. He has great difficulty in mixing with other children and in standing up for himself.

(c) Inconsistency

Few parents are entirely consistent in their behaviour towards their children, and indeed a certain amount of flexibility is to be preferred to rigidity in child-rearing practices. However, grossly inconsistent attitudes and behaviour on the part of the parents are likely to be damaging to children.

If the standards set by either parent are fluctuating and unpredictable, or if the parents do not have a reasonably common policy, children will not know where they stand and so will find themselves in an impossible position. They will not be able to learn which of their actions will meet with approval or condemnation, and may as a result develop into indecisive, conflict-ridden individuals. Nursery staff, if they are consistent, can help to provide children with a more coherent framework to their lives, though this will not necessarily help a child's relationship with his parents.

> Ian (aged 4) is overactive, demanding and aggressive. Mother is reluctant to discipline the child in any way and is fearful of the father's disapproval of her actions; father is strict, and resents any interference or attempts by others to help Ian. He appears to ignore the mother's attempts to deal with the boy, who hits his younger sister (aged 3) if she has anything he wants.

Jealousy and sibling rivalry (see Ian). By the age of three, the child may have made great strides in learning to relate to and play with brothers or sisters, and will usually get much satisfaction and pleasure from their company. However, it is very common for a certain amount of rivalry to exist among children in the same family, who will vie for their parents' love and attention. Nearly every child, too, under five or six will experience fairly intense feelings of jealousy when a new baby arrives on the scene and demands a lot of parents' time. Rivalry and jealousy will be exacerbated when parents have not prepared their child for the new arrival, particularly when this event coincides with entry into the nursery group. Difficulties may also be created when the parents (consciously or unconsciously) give markedly preferential treatment to one of their children.

A child who feels displaced or inferior in the family circle may compensate by seeking a lot of attention from nursery staff, and may be very demanding and difficult to handle, at least for a period. It is helpful to nursery staff to know something about the child's relationships with siblings and to find out when there is an addition to the family.

(c) A Cautionary Note
In concluding this section on factors associated with
behaviour problems in young children, it is perhaps
necessary to stress that the above discussion of
possible causative factors is not meant to be comprehensive. Much more could be said about each of
the factors listed, and it should also be emphasised
once again that conclusions about the causation of
behaviour problems should not be arrived at too
readily. The total picture may take a long time
to emerge, and in most cases you are likely to have
only a hazy idea of what the parents are really
like. Remember that a child coming from a poverty-
stricken home may have plenty of loving care, and
that some children from affluent backgrounds may be
rejected or over-protected, or subjected to pressures
of varying kinds. Be mindful, too, that some
parents may be experiencing a great deal of stress
and strain in their own lives and need understanding
and support rather than criticism or blame.

(d) Keeping Records
Once you have embarked upon the process of assessing
and planning a programme for a child, it is essential
for a variety of reasons, that you keep accurate
records of what you are doing:

1. gathering and collating a written record
    will help clarify your thoughts and
    enable you to gain a more coherent
    picture of a child. This will be of
    use when you are deciding upon a plan
    of action;
2. some system or record keeping is imp-
    ortant when observing and assessing a
    child as you cannot rely upon your
    memory to retain the information over
    a period of time, much less recall
    it accurately months later;
3. records will indicate whether your
    chosen approach is being successful
    and if not, where alterations need to
    be made;
4. with records you will notice small
    but significant changes in behaviour
    which might otherwise be over-looked
    and perhaps result in a successful
    approach being abandoned prematurely.

Understanding the Problem

To simplify your record keeping we have
designed a Record Booklet (see Appendix B), further
copies of which can be reproduced by any means convenient to you.   The booklet comprises four
sections; the purpose of each will be described below.

Section I

This first section is for you to make an
orderly summary of the information you have
gained about a child in the assessment
phase.   Taking each of the assessment
schedules in turn, the relevant information
is condensed and transferred to the
appropriate pages of the record book.

Section II

Once the assessment phase has been completed
and recorded you should then write down the
aims and objectives of your plan of action
and select the most suitable approach(es)for
yourself and the child.   In this section
you are required to note the most worrying
aspects of the child's behaviour and the
order in which they will be tackled together with the changes you hope to achieve
and the approaches that will be employed.
It is important to write the plan in some
detail, specifying when, where and how
much time will be devoted to a particular
approach, which activities (in what order)
will be tried and who will be responsible
for carrying out the programme and keeping
the records.   If you are at all unsure
about how to go about designing and writing
a plan of action then please refer to
Chapter 6, Making a Plan of Action (pp.203-254),
which includes examples of plans designed
and used successfully by adults working in
nursery groups.

Section III

This section consists of a series of blank
sheets on which to monitor your progress at
weekly intervals.   During the week you may
find it useful to carry around a small note-
book in which to jot down quickly any
important observations as they occur and
then it is an easy matter to summarise these
more neatly in the Record Book at the end
of the week.   Careful record keeping will

indicate whether or not you are succeeding
in your aims and should it appear that
the child is not making progress then you
will have to re-appraise both your methods
and your application of them. You should,
however, be careful to give your chosen
approach sufficient time to have some
effect as long standing difficulties will
not vanish overnight. It is sometimes
helpful to involve another adult in monitoring as well as yourself, as it is
difficult to retain a sense of objectivity
when closely involved with a child.

Section IV Re-assessment

At the end of each term it is useful to re-
assess the child using Schedules 1 and 2,
as comparison with the results of previous
assessments will provide another valuable
yardstick with which to measure the child's
progress. Space has also been left for
you to note down your impressions of the
term's progress.

If the child should leave your care
whilst you are still working with him/her,
please pass on the Record Book and materials
to his/her new teacher or group leader
so that she understands what you are trying
to accomplish and will be able to take over
where you left off.

FURTHER READING

Bower, E.M. (1969) Early Identification of Emotionally Handicapped Children in School. Spring-
field, Ill. : C.C. Thomas.
Chazan, M. (1976) The early identification of
children with adjustment problems. Chapter 5
in Wedell,K. and Raybould, E.C. (eds., 1976)
The Early Identification of Educationally
'at risk' Children. Educational Review
Occasional Publication, Number Six, School of
Education, University of Birmingham.
Lee, C. (1977, 2nd ed.) The Growth and Development
of Children. London : Longman.
Mussen, P.H., Conger, J.J. and Kagan, J. (latest
edition) Child Development and Personality
(especially Parts 1 to 4). New York : Harper
and Row.

Richman, N., Stevenson, J. and Graham, P.J. (1982)
    Pre-School to School : a behavioural study.
    London : Academic Press.
Rutter, M. (1975) Helping Troubled Children.
    Harmondsworth : Penguin Books.

B.   PRACTICAL STEPS

(e) Behaviour Assessment (Schedule 2)
Schedule 2 (Behaviour Assessment) is designed to
enable you to describe and record in some detail the
behaviour shown by a child whom you wish to help.
Too often, we are satisfied with a somewhat vague
description of a behaviour problem, for example
referring to a child as 'aggressive', 'destructive'
or 'withdrawn' without further elaboration.   Such
labels are not much help to you when it comes to
planning action.   What one person means by
'aggressive' is different from someone else's
opinion, and the word 'aggressive' is not so much
a description of behaviour but more the meaning that
someone attaches to a behaviour.   Also, it is all
too easy to label a child on the basis of first
impressions which may be totally erroneous, as can
be demonstrated by Mrs. S.   She was concerned
about a child in her group who she felt was not
getting the most from his nursery experience.
     Although James enjoyed outside activities and
boisterous games Mrs. S. thought he should be
encouraged to try out some of the quieter pursuits
on offer such as painting, small constructional toys
and jigsaws.   She perceived him as a somewhat shy
child with few friends, who was easily led and
bossed about.   After a period of observing him
Mrs. S. was forced to revise her opinion of James.
Contrary to her immediate impressions he did, in
fact, show interest in a wide variety of activities
and was observed participating in almost the entire
range provided by the nursery.   His social contacts
were much broader than at first thought and he was
seen to join several different groups, sometimes as
a leader and sometimes as a follower.   Without
this period of close observation James would have
been labelled by his teacher as shy and lacking in
confidence when, in fact, he proved to be an average
four-year-old, no different from his peers.
     Before you can deal constructively with a
problem you need to know as much as possible about
the behaviour you want to change and this can only
be achieved by close observation of the child in
question.   You may then find, like Mrs. S., that
the problem is not as serious as you first thought.
Observation without record keeping is a waste of
time, as it is simply not possible for anyone to
remember the information observed over a period of
time and recall it accurately at a later date.
Without making some sort of record of what is going

on it will be difficult for you to get to know enough about a child and his behaviour to reorganise and manage the situation successfully in future. Observation and recording will also be important later on when you are trying to see what effect your intervention is having on the child.   To aid and simplify your record keeping we have produced Behaviour Recording Sheets.

Part I. Behaviour Recording Sheets. These provide a means of ensuring that the same kinds of inform- ation are always collected, as haphazard and casual observations will be of little use when it comes to devising strategies to help the child.   Using the sheets you should observe the child systematically for at least a week, noting down as exactly as you can how he behaves.   (Generally speaking, the longer the period over which observations are made the more reliable the information you gather is likely to be.)   It is insufficient, for instance, to record "Freddy was aggressive all morning". You need to know whether he kicks, scratches, bites, pinches.   What or whom does he do it to?   What happens beforehand?   In what circumstances does he quieten down?   Similarly "all morning" is unlikely to mean the entire morning.   You will need to know how often and for how long the behaviour occurs and whether there is a regular pattern.   Is it worse in the mornings or afternoons for instance?   Does it happen more often outdoors than in?   It is also important to make a note of the times when Freddy is behaving normally and positively.   What act- ivities, for instance, hold his attention?   Which children does he play co-operatively with?   Does he enjoy adult-directed activities?
      Set out overleaf is a sample recording sheet which represents a morning's observations of Howard who, unlike Freddy, is a shy, withdrawn, dependent little boy.   As you can see the date and time of each observation are carefully recorded, as are the settings (play house, block corner, milk table) where Howard was playing, together with the names of any adults or other children in the immediate vicinity.   The recordings are not continuous but are made at varying intervals during the morning until five separate observations have been gathered. You may find it easier to take notes if you devise for yourself some form of personal shorthand or coding, which will allow you to record large amounts of information more rapidly.   Such a personal brand of shorthand, providing it is not too complicated,

can greatly increase the efficiency of your
observations. At the end of the week you should
have collected twenty-five observations for a child
attending part-time such as Howard (fifty for a
child attending full-time) and be ready to move
onto the second part of behaviour assessment, which
is a checklist.

Part II. Behaviour Assessment Checklist. This is
a checklist which describes in some detail the kind
of problem behaviour which you have identified. The
descriptions should be read carefully and those
which apply to the child in question should be
ticked. The descriptions may not fit exactly, but
you should find it possible to tick an item which
seems to match fairly closely the typical behaviour
of the child. Make any additional notes which
seem called for at the time you are completing
the checklist. It is not easy to say what is
'normal' behaviour, and in completing this Schedule
you will need to use your knowledge of the ways in
which children usually behave in the nursery group.
You should also bear in mind the actual age of the
child.

BEHAVIOUR RECORDING SHEET

NAME: HOWARD   DATE: 28.1.81   MONDAY A.M.

TIME	SETTING	ADULTS CHILDREN PRESENT	DESCRIPTION OF BEHAVIOUR
9.30	Block Play	NNEB Gareth James Steven	NNEB and children are building a motorway. Howard is watching with great interest but when NNEB tries to include him he covers his face with his arm and walks away.
9.45	Home Corner	Cathy Bethan Sarah	The girls are playing birthday parties. Howard peeps around the corner; they want him to sit down and join in but he runs away and sits in the Quiet Room on his own.
10.00	Milk Table	NNEB Paul Daniel Gareth	Howard is standing at side of table sucking his thumb. Mrs. A. offers him a mug of milk, he gets under the table and will not come out - cries bitterly.
10.30	Music and Movement	Mrs.G. and large group	The group are playing 'The Farmer's in his Den'. Anthony chooses Howard who turns away and hides his face for the rest of the session.
11.15	Story Time	Mrs.L. and group of younger children	Howard cannot be found. NNEB locates him in the cloakroom where he is hiding behind the coats. He comes in and buries his head in the chair throughout story time.

contd...

MONDAY P.M.

TIME	SETTING	ADULTS CHILDREN PRESENT	DESCRIPTION OF BEHAVIOUR

(f) General Assessment (Schedule 3)

Schedule 3 will enable you to systematise your impressions and observations of the child in the nursery group. Behaviour problems need to be viewed in the context of the child's general development, and Schedule 3 will help you to pin-point the child's strengths and weaknesses, and to take appropriate action. For example, if the child shows weaknesses in areas such as self-help or language skills, you need to consider what help may be given to develop such skills. Specific help of this kind, although not necessarily directed at the behaviour problem, is likely to contribute to the child's better adjustment in the group. Schedule 3 will also help you to decide whether the child needs a more detailed assessment, e.g. for defects in vision or hearing, or perhaps to confirm your view that the child is well below the norm in general learning ability.

Read through Schedule 3 carefully and, before completing any section, try to observe the child

in as many different situations as possible and
at various times of the day. It is suprising how
differently children can react in different contexts.
See what happens when the child is attempting a task
or playing independently, and also when with another
child or in a group. But do not assume that children are unable to succeed at a task because they
are not actually doing it - they may not have had
the chance to try. So experiment with all sorts
of games and activities, at a level that will
present children with something of a challenge without being too difficult for them. The Schedule
itself gives you some idea of what kinds of activities to engage in. Make careful notes of the
child's response both to others and in carrying out
a variety of activities.

You may find it difficult to assess what is
'normal' functioning. As far as possible, the
Schedule requires you to record whether the child
performs specific skills successfully, partially
or not at all. Your own experience with children
of nursery age will help you to judge what can be
expected of any child but remember, when comparing
the child with others, that a few months of
chronological age can make a lot of difference in
the case of young children. If you can, discuss
your own observations with a colleague who also
knows the child well.

It is far from easy to make detailed and
accurate observations of children, especially as in
the nursery group they tend to flit from one
activity to another and also you yourself will be
perpetually busy with other things. But you will
find that you become a better observer as you
practise making a record of behaviour as required
by Schedule 3. This Schedule asks you to observe
the way in which the child moves around (Section I -
Mobility) and hand-eye co-ordination (Section 2).
Neither of these sections should present you with
much difficulty. It is more difficult to assess
children's vision and hearing (Sections 3 and 4),
and to judge whether their functioning in the group
is impaired by a sensory defect; if you are in the
slightest doubt whether this is the case, do not
hesitate to seek a specialist opinion.

Self-help skills (Section 5) are reasonably
easy to assess, though you will need to ensure that
children are given ample opportunity to demonstrate
how independent they are in carrying out the tasks
listed in this section. The assessment of a child's

38

language development (Sections 6 and 7) may prove
less easy, and usually requires extensive periods of
observation. Most young children have rather
better receptive than expressive language skills,
and some will need considerable encouragement before
they will talk readily to adults, even when they
are able to express themselves adequately. Some
will talk only or mainly when they are on their
own with one adult whom they know well, but say
little or nothing in the group. So it is necessary to give children varied opportunities in which
to show their language ability, but, of course,
trying too hard to elicit a response may put off a
child reluctant to talk.
      The final two sections provide for a record of
children's responses in various play situations
(Section 8) and also their general response to the
opportunities for learning that they are provided
with in the nursery group (Section 9 - Response
to Learning/Adaptability). In most (though not all)
groups one or two children will stand out as being
slow to learn as compared to the others, and these
may well be retarded in their general development.
But in a number of cases, it will not be clear
whether the children are less capable of learning
than other children, or whether they need extra
attention and encouragement from adults before
showing what they can do. Quite a few children
are prematurely judged to be below the norm in
ability, when all they need is time to adjust and
appropriate stimulation. Do not, therefore,
hesitate to suspend judgement and to make only a
tentative assessment when you are in any doubt.
Refrain, also, from putting too much emphasis on
the things the child cannot do. As noted at the
end of Schedule 3, "Now that you are aware of the
child's strong points it may be possible to use
them as a basis for tackling his problem behaviour".

(g) Talking to Parents
Introduction
It is difficult, often, to know where to begin your
discussion of a child with the parents (or other
caretakers) and to know how far to go in your talks
with them. A discussion can easly become too
wide-ranging or involve you more deeply than is
necessary or desirable.
      It is important that you start off with a
clear idea of what you want to achieve in talking
to the parents about their child's behaviour. A

useful first step is to try and form in your mind a picture of the total problem area to be covered. For example, one child may show a particular pattern of problem behaviour in the nursery and you may want to know whether this pattern holds true for the home as well. Additionally, contact with the parents will be an opportunity to ask for specific details of any physical illnesses, injuries or other problems that cannot be obtained from the school records.

Aims

The main aims of talking to parents are:

(a) to seek and to give information about the child's development, so as to promote a better understanding of the child on both sides;

(b) to find out whether the family has had, or needs, contact with support services;

(c) to see to what extent and in what ways you can work with the parents in the management of the problem.

If you are a good listener and avoid rushing to give advice about family problems that may be the proper concern, say, of a health visitor, the discussion could prove to be constructive and useful.

A Delicate Relationship

After what has been said already about the importance of the home in meeting the young child's basic needs and about the extent to which the child's problem behaviour may stem from the family situation, the desirability of full parental involvement in dealing with the problem cannot be over-emphasised. In the case of playgroups, the parents are often very much involved already but getting the parents involved in nursery schools or classes may be a much lengthier process. Although parents nowadays are spending more time in nursery schools, teachers and parents do not always find it easy to relate to one another. Teachers may be unsure how far they should go in asking questions of the parents, and some may start off the relationship badly by implying, even if very indirectly, that the parents are to blame for a child's difficulties. Again, some parents may be over-sensitive about their child and resent any questions about their family life. Take, for example, the case of Ian's parents:

Ian is an aggressive, demanding child who frequently attacks the other children in the nursery, sometimes for no particular reason and on other occasions when he is thwarted in his attempts to obtain a favourite toy or to indulge in a particular activity. Ian's teacher is very concerned about his behaviour and has sought the advice of the headmistress about what she should do. They decide to approach Ian's mother about his behaviour to try and establish whether he behaves similarly at home, and what can be done to help him.

The mother appears to be a rather timid, ineffectual person who rarely rebukes Ian, even when he is misbehaving on school premises at collecting time. The father, on the other hand, is a very dominant character who will brook no interference with his child. A health visitor who visited the home was dealt with in a very peremptory fashion by the father who demanded to know exactly what she was 'up to' with Ian. The mother is grateful for the concern shown by Ian's teachers and is glad to accept any help, but she is terrified that the father will learn of this and blame her for going behind his back.

In this situation it is very difficult for a teacher to know what to do. She may well cause considerable problems for Ian's mother and create greater tensions in the home by seeking to involve the father even though it appears that the home situation is critical to the understanding of Ian's behaviour. He has a sister a year younger than himself whom he completely dominates at home. He will hit her or bully her to obtain a toy or to get his own way. The mother does not attempt to interfere because of the father's attitude.

41

The father was approached by the teachers in this case and eventually agreed that they should try to change Ian's behaviour. The nursery staff planned a programme of help for Ian, with some success, but the long-term effect was not a happy one, as we shall find out later.

In the example given above the father's attitude was extreme. In fact, most parents are happy to cooperate with the teacher as they realise that it is for the child's benefit that the nursery staff are paying attention to their child. If the nursery staff are careful and diplomatic in the way that they approach parents, then considerable mutual benefit can be gained from the relationship.

Great care should be exercised to avoid making parents feel guilty about their child's behaviour. Most parents want to do their best for their children, but many live under very difficult conditions which are not of their own choosing. The father might be unemployed and unable to look after his family's needs as he would like, and a sensitive approach by the teacher would be needed to avoid further tensions in the home. Again, mothers with pre-school children are particularly vulnerable to stress, and a high incidence of depression has been found amongst those with several young children who have also to face severe financial and social constraints.

On the parents' side they may feel uncomfortable about talking to teachers, perhaps because they, themselves, have had mainly negative experiences of school in the past. They may be on the defensive when discussing their child's difficult behaviour, and not a few will give the rosiest possible picture of their child's behaviour at home, even when this is blatantly untrue. Again, individuals differ in the extent to which they are willing to part with any information about themselves that they regard as personal or private, even though this information maybe of crucial importance in understanding their child's behaviour.

Some of the questions you ask may deal with matters that the mother and father are deeply concerned about. It will be necessary to phrase questions in such a way as to avoid upsetting the parents unduly, but which will enable them to speak freely about their child's problems. You may well find that the parents will be only too happy to unburden themselves, and that both you and they will gain relief from talking. Of course, their initial response may be complete denial that the child has any problem at all, but a little probing may uncover a source of worry.

There again, care should be exercised to avoid putting ideas in the parents' minds. It is only too easy to start people worrying that there may be something wrong with their child by phrasing a question badly or by being too formal in your approach. You should aim to help the parents feel relaxed and get them chatting in a free, informal manner. Getting someone to talk openly is a definite skill that can be learned and improved with practice. We will give some hints later on as to how this skill may be improved.

It is important for you to realise that you have a unique perspective of the child's behaviour. Obviously, you see the child for longer periods than other professionals and you may have closer and more frequent contact with the parents. Often it is to you that parents will unburden themselves, although some may view you as a high status 'authority-figure' and may be reluctant to approach you initially. Again, some individual staff may wish to preserve their position and find it difficult to talk easily to parents. It may not be easy to achieve the desired relationship with parents but improved communication is always possible.

You may have strong feelings about the child - or even the parents - but it is important that these feelings should not obtrude or prevent you from being reasonably objective. Some parents will come from a social background which is different from yours, and you will need to have a sympathetic understanding of this background. Even without saying anything, it is very easy to convey to parents that you are reacting negatively to their appearance or speech. Parents living in very poor circumstances often provide their children with ample warmth and affection, while parents who are advantaged in terms of wealth and education sometimes fail to satisfy the basic emotional needs of their children.

To sum up, trying to make a relationship with parents and to work constructively with them to solve a problem is not a simple task, but one often fraught with difficulties. You should not, however, be put off by these difficulties but regard them as almost inevitable in the kind of relationship you are attempting to create and deal with them in a positive manner as they arise.

Direct and Indirect Information

There will be some items of information about the child's home background and behaviour away from the nursery that you will feel able to ask the parents about <u>directly</u>. Details relating to the child's health or position in the family, for example, may be asked without incurring hostility. However, there will be some items, such as emotional difficulties between parents or between the child and siblings, that may have to be approached very delicately or not at all, depending on how you gauge the situation and the likely response of the parents in question. Considerable judgement will have to be exercised on your part when talking to individual parents, but very often you may be surprised and pleased by their frankness once you have broken the ice and got them talking freely about the child and family. Where you encounter open hostility or feel that you may exacerbate a problem by raising it, it may well be best to avoid putting the question in the first place. In order to sustain a good relationship with the parents you may have to do without certain information which you would like to have. Information about the home situation may be available from other professionals (see 'Help from Others', pp. 49-57).

The First Meeting with the Parents

The first meeting with the parents will be particularly important as the first impressions gained by them will often dictate their subsequent attitudes to you. On this occasion, the parents might be invited to the school at a time convenient for them and you.

Opportunites for a Continuing Relationship

Think about other likely occasions when you will be able to have a relaxed chat with the parents, though you may well be able to ask a few questions of them in a very brief meeting. Opportunities for a proper talk may present themselves as follows:

(a) when a child is brought to or taken home from school;

(b) when the child has to be taken home for some reason such as illness, an act for which the parent will probably be grateful and therefore more amenable to questioning;

(c) when there may be another reason for calling in the child's home area and you have some time to spare;

(d) when you meet casually on the street or in other circumstances. In many cases the parents will be more forthcoming when they meet you socially or on another occasion which is not seen as official or formal.

Ways of Approaching Parents

Your talks with parents should aim to be relaxed and informal, but should also ensure that you are able to obtain the information that you are seeking. There is no set of formal rules that should be rigidly adhered to but the following points may help to guide you:

(i) decide beforehand the areas of the child's behaviour or family background that you are going to ask about on this particular occasion. Make a note of these and decide how each question should be put;

(ii) ask fairly straightforward questions initially, so that the parents do not develop a resistance to being questioned early on in your talk;

(iii) when you feel that the moment is right, put any questions to the parents about more delicate matters, such as the child's relations with brothers or sisters, or enquire in a general way whether there are any aspects of behaviour that the parents find worrying;

(iv) allow the parents to expand upon the information they give you and probe very gently about any details that may be of specific interest to you. It may transpire that the parents will talk very frankly to you once a subject has been broached and be glad to unburden themselves of certain worries about their child. You should allow them to do this by listening sympathetically to what they have to say and maybe offering some support by making the occasional understanding remark such as ...... "quite a few children of his age are like that of course ..." or ... "that is not all that unusual". Thus you may assuage some of their anxiety and convey that you share their concern for the child. Occasionally fairly neutral comments will help to keep the conversation flowing and dispel any impression that the parents might have that they are talking in a vacuum. Essentially, what we are saying here is that you should remember that the act of talking to parents is an <u>interaction</u> between them and yourself. Try to be both a good listener and to offer advice sympathetically;

(v) avoid letting the talk become too chatty and irrelevant. It is only too easy to get side-tracked by some fairly trivial detail and spend a great deal of time talking about something which has little to do with the child's difficulties. Avoid making too many comments on your own, but try to guide the conversation into more relevant paths;

(vi) do not be unduly surprised if on subsequent occasions the parents contradict what they have said to you earlier. It is easy to give a wrong impression unintentionally and virtually impossible to be totally objective about one's own child. Thus parents commonly overrate their child's abilities and underplay shortcomings. A few may underestimate their child's good points and be over-critical. Try to keep a sense of balance and be as objective as you possibly can. Note what you consider to be over-exaggeration on the parents' part, or an undue emphasis on attainments that may be unrealistic for their child. Remember that contradictions in information may be merely due to poor recall. Distant events in particular can become distorted. Thus always balance what the parents said during one talk against what they said on subsequent occasions;

(vii) be careful how you actually phrase a question. It is only too easy to ask a 'loaded' question - that is, to pre-determine the likely response. This may often be due to certain key words being included or excluded from the question. Thus the question "Does your child often have temper tantrums?" is likely to evoke a rather different response from the parents than the question "Some children often have temper tantrums, does your child?". The first question may trigger off a denial, whilst the second question is less likely to cause resentment because it acknowledges that other children have temper tantrums. Try to make it clear by your phrasing of the question that a particular difficulty is not something which applies just to them and their child alone but may be a fairly common occurrence among children of this age group;

(viii) whenever possible, try to be positive and offer concrete suggestions about how to help the child. Praise good points as well as pointing out shortcomings. When you have decided upon a plan of action discuss this with the parents and describe what you would like to do to try to help their child.

Try to get the parents on your side, and view the intervention as a cooperative venture where you keep them informed and seek their approval for any course of action that you propose to take.

A Summary of Points to Remember when Talking with Parents

1. Have a clear idea about what information you want.
2. Prepare some questions beforehand and phrase these carefully.
3. Establish a free, relaxed atmosphere - get rapport.
4. Try to avoid spending too much time on irrelevant matters.
5. Probe deeper when the parents are receptive and obviously willing to talk about a particular problem.

47

6. Do not press on matters of delicacy when the parents clearly do not want the matter pursued.
7. Be prepared to talk with parents on several occasions and in different situations; balance what is said on one occasion against the total picture.
8. Show your concern for and interest in the child, and seek approval for your intended course of action.
9. Be positive, praise good points as well as describing difficulties.
10. Be specific - talk in concrete terms about what the child actually does and what might be practical courses of helpful action.
11. At all times be sympathetic and prepared to listen closely to what the parents have to say, and encourage them to express their ideas and help in concrete ways with the child.

The Swansea Assessment Schedule No. 4 : Talking to Parents

To help you when talking to parents, a schedule entitled 'Talking to Parents' (see Appendix A) has been drawn up. This is divided into three parts.

Part I denotes some general areas of interest and lists some items under each of these that you may wish to ask the parents about. Most of these items refer to fairly innocuous matters about which you should feel able to ask the parents a direct question. However, bear in mind what has been said about phrasing questions so as to avoid bias.

Part II consists of a list of items which refer to more delicate matters about the family and home background. You should exercise great care in how you approach the parents on these points, and should choose a time when they are being frank and obviously prepared to discuss matters openly.

Part III of the Schedule requires you to give a brief description of the child's home and family background. You will, of course, be repeating some information that will have been given in Parts I and II but this does not matter. It will be an asset to have a total picture of the home situation to act as a summary of the various bits of information noted elsewhere.

To re-emphasise an important point - all the
items in the Schedule are merely suggestions as to
what information should be sought. There may be
other items that will occur to you. The way that
you phrase the questions and the order in which you
ask them are left to your judgement.
Talking to parents should not be thought of as
a formal interview situation but some valuable
tips may be gained from reading one or two of the
references given below.

REFERENCES

Cannell, C.F. and Kahn, R.L. (1968) Interviewing.
    In Lindsey, G. and Aronson, E. (eds.) The
    Handbook of Social Psychology, vol.2, Research
    Methods. New York : Addison Wesley.
Cohen, L. and Manion, L. (1980) The Interview.   In
    Research Methods in Education. London :
    Croom Helm.
Price Williams, P.R. (1962) Interviews.   In
    Humphrey, G. and Argyle, M. (eds.) Social
    Psychology through Experiment. London: Methuen.

(h) Help from Others
If help is needed from others outside the classroom
or group, you are particularly well positioned to
seek out and co-ordinate this help. Fitzherbert
(1977) says, "I would see the teacher's (or leader's)
role as that of the conductor of the orchestra who
brings in various instruments at the appropriate
time". This co-ordinating role derives from the
close and continuing contact you have with the children in your group, from the possibility of involving
parents because you know them well and from the fact
that you can speak to other professionals as equals.
It is true, of course, that children's difficulties
may not only be evident in the group setting. They
may well be the source of worry and concern at home
and children and their families may need help of
a more continuous kind than it is possible for you
to give. It is, therefore, very wise to work
closely with the health visitor/school nurse and,
through her, with the family health visitor who will
probably have known the family over a number of
years. Other people may also be able to offer
support, and the purpose of this section is to discuss what help is available and how staff can gain

access to it. An explanation of some of the terms used is given in Appendix C (pp.303-306).

Why Refer Children?

It is a mistake to wait until a problem is well established before doing something about it. The more long-standing the difficulty, the harder it is to alter it. What you should aim for is to have the kind of relationship with other professionals which enables you (or the head teacher/ group leader) to discuss with them your concern about any child, whether or not that concern proves to be justified in the long run. Such discussions when the problem is first noticed are better than waiting for a crisis to develop.

The reasons for referring children can be categorised as follows:

(a) <u>when you feel that help is needed in an area in which you are not an expert.</u> For example, a withdrawn child may never speak to you. Discussion with the mother indicates that the child has some speech at home but you suspect from what you are told that it is very immature and babyish. Referral to a speech therapist would be the right move in this case, either directly or through the health visitor or school nurse.

(b) <u>when difficulties in the home are affecting the child.</u> You may know through a visit to the home or talking to the parents or observation of the child that there is hardship in the family or very poor living conditions or parental ill-health or even possible abuse. These problems are not really for you to deal with but you have a responsibility to contact (or to encourage the parents to contact) those who can help, e.g. the health visitor, the family doctor, or the social worker if appropriate.

(c) <u>when you are unable to meet the parents.</u> It may be that, despite all your efforts to see the mother of a child who is presenting a problem, you fail to make contact with her. The health visitor/school nurse would be a very useful ally here as a source of information and possible action.

(d) <u>when the child fails to progress in the same way as others in the group</u>. For example, a child may seem to you to be very slow to pick up new skills or to be unduly clumsy, aggressive, over-active, un-co-operative or lacking in interest. The best person to contact in such cases is the educational psychologist, who can help you to find out exactly where the main problem lies and perhaps in conjunction with the school doctor or paediatrician give advice as to how to tackle it.

Who Can Help?

A number of professionals concerned with young children have already been mentioned and completion of Swansea Assessment Schedule 5 (see Appendix A, pp. 284-289)might indicate others from whom help is available. Some of these professionals, for example the school nurse, make regular visits to the school. Others may have to be contacted specially (see next sub-section). Remember that the problem may not be a new one, although sometimes difficulties arise for the first time with entry to a group. You may find that others, especially the health visitor, are already working with the family and your concern and co-operation would be useful.

The kind of information which can be obtained from various professionals is indicated in Table 3.1. This diagram gives an outline of the help available and the information which can be 'fed in' about children and their behaviour and development. It does not show the interlinking, which is consider-able, within the various groups of professionals. Co-operation between the groups could often, it is true, be improved (see Court Report) and if you want to work with others you must be prepared for set-backs and difficulties. With perseverance, these may gradually disappear as people get to know one another.

How to Refer a Child

Usually a child is referred through the headteacher/ group leader after the difficulty has been fully discussed with the member of staff most closely involved. It is helpful for everyone concerned if a written report is drawn up giving specific details of the child (full name, age, position in family, adress etc.) and of the problem (how long has the behaviour been going on, how often does it happen, what has been done about it, what effect it is having on the child's development and on other children etc.). The Behaviour Assessment Schedule 2 (see pp.262-268) would help here as it involves a careful breakdown of the problem. Be precise rather than vague (e.g. do not just say, "Richard is withdrawn" but say what he does and does not do), as this impresses on other agencies that you have really thought about the difficulty and believe them able to help. A telephone call giving the details may be acceptable but it is better to put everything down in writing. If you get no response from the outside agency, get in touch again. You may have to be persistent for the sake of the child. But do remember that often these professionals are considerably overworked and lack of response does not always mean lack of interest.

Following up Referrals

Bringing children to the notice of outside agencies is a beginning but your responsibility does not end there. Reports should be sent to you on the children and the information they contain has to be acted upon. Some information may be confidential and the headteacher may decide that it should not be passed on, but at least the outlines of the situation should be available to those working with the children. You have to know if things are difficult at home even if you do not necessarily need to know the exact details of any illness or the marital relationship or the family's income. Ask the headteacher for the results of the referral if you are given no information, as this may serve as a reminder to get in touch with the outside professional again.

It may be necessary to work out and implement a special programme. Nursery staff should be involved in planning any such programme as only they know whether they have the opportunity to carry it out. Ask to see the therapist or the psychologist so that you can talk over the programme. Often it is easy enough to say what the problem is but a great deal of ingenuity and imagination may be necessary to see what can be done about it.

Confidentiality

If information comes your way which is of a private nature, then you should make sure that you are not going to be the one to gossip about it. Try to be

Table 3.1   Help for Children with Special Needs

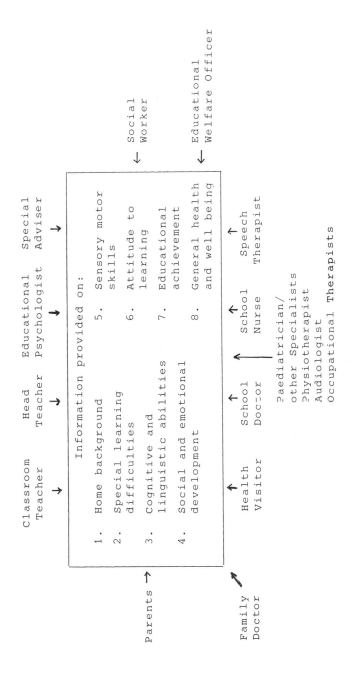

	Classroom Teacher	Head Teacher	Educational Psychologist	Special Adviser

Information provided on:

1. Home background
2. Special learning difficulties
3. Cognitive and linguistic abilities
4. Social and emotional development
5. Sensory motor skills
6. Attitude to learning
7. Educational achievement
8. General health and well being

Parents

Social Worker

Educational Welfare Officer

Family Doctor	Health Visitor	School Doctor	School Nurse	Speech Therapist

Paediatrician/ other Specialists
Physiotherapist
Audiologist
Occupational Therapists

objective, too, about any information you receive so that you do not jump to conclusions too soon and treat as fact what may only be your opinion. Some agencies are particularly reluctant to pass on information as they regard the keeping of confidences to be essential to their relationship with the family. Such a view must be respected but, as has already been said, if you have developed good communication with the service usually the general outlines of the situation will be passed on. Trust will develop only when it can be seen by all that the welfare of the children and their families is the first priority.

More than One Agency Involved?

When more than one professional becomes involved with a child, the 'teacher as conductor of the orchestra' has even greater responsibilities. It is often the case that the child as a whole gets over-looked when a number of specialists are concentrating exclusively on their own particular concern. Sometimes this has had disastrous results, as in some cases of child abuse where everyone was working in his or her own field but no one was putting all the information together.

The task of co-ordinating information or help from a number of sources frequently falls on the nursery staff. Of course they will need to work closely with the parents, so that there are no breaks in the treatment or programme being offered to children. Not only will this make any help more effective, but it will also encourage discussion of any misunderstandings that may have arisen and highlight gaps which might be filled by contacting someone else. The extent to which staff can assume the responsibility of co-ordination depends on ease of communication with the various agencies. Time spent improving relationships with others is a good investment. Other professionals could be invited to the school or group for informal chats or on formal occasions so that all the adults concerned get to know each other. Professionals naturally tend to concentrate on their own service and to see it as having priority in working with the child. Teachers may be in the position to take an overview of the situation as they spend longer time with the children than any other professional and often have fairly frequent opportunities to meet the parents.

The School and the Health Services

What is normally provided for all pupils is a routine
medical examination on entry to school and subsequent
examinations if need arises. There should be
continuous health surveillance of children at home
and in clinics, health centres etc., and the pre-
school assessment of nursery school or class children is part of this. Any child with a handicap
can be seen by the school health service from the
age of two years onwards and children whose special
needs are in the area of emotional development can
be included in this category.

As far as advice on health problems goes, the
key person is the health visitor/school nurse. She
may be instrumental in contacting outside agencies
in the first place and can carry out 'follow-up'
visits to the home as considered necessary. The
latter give her access to information helpful in
the day-to-day handling of the child. She can also
obtain information from the family's own health
visitor and family doctor who should know about the
child's general development since birth.

The School and the Social Services Department

Social workers are often not so involved with nursery
staff or with young, handicapped children as they
would like to be. Their role is to help families
who are faced with considerable stress, whatever
the nature of that stress, and a child with behavioural problems or emotional difficulties is in practically every case stressful. It may be your job,
therefore, to realise that help could be given from
this quarter and to alert the Social Services
Department. Links with the social worker are also
invaluable in promoting co-operation between the
home and the group the child attends.

Young children are particulary vulnerable to
child abuse or neglect. If you have any reason
from your observation of children or their behaviour
to suspect that their well-being may be at risk
in this way, the Social Services Department must be
contacted. If you find it difficult to tolerate
certain behaviour during the fairly brief time the
children are in the group, then you should consider
that parents may be much more stressed or less
able to cope with such stresses. Children with
behavioural disturbance may be especially likely
to become the victims of abuse; indeed, their
difficult or withdrawn behaviour in the group may
be a reaction to adverse handling at home.

The School and the Educational Services

No nursery school or class should have difficulty in obtaining help from specialists within the educational service itself. In some areas, for example, there are advisory teachers with special responsibility for the nursery and infant age ranges. They may well prove helpful in discussing behaviour problems and can act as a liaison between schools and outside agencies.

Educational welfare officers also perform a useful liaison service. Their responsibilities include not only problems of attendance in older children but, in addition, other aspects of family welfare, such as negotiating material assistance, advising parents on educational matters and bringing together the home, the community and the school. In some areas the service is less well developed than in others but it is worth while making contact with your EWO (or the one attached to the primary school which you feed) to find out what help he can offer.

The School and the Psychological Services

Children may be referred to an educational/clinical psychologist by their parents, their teachers, their doctors or any member of another profession concerned with them. Clearly it is simpler to refer children who are in school but the fact that children are not at school does not prevent referral. They can always be referred by their parents or their name can be put forward by any play group leader through the Social Services Department.

The educational psychologist is able to offer advice on the management of children, on the type of programmes which might prove helpful in individual cases and on developmental objectives. Recent research has emphasised the vital importance of the early years in children's development and in many areas the educational psychologists are becoming increasingly anxious to work with young children before problem behaviour has become firly established. The skills which they possess are very much in tune with the needs of young children and there is a growing interest in the profession in working with those who are involved daily with the problem. Clinical psychologists, who work within the Health Service, also offer help, mostly in a hospital setting, to children with behaviour problems.

It has to be said that the demand for psychological services from the schools is high and it

is also true that very young children are not the
easiest of clients, especially if their language
development is retarded. There may, therefore,
be a tendency to postpone seeing children until
after they reach compulsory school age. But if
you feel that a child requires the kind of help
which psychologists can give, then you should not
hesitate to make contact with the School Psychological Service.

With young children, it is always difficult
to know whether their developmental difficulties
are temporary or indicative of a long-lasting
problem. It is tempting, therefore, to postpone
action in order to allow the condition either to
disappear or to develop. While some passage of
time may be necessary on occasion before firm
decisions can be taken about the need for special
action, it is unwise for nursery staff to regard
time as the 'great healer' in every case. Delay
in offering help and in contacting the relevant
agencies where necessary may allow the problem to
establish itself and become increasingly difficult
to alleviate.

FURTHER READING

Bryant, B., Harris, M. and Newton, D. (1980)
    Children and Minders. London : Grant McIntyre.
Chazan, M., Laing, A.F., Shackleton Bailey, M. and
    Jones, G. (1980) Some of Our Children. London:
    Open Books.
Family Welfare Association (501-503 Kingsland Road,
    Dalston, London E8 4AU) Guide to the Social
    Services. London: MacDonald and Evans
    (published annually).
Fitzherbert, K. (1977) Child Care Services and the
    Teacher. London:Temple Smith.
Garland, C. and White, S. (1980) Children and Day
    Nurseries. London : Grant McIntyre.
National Council of Social Services (1978) Voluntary
    Social Services - a Directory of National
    Organisations.
Pringle, M.L. Kellmer, Davie, R. and Hancock, L.E.
    (1969) Directory of Voluntary Organisations
    Concerned with Children. London : Longman
    (in association with National Children's
    Bureau).
Sainsbury, E. (1977) The Personal Social Services.
    London : Pitman Publishing Co.
Stroud, J. (1975) Where to get Help : a guide to the
    support services. London:Ward Lock Educational.

<u>PART TWO</u>

<u>DECIDING WHAT TO DO</u>

Chapter 3

USING CREATIVE AND LANGUAGE ACTIVITIES

The normal programme offered in nursery classes and
play groups does much to help young children develop
social and emotional control.   It might be worthwhile for you to consider how fairly slight changes
to your ordinary pattern of work could help children
cope with behavioural difficulties, especially when
these difficulties are not very pronounced. By
changing the emphasis or extending the time alloca-
ted to certain activities, you might find that
difficulties can be overcome before they have a
chance to grow into problems.   Two aspects in
particular can do much in this respect:

    (a) creative activities

    (b) language activities

(a) CREATIVE ACTIVITIES

Introduction
By being given the freedom to manipulate a variety
of materials, children can express their feelings
one moment and erase them the next; for example, a
child may spend a considerable amount of time and
energy pummelling and shaping a piece of clay,only
to squash it and flatten it out of recognition the
next.   This can be frustrating to a teacher
wishing to 'save' the end product, but if the child
has received some satisfaction from the task, this
in itself is a worthwhile 'end product'.   This
kind of activity is particularly helpful for a child
who is suffering from tension or stress, but there
are other children who need a more powerful energetic
outlet.   For this type of child some sessions of
expressive movement would be particularly helpful.

In flinging their bodies around, they release pent-up energies which may act as a safety valve for their emotions. Sometimes children who are experiencing difficulties at home and are under strain, can lose themselves in an imaginative situation.

Nicola is a generally happy carefree child, but tends to show some signs of insecurity, e.g. thumb sucking and chewing toys. This insecurity was aggravated by the break-up of her parents' marriage and Nicola became restless and lacking in concentration. Included in some of the activities in the nursery were many sessions of imaginative play. The teacher would suggest a theme e.g. a visit to the seaside or a picnic and then the children would act out all the imaginary actions. A visit to the seaside might involve running to catch the train, travelling, arriving and seeing the sea - undressing and running into the water, splashing, swimming and so on. Nicola appeared to enjoy these activities very much. For a while afterwards she would be "smiling and happy with a look of wonderment on her face". Through these activities this little girl was able to transport herself to an imaginary world. This was satisfying to her if only offering a few minutes' respite from the stresses of her real world.

Howard is a shy, withdrawn little boy. He clings to his mother, is passive and lacks confidence. Having observed Howard's behaviour over a period of time, the teacher sees that the quality of his play is poor, he is an 'onlooker' and does not stand up for himself in confrontations with other children. He cannot relate to his peers, and his lack of language would seem to aggravate this. On the other hand, he has good mobility, being quite agile. He enjoys listening to stories and understands most of what is being said.

It would seem that Howard needs an outlet for self-expression. A conversation with father reveals that Howard is his constant companion in his D.I.Y. activities. This being so, the teacher could arrange opportunities for him to work at a

woodwork bench, which should be satisfying for him.
If he has any expertise in the matter, he would
achieve some standing amongst his peers. The
teacher can also capitalise on an interest shown in
sand and water play and allow him free rein in those
areas. Being agile and well co-ordinated, Howard
should enjoy some sessions of energetic music and
movement if he can be persuaded to join in. He
would inevitably be an 'onlooker' for the first
few sessions, but if they are lively and fun he
might be drawn to them in spite of himself. In
movement sessions no individual is singled out for
attention, and this would suit Howard.

Sometimes the novelty of using percussion
instruments will break down the barriers of shyness
in a child. The desire to touch and to play can
be stronger than the anti-social feelings. Whilst
a boy like Howard might not open his mouth to sing
he can play his chosen instrument safe in the
knowledge that no-one else is listening - all the
other children are too absorbed in their own music
making!

Difficult Children or Creative Children?

Sometimes nursery teachers place undue emphasis on
the need for children to conform, and when they find
them reluctant to do this they label them 'difficult'.
This is not necessarily a correct description; it
may be that these children have a highly creative
nature and will seldom conform or be identified
with the majority.

Rachel is one such child. After a short period
in the nursery, she would stay at an activity
heedless of adults urging her to hurry up
and finish. When the others would be putting
on their coats for outdoor play she could
be found playing a game by herself in the
cloakroom. During some collage work she
would not be content with any piece of material
provided, but would stipulate the colour and
texture of the piece required for her use.

This type of behaviour can sometimes lead to
head-on collisions with nursery staff, unless time
is spent observing the child and perhaps realising
that her creativity cannot be confined within the
normal routine. This does not necessarily mean
that the 'rules' of the nursery must be changed
solely for her benefit. Rather it calls for an

understanding attitude on the teacher's part, and
perhaps more thought given to the creative content
of the nursery day.

Stimulating Creative Behaviour

It is possible for parents and adults to stimulate
behaviour, and allow children to release whatever
creative ability they may possess. Children need
to express their feelings, but at this stage of
development, verbal communication is limited, and
they will need to find other means of communicating.
Some will revel in artistic expression, others will
find fulfilment in music and rhythm. Yet others
will enjoy shaping and moulding clay, or sorting
out pleasurable pictures and patterns to their
satisfaction.

For most people the completion of a creative
act provides a thrill. It is a pleasurable experience, and if the completed act gives someone
else pleasure, then the impact on the creator is
strong.

A teacher ...."should act as a catalyst in
bringing about children's growth in
creativity. Her catalyctic potential
may lie in part in her understanding
of children, and her warm honest acceptance
of their products" (Helen Merritt, 1967).

Care must be taken not to hurry the process
of assimilation. Children need time to explore
and discover, handle and experiment with materials
and then repeat the performance many times over.
When embarking on creative projects, they will need
time to complete their creative activity to their
own satisfaction. When children have made important
discoveries about the materials and are given freedom of expression, they will then be in a position
to handle the materials in a truly creative manner.

A. Creativity through the Medium of Art and Crafts

Painting and drawing offer children, whether they
are having behaviour problems or not, a satisfying
outlet for expression. The opportunity to indulge
in messy activities without fear of reprisal is a
new experience, and a necessary stage in their
creative development. Finger painting in particular is satisfying inasmuch that it allows
children to have direct control over the flow of

movement, and the feel and touch of the paint sub-
stance is a very direct experience. For aggressive
and over-active children, where painting at an easel
with brushes may be too much of a temptation to
act wildly, finger painting could prove to be
immensely satisfying as they can see visible traces
of their actions. They will easily create patterns,
erase them and change direction continuously.

<u>Working with clay</u>. This is a medium helpful to <u>all</u>
children. For the aggressive child it is something
to pound and pummel, flatten and squeeze, thereby
allowing acceptable release of any hostilities the
child may be feeling. Shy, withdrawn children
may not be using the medium in this energetic manner,
but may be more gentle and probing and they may
discover that clay responds to even the most gentle
imprint of finger or clay tool.

<u>Working with wood</u>. Although most nurseries have
a woodwork bench as part of their basic equipment,
many teachers are reluctant to make full use of it.
It may be that the noise level around the woodwork
table disrupts other activities, or perhaps the
teacher is unsure of the safety of the activities.

B. <u>Creativity through the Medium of Music</u>
For children and adults, musical sounds and experiences can be thoroughly satisfying as well as
therapeutic. Music affords children many opportunities for self-expression; for some, music may
generate a feeling of well-being and satisfaction,
for others it will provide a release for pent-up
or disagreeable emotions.
     As many children may have had little experience
of music before starting in the nursery playgroup,
there is much that can be done to remedy this. Even
non-musical teachers can provide the right environment and stimulus to make children aware of music.
The ability to re-create music composed by others
and to create music themselves develops later. The
prime concern is to allow children to enjoy music,
the emphasis being on the <u>enjoyment</u> rather than on
any particular skills, and on the <u>experience</u>, not
any end product.

     <u>Margaret</u> (4½ years) was a little girl who
     caused her nursery teacher some concern,
     as she would not communicate verbally with
     either adults or peers. This was not a

case of language delay, as the teacher knew
that the child spoke fluently at home.
She was advanced in all other aspects of
her development, and responded well to
instructions in a non-verbal manner. During
a singing together session, the teacher
noticed Margaret's lips move, but was unable
to perceive actual sounds. By halving the
group she was able to hear the child's
voice, and praised her for her singing.
Gradually she decreased the numbers of
children singing together at one time until
Margaret was singing with one other child.
Knowing by this stage that Margaret shied
away from too much attention she did not
ask her to sing alone, but on the next
occasion asked for a volunteer and Margaret
came forward and sang by herself. After
this, Margaret showed a willingness to
respond verbally on other occasions and
situations.

This example shows how important some singing
activities can be in encouraging the shy child to
make a contribution. Another child, <u>Christopher</u>
(aged 4), who was immature and had language problems
also benefited from singing in a group. In this
instance the teacher used a tape recorder to record
the children's voices individually. When it was
his turn Christopher was prepared to record his
voice and immature speech. These sessions helped
him to make an effort to communicate with others,
thus in turn reducing the temper tantrums he had
previously been exhibiting.

<u>Percussion instruments</u>. Because of their enthus-
iasm children often become excitable and difficult
to control in a music-making session. This often
results in the nursery staff being reluctant to allow
the children to use the instruments. When they do,
the unfamiliarity produces excitability and so it
becomes a vicious circle. Good organisation is
the key to enjoyable music making, and good provision of instruments. Sometimes a child will sulk
if not given a favourite instrument, but if the
children exchange instruments during the session,
they will learn to be patient, and gain experience
of a variety of instruments.
No music table ever has sufficient instruments,
and it is sometimes necessary to make some. This
can be a satisfying task if the children participate.

65

Most teachers are familiar with making these, from paper plates with bottle tops attached, or dowelling rods with bottle tops, to simple plastic containers filled with peas, rice, etc. The instruments should not be confined solely to the music area. They can be useful in story telling, e.g. the story of the Elves and the Shoemaker calls for a number of tapping noises, or the noise of the clock striking. Used in this way the children can see the imaginative potential of the instruments.

A timid child may be reluctant at first to hold a percussion instrument, let alone produce any sounds with it. Usually, however, any reservations will be overcome by the novelty and appeal of the music making. Children soon realise that they have freedom to experiment with their instruments and that no special expertise is needed in order to achieve some satisfying sounds.

C. Creativity through the Medium of Movement
Movement is at its most creative when children are able to interpret music in a highly individual way. But before reaching this advanced stage of expressive movement, children must be made aware of the infinite variety of body movements. In this way they will begin to understand themselves and realise that certain moods and feelings are bound up with expressive movement. The movements of a happy child contrast strongly with those of a child who is fearful and worried. It may be that children who are not receiving satisfaction from other media will find that this is the medium to which they can respond.

For some children, participating in a session of movement with an imaginative theme can allow for a release of energy that is unacceptable in other spheres. Boisterous aggressive children will delight in being fearsome giants or brave explorers hacking their way through the jungle. At the same time, shy withdrawn children, while reluctant to join in the activities, may enjoy watching the others, and sometimes will re-enact the themes or movements when playing elsewhere. This was true of Howard (aged 4), a timid, over-protected little boy. After a long period in the nursery he became attached to a boy who was the exact opposite of himself, extroverted and boisterous. Both boys had been engaged on some constructive block play which led to a space rocket theme. The nursery teacher then continued this theme later in music and movement, where they all participated in flying to the moon. Howard did not join in any of these movement sessions, merely observing the others. However, later that day, when the children played outdoors, the nursery staff saw that they were continuing the space theme, and that Howard was joining in enthusiastically.

Conclusion

Nurseries have the resources to facilitate creative ideas, and many teachers possess an artistic ability or preference for a certain aspect of creativity which will inevitably be passed on to the children. It has not been possible to describe creative activities in great detail, but listed below are some books which may extend your knowledge if you decide to use a creative approach to help a child with behaviour difficulties.

REFERENCES AND FURTHER READING

Chazan, M. (ed.) (1973)Education in the Early Years. Swansea : Faculty of Education, University College of Swansea.

Eliason, C.F. and Jenkins, L.T., (1977) A Practical Guide to Early Childhood Curriculum. St. Louis: C.V. Mosby.

Merritt, H. (1964) Guiding Free Expression in Children's Art. New York; Holt, Rinehart and Winston Inc.

Pickering, D. and M. (1974) Pre-School Activities. London: Batsford Books.

Yardley, A. (1970) Senses and Sensitivity. London: Evans Bros.

(b) LANGUAGE ACTIVITIES

Introduction

The role of language in early childhood education is currently receiving a good deal of attention (Cazden, 1979). We still do not fully understand the complex relationship between language and learning, and we must be careful not to over-estimate the role of language in early development: Piaget has warned us that lanugage can be used without real understanding, especially if sensory and motor

experience is lacking. However, it is clear that
many aspects of children's thinking are dependent
on the acquisition of basic language skills. Language, in its oral and written forms, is the main
medium of teaching in schools, and children
need linguistic competence if they are to derive
full benefit from their school years. Early childhood is characterised by very rapid language development, and it is desirable that children should
get off to a good start (Woodhead, 1976a). Although
the family has a major role in fostering language
growth, nursery groups can contribute much to
linguistic development in young children, and most
nursery staff would place the encouragement of
expressive and receptive language skills high on
their list of goals.

How Language helps Emotional and Social Development
Up till now it is the role of language in cognitive
development and school achievement which has
received most attention. We tend to overlook the
place of language in emotional and social development, and relatively little work has been carried
out on this topic. Yet children's feelings and
social skills are closely linked with their
language development, and although interaction with
others is not entirely dependent on verbal communication, it does not greatly progress without
language. Smiles and gestures, whether from child
or adult, make quite a lot of impact, but communication is on a different level once the child
has some language. The child who says little or
nothing soon ceases to obtain the fullest positive
feedback even from loving parents; probably the same
sort of thing happens in the nursery group. The
acquisition, development and use of language are
related to emotional and social development in a
number of ways (Herriot, 1971; Tough, 1977).
These are outlined below.

  1. Language helps children to regulate their
     own behaviour and that of others. It
     enables children to direct their attention
     to their own actions, bringing them under
     their control, as well as to wield some
     sort of power over others, e.g. by
     expressing their needs or by issuing
     commands.
  2. Language facilitates the development
     of a concept of self. Being involved in

verbal exchange, whether adult-child or
child-child, helps children to be aware
of their importance and value as individuals. Further, both the extent
to which children understand descriptive
and evaluative words such as 'good',
'bad', 'naughty' or 'nice' and the ways
in which these words are applied to
them will affect their perception of
themselves as separate individuals.

3. Language influences the development
   of attitudes. The context in which
   words indicating values (e.g. 'right',
   'wrong', 'wicked', 'lovely') are used
   by parents, nursery staff and others
   will, over time, contribute to the
   formation of the child's attitudes.
   Particularly in the early years,
   children are likely to imitate and
   internalise the behaviour and values
   of others.

4. Language helps the child to an increasing
   understanding of the feelings and reactions of other adults and children. This
   understanding comes slowly, but it is an
   important component of emotional and
   social development. Lewis has suggested
   that deficiencies in children's vocabu-
   laries relating to personal characteristics (e.g. 'happy','glad', 'sad') may
   retard personality development.

5. Language enables children to express
   themselves emotionally and socially in
   play to a fuller extent than is possible
   without it. Language helps the development of complex and imaginative forms of
   play, which might otherwise remain at a
   low level. Some kinds of play,
   accompanied by verbal expression
   (especially role playing) may be a means
   of working through conflicts. Ways of
   using language in play are suggested in
   the section on 'Play Activities'(pp.92-128).

6. Language assists the child to become
   aware that there is more than one possible
   response to most situations, and is an
   essential tool in the problem-solving
   strategies discussed in the Handbook.
   It can help the child to learn how to
   substitute more socially acceptable
   responses for physical aggression. On the

whole in our society, verbal attacks incur less displeasure from others than physical assault.

The Role of the Nursery Group in Fostering Language

There has been much discussion lately about the contribution which can be made by the nursery group to fostering language development. We cannot assume that participation in nursery school or play-group necessarily provides adequate opportunities for young children to advance their language. In a small-scale study in South-East England, Valerie Thomas (1973) found that many of the questions put to children by the adults in a nursery class were not answered - the children either did not listen at all, tuned out before the completion of the question, considered a one-word answer sufficient or did not think the question worth an answer. As there was no pressure to reply, they probably did not think anyone cared whether they answered or not. A considerable proportion of the adults' speech was in the form of commands, or emotionally-toned remarks such as 'Naughty' or 'I am surprised at you!' or phrases such as 'Jolly good!' and 'Oh, pretty!'. Minimum verbalisation was accepted by the staff, and no child was expected to repeat, clarify or extend a statement; few remarks from the child developed into a conversation.

The results of this limited study cannot be generalised to all nursery groups, and the situation is always changing, with an increasing emphasis on planned adult-child verbal interactions. However, Barbara Tizard (1976),in looking at staff behaviour in pre-school centres, found that while the adults talked a great deal to the children, often the talk was at a lower level than it might have been. The Oxford Pre-school Research Project (Sylva et al., 1980), too, found that although the pre-schools involved in the study appeared to be alive with talk, conversations between adults and children were very fleeting. Real exchanges about a single topic were rarely conducted. Further, the children engaged in little conversational exchange amongst themselves.

Some General Principles

On the basis of work carried out in a variety of contexts, and the recommendations of the Bullock

Report (1975), which gave considerable attention to
language in the early years, it would seem desirable
that nursery staff should:

1) give planned attention to children's
   language development. Without a
   deliberate language policy, it is
   likely that the level of verbal interaction in the nursery group will be
   lower than it need be;
2) provide as many opportunities as
   possible for children to be in a one-
   to-one relationship with adults in
   the nursery group. This will mean
   encouraging, in a controlled manner,
   the participation of adults additional
   to the usual staff in the group;
3) as far as they can, provide appropriate
   settings for adults to work with individual children and small groups.
   Sylva et al. (1980) comment that
   'dialogue-inducing' settings are
   likely to be small, quiet rooms, intimate
   and home-like, with two or three
   children. In the Oxford study, some
   of the richest conversations took place
   in the home corner, or 'dens' which a
   small group of children had constructed
   on their own. Downes (1978) discusses
   how language can be encouraged in the
   normal 'work areas' found in the nursery
   group e.g. the sand area or home corner.
   Unfortunately, many nursery groups lack
   natural spaces where individual or small
   group activity can take place away from
   the usual bustle associated with a large
   number of children, and ingenuity is
   needed to create suitable settings;
4) seek a close partnership with parents,
   who play a major part in the child's
   language development.

Planned attention to language, a one-to-one
relationship with adults, appropriate settings and
parental involvement are particularly important in
the case of children with emotional or social
difficulties. Some children, especially those with
a poor self-image, will benefit from being involved
in varied language activities which introduce, at a
level appropriate to the individual child, vocabulary
and concepts relating to the self (see section on

'Play Activities').

Language Schemes and Programmes

The Bullock Report (1975) suggested that language should be learned in the course of using it in, and about, the daily experiences of the classroom and the home, but within this framework teachers might find support in some language programmes. Nursery staff in Britain are not greatly attracted to language schemes or programmes of a structured nature, such as have been produced in the U.S.A. Nevertheless, even if one does not accept a scheme in its entirety, or subscribe to the rationale behind it, many useful ideas can be gleaned from the available programmes, which may be discussed under four headings, although some of the schemes do not clearly come within a particular category:

1. traditional (informal) enrichment
2. planned language stimulation, not using one specific scheme
3. direct instruction
4. instructional dialogue

It is likely that most nursery staff, rather than choosing a particular emphasis, will prefer to combine all four of these approaches in varying ways.

1. Traditional (informal) Enrichment

This model sees help and encouragement from adults as providing the best opportunity for children to increase their linguistic skills (Parry and Archer, 1974). The emphasis is on flexibility of approach, free play and self-expression, incidental language learning in a appropriate environment rather than on specific language lessons with highly structured materials or situations, and on unobtrusive guidance rather than direction by the teacher. Most educationists would agree that, for some part at least of the school day, informal approaches and child-directed activities are desirable for young children, and many informal activities are included in the schemes discussed under 'direct instruction' and 'instructional dialogue'. However, nursery staff guided predominantly by the 'traditional enrichment' philosophy must be careful to ensure that language learning actually does occur. There are indeed many opportunities in the nursery group for such learning to take place.

Using Creative and Language Activities

Publications of Relevance

Schools Council Pre-School Education Project
Marianne Parry and Hilda Archer

1974a Pre-School Education London : Macmillan
Education.

This is a report on the project's survey of 'good
practice' in various nursery groups.

1974b Two to Five London : Macmillan Education.

A guide for nursery staff, which considers play
experiences, particulary in the context of language
development, and the use of basic materials in the
nursery group. The guide is accompanied by four
16 mm. colour films.

2. Planned Language Stimulation (not using a pre-
packaged scheme)
Some nursery groups, while not wishing to be tied
to a specific language scheme, want to do more than
rely on incidental language learning during the
normal activities of the day. They prefer to
devote some time, as a team, to the planning of
language stimulation and thereby to ensure that each
child is definitely involved in language activity.
This approach has been adopted particularly in
relation to socially disadvantaged children, and is
illustrated by the work undertaken by S. Harvey and
T.R. Lee. An account of this work, 'An Experimental Study of Educational Compensation' is given
in Educational Priority, Volume 5 : EPA - A Scottish
Study (London, HMSO, 1974). In this project,
carried out in pre-schools in Dundee, there was no
specific language programme, but language development was encouraged in the framework of an integrated
scheme designed to enhance general cognitive
development. 'Themes' were planned, usually lasting
for a full week and maintaining continuity of
emphasis on a single cognitive concept. Each theme
was introduced by an activity or experience, and
then the selected concept was dealt with from
different points of view, i.e. through different
senses, using varied play material, differently
contrived situations and a wide range of songs,
nursery rhymes and stories.
The 'cognitive discovery' approach, too,
inspired by Piaget's work, involves the planning of

appropriate activities by adults rather than the
use of a pre-packaged scheme.   Kamii and Radin
(1970) and Kamii (1971 and 1973) describe the pre-
school curriculum which they devised for four-year-
old chilren.   The general procedure was for the
teacher to set up a situation or propose an activity,
and to see how the children reacted before deciding
what to pick upon in order to extend the child's
thinking.   Understanding through exploration and
activity is stressed rather than the use of language
for its own sake, the language being linked to the
experiences offered.

3. Direct Instruction
A direct teaching model has been used by Bereiter
and Engelmann in the U.S.A. (see 'Teaching Disadvantaged Children in the Preschool, 1966) and in
later work by Engelmann and his associates (1970).
This model, based on behaviour modification theory,
aims at promoting language development through
direct teaching of specific skills.   It uses a
demanding rather than a persuasive approach and
requires imitative and structured, rather than
individual and intuitive, responses from the children.   The teacher takes on a highly directive role,
making use of patterned repetition and extrinsic
reinforcement as much as possible; children's
success is judged in terms of how accurately they
imitate the teacher's language model.
      Another American programme using a direct
instruction model is the Peabody Language Development
Kit (PLDK) devised by L.M. Dunn and L.O. Smith in
1964 (Level P is designed for pre-school children).
The PLDK is designed, through a series of 180
carefully sequenced daily lessons, to stimulate oral
language development.   It provides a variety of
teaching aids, including pictorial material, puppets,
life-sized plastic fruits and vegetables, magnetic
shapes and strips, and recordings of different sounds.
It aims to encourage creative responses as well as
convergent thinking, and offers varied types of
activities, including general vocabulary enrichment,
the teaching of key sentence patterns and the use
of language to serve many functions, ranging from
logical and mathematical to social and emotional.
A revision of the PLDK has been undertaken by the
National Foundation for Educational Research, which
has published a British Manual (Quigley and Hudson,
1974).

GOAL - Game Oriented Activities for Learning - is another American structured language development pack devised by M. Karnes, which although expensive is less so than the Peabody Kit. The publishers claim that GOAL is suitable for all children between the ages of 3 and 5 regardless of intelligence, background and handicap and can be used with children who have visual and hearing impairments. Six points are noted in the teacher guide to explain what GOAL does : it develops a desire to learn; it develops a positive self-concept and good emotional development; it develops good social skills; it enhances creative and problem-solving abilities; it promotes motor skills;and it encourages teachers and parents to focus on the language development of children. Reports from schools known to be using GOAL indicate that it offers considerable potential for teachers wishing to design programmes to meet the needs of individual children or small groups.

Some of the ideas from the direct instruction programmes have been incorporated in a more eclectic language programme described by D.M. and G.A. Gahagan in their book 'Talk Reform'(1970). Although the Gahagans worked in London infant schools, many of their suggestions can be adapted for nursery groups. 'Talk Reform' describes a language training programme (20 minutes per day) advocating a variety of activities, including games, picture stories, drama, small group discussions and direct instruction, with the main aim of improving (a) attention and auditory discrimination; (b) speech; (c) structure and vocabulary.

'Teach Them to Speak' (by G.M. Shiach, 1972) is another programme devised in Britain which relies heavily on formal training in language skills. The book presents a series of 200 lessons which aim to develop oral language in children aged four to seven years. No special kit is provided, and the materials needed can easily be collected or bought, e.g. picture cards, posters, colour cubes, hand puppets and various objects. The lessons, one for each day, last for about half an hour, and are designed to give a feeling of success through graded steps. There is constant revision, drill and repetition, with the emphasis on descriptions and explanations in well-structured grammatically complete and correct sentences. Stress is put on 'expansion'by the teacher, that is, modifying and extending the child's oral responses to achieve a desired sentence form. Some of the activities are somewhat stereotyped and unimaginative, and could be dull for both adults and children; but there is much useful material here for nursery staff to consider.

4. Instructional Dialogue
'Instructional dialogue' strategies have been developed in the U.S.A. by Marion Blank (1973) and in Britain by Joan Tough (1977b). The handbook of suggestions on language activities for disadvantaged children in their first year in the infant school (Downes, 1978), too, while adopting an eclectic stance, owes something to the 'instructional dialogue' approach.

Marion Blank's tutorial language programme is based on dialogue between teacher and child for about fifteen to twenty minutes each day. The main aim of this individual tutoring programme is to help the child to progress towards abstract thinking. The teacher uses no gestures, but helps the child to use language to complete the task set. The child is encouraged to extend his thinking beyond the concrete situation, by, for example, discussing alternative courses of action or attempting explanations of events. Errors made by the child in his verbal responses are used as a basis for developing thinking skills. Inexpensive and readily-available objects (e.g. paper, crayons, blocks, toys, simple books) are all that is needed for the programme. This approach, however, requires more adults to be available than is usually the case in most nursery groups.

Joan Tough's work as Director of the Schools Council 'Communication Skills in Early Childhood Project', focusses on ways of discovering what children can do with language and how the teacher can stimulate children to use language for a variety of purposes meaningful to them and for extending their thinking. The following publications relating to this work are available (all by Joan Tough):

    A.   Books discussing rationale
          1973. Focus on Meaning. London: Allen and Unwin.
          1977a. The Development of Meaning. London : Allen and Unwin.

    B.   A Guide to the Appraisal of Children's Use of Language
          1976. Listening to Children Talking. London : Ward Lock Educational (for Schools

Council).

C. A Guide to Fostering Communication Skills
1977b. Talking and Learning. London :
Ward Lock Educational (for Schools Council).

(A set of video-tapes is also available, published by
Drake Educational Associates and Ward Lock Educational). The handbook by Galen Downes (1978) focusses
upon the vocabulary and language structures
associated with logical thinking and reasoning. Its
main aim is to help children to develop more elaborated speech, including more accurate descriptions and
explanations and the use of questions to elicit
information. It discusses the development of seven
language skills (listening, naming, categorising,
describing, denoting position, sequencing and
reasoning) through activities and materials. The
handbook contains a set of guidelines and suggested
activities and games from which a selection can be
made rather than a detailed, pre-sequenced 'package'
of language activities. Teachers are encouraged to
use the normal resources of the classroom to provide
stimulation for language development, in addition
to producing simple but imaginative materials
themselves. Although designed for disadvantaged
children in the early stages of formal schooling,
many of the suggestions contained in the handbook are
applicable to nursery groups.

Children with Severe Language Difficulties

Children with severe speech or language difficulties
in the nursery group will need careful assessment,
involving speech therapist, psychologist, medical
officer or other professionals. In some cases,
the emphasis will need to be on fundamental sensori-
motor skills rather than on formal language training,
and then on building up a basis of receptive language
before systematic attempts are made to encourage
speech (Reynell, 1973). Where the child has very
poor language skills, schemes which assume a low
starting point will be found useful. Two such
schemes are:

1. 'Let Me Speak' by D.M. Jeffree and
   R. McConkey, published by Souvenir
   Press, London, 1976.
2. 'The First Words Language Programme', by
   B. Gillham, published by Allen and Unwin,

London, and University Park Press,
Baltimore, 1979.

Conclusion

We have stressed that nursery staff can do much to
promote language skills in the course of their
daily work, and that they need to give a lot of
thought to planning appropriate individual and group
activities. Growing competence in understanding
and using language will give the child much confidence and pleasure. We would also emphasise that
the influence of the home on early language development is so important that nursery staff should
seek to support the parents to the fullest extent,
and encourage parental involvement as much as possible.
Parents already play a considerable part in playgroups.
Nursery schools should actively contribute to toy
and book library schemes, and be concerned with a
wide range of activities designed to encourage
parents to interact naturally but purposefully with
their children. Such positive interaction will be
of great benefit to the child in his emotional and
social development.

REFERENCES AND FURTHER READING

Bereiter, C.E. and Engelmann, S. (1966) Teaching
    Disadvantaged Children in the Pre-school.
    Englewood Cliffs, N.J. : Prentice-Hall.
Blank, M. (1973) Teaching Learning in the Pre-school:
    a Dialogue Approach. Columbus Ohio : Charles
    E. Merrill.
Bullock Report (Department of Education and Science,
    1975) A Language for Life. London ; HMSO.
Cazden, C.B. and Harvey, D. (eds., 1979) Language
    in Early Childhood Education. Washington, DC :
    National Association for the Education of
    Young Children.
Downes, G. (1978) Language Development and the
    Disadvantaged Child. Edinburgh : Holmes-
    McDougall.
Dunn, L.M. and Smith, L.O. (1964) Peabody Language
    Development Kit. Nashville, Tennessee :
    Institute for Mental Retardation and Intellectual
    Development, George Peabody College for Teachers
    (distributed by NFER, The Mere, Upton Park,
    Slough, Berks SL12DQ).

Engelmann, S., Osborn, J. and Engelmann, T. (1970) Distar Language I and II. Chicago:Science Research Associates.

Gahagan, D.M. and Gahagan, G.A. (1970) Talk Reform. London: Routledge and Kegan Paul.

Gillham, B. (1979) The First Words Language Programme. London: Allen and Unwin.

Halsey, A.H. (ed., 1972) Educational Priority, Vol.1 EPA Problems and Policies. London:HMSO.

Harvey, S. and Lee, T.R. (1974) An experimental study of educational compensation. In Educational Priority, Vol. 5: EPA - A Scottish Study. London: HMSO.

Herriot, P. (1970) An Introduction to the Psychology of Language. London:Methuen.

Jeffree, D.M. and McConkey, R. (1976) Let Me Speak. London: Souvenir Press.

Kamii, C. (1971) Evaluation of learning in pre-school education; socio-emotional, perceptual-motor and cognitive development. In Bloom, B.S. Hastings, J.T. and Madaus, G.F.(eds.) Handbook on Formative and Summative Evaluation of Student Learning. New York: McGraw-Hill.

Kamii, C. (1973) A sketch of the Piaget-derived pre-school curriculum developed by the Ypsilanti Early Education Program. In Spodek, B. (ed.) Early Childhood Education. Englewood Cliffs, N.J.:Prentice-Hall.

Kamii, C. and Radin, N. (1970) A framework for a pre-school curriculum based on some Piagetian concepts. In Athey, I.J. and Rubadeau, D.O. (eds.) Educational Implications of Piaget's Theory. New York:Wiley.

Karnes, M. Goal Language Development Kit available from LBA, Park Works, Norwich Road, Wisbech, Cambridgeshire.

Lewis, M.M. (1968) Language and Personality in Deaf Children. Slough:NFER.

Myklebust, H.R. (1964) The Psychology of Deafness. New York:Grune and Stratton.

Parry, M. and Archer, H. (1974a) Pre-school Education. London:Macmillan Education

Parry, M. and Archer, H. (1974b) Two to Five. London:MacMillan Education.

Quigley, H. and Hudson, M. (1974) British Manual to the Peabody Language Development Kit (Level P) Windsor:Test Division, NFER Publishing Co.

Reynell, J.K. (1973) Planning treatment programmes for pre-school children. In Mittler, P. (ed.) Assessment for Learning in the Mentally Handicapped. Edinburgh and London:Churchill Livingstone.

Shiach, G.M. (1972) Teach Them to Speak. London :
     Ward Lock Educational.
Sylva, K., Roy, C. and Painter, M. (1980) Child-
     watching at Playgroup and Nursery School.
     London : Grant McIntyre.
Thomas, V. (1973) Children's use of language in the
     nursery. Educational Research, 15, 3, 209-16.
Tizard, B., Philps, J. and Plewis, I. (1976) Staff
     behaviour in pre-school centres. J. Child
     Psychol. Psychiat., 17. 21-33.
Tough, J. (1973) Focus on Meaning, London : Allen
     and Unwin.
Tough, J. (1976) Listening to Children Talking.
     London : Ward Lock Educational.
Tough, J. (1977a) The Development of Meaning.
     London : Allen and Unwin.
Tough, J. (1977b) Talking and Learning. London :
     Ward Lock Educational.
Woodhead, M. (1976a) Intervening in Disadvantage :
     a challenge for nursery education. Windsor :
     NFER Publishing Co.
Woodhead, M. (ed., 1976b) An Experiment in Nursery
     Education. Windsor : NFER Publishing Co.

CHAPTER 5

SPECIAL HELP IN THE CLASSROOM

Introduction

In previous sections of this book, a number of children have been discussed. Richard is shy and withdrawn, lacking in confidence and uninterested in other children. Jonathan clings to the teacher for reassurance but also has temper tantrums and outbursts of rather babyish behaviour. William is overactive, never settling to anything and constantly interfering with other children. Eric is disobedient, rude and aggressive. These four boys pose real but different problems to their teachers. What should they do about them?

Later on in this section you will find descriptions of a number of possible approaches. To start with, however, there will be a discussion of some general principles. Let us suppose first of all that you are faced with Brian in your group. What would you do to help him?

Brian was recommended for speech therapy by his family health visitor at the age of two years six months. He appeared behind in all aspects of development, especially his speech, and he was given a priority place at nursery school, attending full-time from the age of three years six months. He has a younger sister, Susan, whom he treats rather roughly although he seems fond of her. He is an overweight, rather lethargic boy usually, but given to fairly violent temper tantrums when he becomes frustrated. As his speech is extremely poor and he is often in difficulties over making himself understood, his tantrums are becoming more frequent and occur at home as well as in school. He is well cared for physically

but the home seems lacking in stimulation
of any kind. His mother is young, but she
too is overweight and is at times 'thumped'
by Brian when he is in one of his tantrums.

There is much more that could be said about
Brian but perhaps the above description enables
some pointers to action with him to be indicated.

1. He needs stimulating, i.e. he needs the
   kind of activities that will attract
   his attention and encourage him to
   spend some time on them.
2. He needs help with his speech. Therapy
   is already being offered but a session
   once a week is not enough for Brian
   to begin to make good his very pronounced
   lag in speech development.
3. He needs to learn how to interact with
   other children so that the possibilities
   of frustration are somewhat reduced
   while, hopefully, his language development begins to catch up.
4. The signs of a coming tantrum or the
   situations which give rise to a tantrum
   need to be recognised so that avoiding
   action can be taken. With tantrums
   prevention is easier than cure.
5. His mother needs some guidance on how
   to cope with him at home.

So far, so good! But the pointers drawn up
above are not very precise. It is not clear
exactly what triggers off the tantrums, nor is it
clear what Brian can do well. Neither his problems
nor his strengths have been exactly noted. The best
way to start to try to help Brian would be to
complete the schedules (copies of which appear
in Appendix A, pp. 257-289),intended to bring
together just the sort of precise information which
is required. Other people are involved, namely
the mother and the speech therapist. The relevant
schedules, when completed, would help to quantify
what is happening at home and in the clinic as well
as indicating who else might be able to help e.g.
health visitor/school nurse (with advice to the
parents) or educational psychologist (with advice
to the teacher and parents).
Perhaps a combination of approaches is required
for, indeed, there is not just one problem but a
number. Descriptions of these approaches are to

be found later in this section).

1. The teacher could use <u>task analysis</u>
   (pp. 163-174) to break down into
   simple steps actions such as putting on
   and taking off his shoes and his coat.
   His increased competence in the nursery
   setting might well help his tantrums.
2. A behaviour modification approach
   (pp. 128-163) could be tried to help
   encourage his speech. Wholehearted
   praise and recognition for his occasional one-word utterances might promote more
   and even longer communication.
3. Simple, imaginative <u>play activities</u>
   (pp. 92-128) might help his social
   development so that he learns to share
   and is confident enough to wait his
   turn.
4. <u>Discussing his problems</u> with Brian
   (pp. 177-202) may <u>not</u> be very helpful
   in this case as difficulties in communication could aggravate rather than
   alleviate the situation.

Sometimes one approach may seem to be the most
likely to succeed, sometimes another, or a combination of approaches. What you have to do now is
to read about the various possible approaches
and decide which one appeals to you. Do not be put
off by the feeling that a suggested approach is very
different from your usual programme. It is usually
possible to fit in a short session with the children
in question on their own (or in a small group) or to
give them the necessary guidance and encouragement
(as when modifying behaviour) when supervising
other activities. If you have a nursery assistant,
the situation is much easier. You can either show
her what you want her to do with particular children
or ask her to cope with the rest of the group while
you work with them.

The vital point is to plan your approach to
the difficulty. The various schedules when completed should give you a good basis for any decisions
you take, and you should note in the Record Book
(pp. 290-302) what you hope to do, what you
actually do, and what you achieve.

It is sometimes the case that behaviour can
change surprisingly quickly when the real problem
is identified and tackled. More often, however,
change may be slow to come and you should be

prepared to spend some time on the approach you have selected. It is difficult to say how long you should spend as this will vary according to the needs of the child you are working with and the techniques you have chosen. A good piece of advice is not to be too ambitious. It is better to work out a series of small objectives which can be comparatively easily reached than to set a goal which is so far from where the child actually is in his behaviour that it may not appear to be even relevant. Rather than setting as your aim, "to improve William's socialisation", it would be better to say, "to encourage William to play for 3 minutes alongside another child". The modest objectives gradually mount up until you realise the tremendous improvement in behaviour when you look back over the record booklet.

If the approach you select does not seem to be working at all, you must first of all consider if you are honestly giving it a chance. If you have decided before you begin that is all a waste of time, then you are very unlikely to succeed. A feeling that the approach is going to work helps you to persevere and achieve your goal. Again, you may not be implementing the approach properly. The methods suggested later in this section all require some changes from normal group procedure. It is unlikely that you are already doing all that they suggest; make sure that you have made the necessary adaptations to your normal approach. But if you have genuinely tried a technique and despite your efforts it has failed, then try another. What works with one child or with one teacher may not be successful with another and you will probably have learned a great deal about the child even if you feel you have not reached your objectives.

It is often argued that teachers and others do not have the time - or the opportunity - to work with one or two children when there are many others clamouring for their attention. Whether this argument is right or not must surely depend on how much time is involved. Children with behavioural problems may take up a lot of time if they are difficult to manage. Very withdrawn children may not be demanding in this respect but they cannot just be ignored. Often what is required is a change of attitude on your part.

Attitudes to Difficulties
Practically every child displays deviant behaviour

at one time or another. Most of these temporary difficulties are coped with adequately by giving unobtrusive support and encouragement. In some cases, however, problems persist or become more marked and children show more than a temporary upset. It is important

1. not to let the problem become magnified. If you look for difficult behaviour, you tend to see it and to miss the occasions on which it may not be in evidence. This is why precise description is so important (see above, pp. 82 and 84);

2. not to let the child's behaviour control your behaviour. Children learn very early how to get an adult's attention, or how to avoid it. It may be better to ignore attention-seeking behaviour, however spectacular, and to praise acceptable behaviour, even if it is minimal to begin with;

3. not to let the difficult behaviour rattle you. It is very seldom effective to have a confrontation with a child who is not behaving as the others are. Apart from the fact that you may not win, a clash of wills can escalate the problem or upset the other children. Rather, avoid the confrontation by the way in which you organise the activities in the nursery group.(see below, pp.87-88);

4. not to let your routine or preferred way of working create difficulties. There are some children who do not take kindly to organisation. They may be dreamy, absorbed in a world of their own, impatient or impulsive. While not arguing for them to be allowed complete freedom, it could be suggested that perhaps their problems about conforming could be realised and the demands, at the beginning anyway, made realistic for them;

5. not to let any labels you attach to children get in the way of your objective view of them. It is possible to label children as 'naughty' and only to see them when they are being naughty.

Some of these points are illustrated by the

following example:

> Karen (aged 4½) is an energetic, talkative
> girl, described by her mother as "rather a
> handful". She was, until recently, an
> only child and has been overindulged by
> her father who sees her infrequently because
> of the nature of his job. In the nursery
> Karen appears to be constantly on the move,
> flitting from activity to activity and
> rarely completing anything. She demands
> her own way in most things and this leads
> to frequent clashes with children and adults
> alike as she will often resort to tantrums
> and physical aggression if checked in any
> way. Much of her behaviour, particularly in
> group situations, is deliberately attention-
> seeking and causes considerable disruption.
> Karen has good language skills and enjoys
> playing with water and constructional toys.

The nursery class which Karen attends is a
large one with over sixty children attending at each
session. The sessions are very tightly structured
and children are expected to take up activities
offered to them at a particular time and leave off
when instructed to make way for other children.
This fairly inflexible routine ensures that each
child at some point in the week experiences all
the activities available but, of course, makes
little allowance for individual interests. Morning
and afternoon sessions are similarly planned with
some variations, depending on the availability of
T.V. programmes for example, and include several
periods when children are expected to sit fairly
passively in groups.
     For many children this organisation may be
perfectly acceptable and it enables the staff to
keep track of a large number of children and make
sure that no aspect of a carefully thought out
programme is being neglected. But for Karen the
organisation is not entirely suitable. She is,
as we have seen, a rather strong-willed little
girl and the demands made upon her by the staff to
take up a particular activity at a certain time
lead to inevitable confrontations, which not infrequently result in loss of temper on both sides.
Being an active child, Karen quickly becomes restless
and bored in the numerous 'quiet' group times, and
she has learned that shouting out and rolling around
the floor quickly attracts the attention she craves.

However, when Karen is interested in an activity she becomes completely absorbed in it and can concentrate for long periods. This too has caused problems, as when she is involved with something Karen does not always attend to requests made to her by staff and her non-compliance is often seen by them as deliberate disobedience. The whole situation is frustrating to the staff and unsuited both to Karen's temperamental and developmental needs. The chances of a tantrum being triggered off are considerably increased and her lack of conformity is acquiring for Karen a reputation of being a naughty, as well as a difficult, child.

There are probably many different solutions to this particular problem, perhaps involving more relaxed individual work building on the good language and co-ordination skills which Karen does have. These possibilities will not be gone into here, although it is interesting to speculate on how a large organisation with a number of staff can be adapted to help individual children. The point is that in this case the school experience was to a large extent being wasted, as Karen was seen as being awkward to cope with, her lack of co-operation was being partly misinterpreted and her 'label', along with the group organisation, was effectively hampering any progress she might otherwise be making. Karen's teachers had adopted certain attitudes towards her, and, unfortuantely, they were not particularly helpful to her.

Some Further Thoughts on Organisation

The role of the nursery staff is primarily to bring about many different kinds of learning in the children with whom they work. They bring professional expertise to bear on the way the room is organised and the decisions taken in it. With young children, the goals set include social and emotional aspects as well as cognitive ones (Clift et al., 1980).

i. Classroom Management

The most obvious facet of classroom management is the organisation of the available space. You should ask yourself whether the way you have arranged the furniture, the storage space, the display areas and so on encourages the kind of controlled, co-operative behaviour wished or whether it invites a lot of movement in which disruption and aggression

Special Help to the Classroom

thrive and withdrawn children are overlooked.
The next point to consider is how effectively
any help available to you in the classroom can be
used, especially N.N.E.B. personnel. Even with
only one other adult present, opportunities for
making individual contacts materialise. You have
to plan carefully to decide which of you will spend
time with children who are having difficulties and
what should be done. In this way, the children
get the attention they may be striving for and they
should also experience success and praise.
Thirdly, the attitudes of the other children
to the children in difficulties need to be considered.
How can situations be arranged so that those children
are seen in the best light by the others? If
children cannot share materials, is it realistic
to expect them to wait until last to get their turn?
How can surplus energy be absorbed while others are
completing a task? Can withdrawn children be
persuaded to play alongside other children as a
preliminary to playing with them? If the children
with special needs can appear to behave in a normal
manner, this may prevent the group from closing
its ranks against them.
Finally, instructions given should be clear
and consistent. Children need to feel they are
being treated fairly and should know what behaviour
is not acceptable. It is better to say, "No",
followed by an instruction to do something specific,
than just to tell children to stop their activity.
Too many negatives should be avoided. Try to
present children with a new activity before they
begin to mess around rather than wait for their
attention to flag and the trouble to start. Vary
the type of activities so that interest is re-
stimulated.

ii. Decisions in the Nursery Group
Decisions in the nursery group are mainly about the
nature of the individual and group programmes to be
offered to the children. As with all other children, the programmes for those with behaviour problems
need to be built around their strengths (see
Assessment Schedule 3, pp.269-276), and to take
account of their preferences while tackling their
weaknesses. Teachers and others have to be
ingenious in contriving materials and situations
which are genuinely attractive to children in
difficulties and which ensure that they will not
fail. It is probably best to set up clear objectives

beforehand which do not expect too much of them.
Decide what you feel might be accomplished in a
week, or a fortnight at the most, and then note
whether or not these objectives are achieved. Not
only do these decisions help to structure your work
and enable others to offer support, they also
simultaneously present you with a record of progress.
If a desired objective is not obtained, consider
why this has happened. Was the objective too
difficult for the children to reach (e.g. you expected them to sit still for five minutes when their
normal behaviour is that they barely sit at all)?
Was the objective irrelevant to them (e.g. you
wanted them to complete a jigsaw when they never
of their own accord choose this activity)? Did they,
in fact, achieve the objective but you missed it
(e.g. the first move of a withdrawn child may be
a tentative stretch of hand towards a toy or another
child)? Would the children obtain the objective
if you tackled it in another way? It is very easy
to assume that, because children cannot or will not
do a thing one way, they are incapable of doing it
at all.

Once the children begin to co-operate with you,
the objectives need not be so short-term. Records
should still be carefully kept so that any slowing
down in progress can be noted (see pp.29-31).

While overactive and disruptive children may
need a number of brief experiences, withdrawn
children may feel more secure if left longer on an
activity, provided they are still involved in it.
To cut down distraction, it may be as well not to
get out too much equipment at any one time and to
absorb the children's energy by getting them to
help when necessary in the organisation. Again,
the demands made on overactive, disruptive children
should not be too high and praise should be given
for co-operation. Withdrawn children are unlikely
to help in this way but care should be taken that
they always have the necessary equipment, so that
they can model the behaviour of the others if they
wish.

Too much emphasis may have been placed in the
past on free choice of activity. The teacher's
role must encompass the reasonable structuring
of the activities to be offered so that all serve
some specific purpose and the whole class gets as
much out of them as they can. Studies of nursery
school children (e.g. Thomas, 1973; Tizard et al.,
1976) have revealed that contacts with adults are
often limited and language experience negligible in

a regime where self-chosen activities predominate. It is not the choosing element which is at fault but the kind of choice offered, so that some children may spend a lot of time on large apparatus, perhaps outside the classroom altogether, while never spending any time in imaginative play or in the book corner. Offering some different activities on different days might help here as would teacher participation, so that the full benefit can be extracted from the activity. Over-structuring should, however, be avoided.

iii. Planning Programmes
When actual planning of specific programmes based on suggested approaches in this book is considered, remember:

> (a) these only apply to a small number of children in the class (as completion of the Behaviour Checklist (pp. 257-261) will reveal);
>
> (b) they need to exist on paper, not just in your head;
>
> (c) the children's progress through them has to be monitored at regular intervals and the programme adapted if necessary;
>
> (d) you must feel that any programmes you adopt are likely to work ,as nothing is gained by half-heartedly implementing something you do not believe in;
>
> (e) have your aims and objectives clearly in mind.

Opportunities to help one particular child may be difficult to find. In open-plan premises in particular, it may not be easy to control an over-active child or establish a close relationship with a withdrawn one. The main opportunities may arise from working or playing with the child in question when he or she turns to suitable activities. Individual sessions lasting 4 or 5 minutes only may be enough to begin to change behaviour.
To sum up what has been said so far. What staff have to do would seem to be to:

Special Help in the Classroom

(a) identify children in difficulty;

(b) assess the nature and extent of the difficulties;

(c) analyse the components of the skills to be acquired so that learning steps can be identified;

(d) plan appropriate programmes at the level of the children's functioning in such a way that they develop more skilled or more acceptable behaviour than shown previously;

(e) manage the group to the benefit of all those in it;

(f) observe the outcome of the programme and keep careful notes on how far it has been successful and what needs to be changed.

The best advice to give to teachers is to look for what children with behavioural problems can do or contribute and build up their strengths through praise until they form the bases from which their difficulties can be tackled.

Which Method of Helping should be Adopted?
We are anxious to avoid suggesting that there is one 'best way' of tackling children's problems. Everyone has different ways of working and children are highly individual. No one method will suit every adult and every child. By reading the following sub-sections of this chapter carefully, and chapter 6, you should be able to decide which method seems most likely to work in the case of the children you are considering. Indeed, a mixture of methods may be required and there is no reason why you should not adopt more than one approach. In this way, you can seize on a variety of opportunities to help.

REFERENCES

Clift, P., Cleave, S. and Griffin, M. (1980) The Aims, Role and Deployment of Staff in the Nursery. Windsor : N.F.E.R.

Tizard, B., Philps, J. and Plewis, I. (1976) Play
     in pre-school centres. I : Play measures and
     their relation to age, sex and IQ. Journal
     of Child Psychology and Psychiatry, 17,
     251-264.
Tizard, B., Philps, J. and Plewis,I. (1976b) Play
     in pre-school centres. II : Effects on play
     on the child's social class and the education-
     al orientation of the centre. Journal of
     Child Psychology and Psychiatry, 17, 265-274.
Thomas, V. (1973) Child's use of language in the
     nursery. Educ. Res., 15, 3, 209-216.

FURTHER READING

Hare, B.A., and Hare, J.,. (1977) Teaching Young
     Handicapped Children. New York ; Grune and
     Stratton.
Jeffree, D., McConkey, R. and Hewson, S. (1977)
     Teaching the Handicapped Child. London :
     Souvenir Press.
Webb, L. (1974) Purpose and Practice in Nursery
     Education. Oxford : Basil Blackwell.

(1) PLAY ACTIVITIES

When it comes to planning action with a particular
child you may like to consider using an approach
based wholly or partly on play activies. One of
the aims of this section is to examine the kinds
of play which have an important role in fostering
the social and emotional development of children.
Suggestions of activities for developing imaginative
and co-operative play are included because they
provide such a rich source of social learning
opportunities for children with adjustment problems.
     This section is in three parts:

     I.   General principles of using a play
          activity approach. Here we emphasise
          the importance of adult participation
          and take a broad look at some general
          principles to bear in mind when organ-
          ising play activities for children with
          behaviour difficulties.

     II. Imaginative Play. A discussion of the

value and functions of imaginative play
for children with behaviour problems,
together with practical advice for
classroom activities.

III. Social Play. Activities for encouraging
      co-operation between children.

Most nursery staff are used to structuring play
activities to suit the developmental level of their
group and find the play approach attractive because
it is so familiar. However, it is worth considering
using some play activities in conjunction with some
of the approaches outlined in other sections.

I. General Principles of Using a Play Activity
Approach
It has always been emphasised in early education that
play should be initiated by the children themselves;
they choose what to play and how to play. They
should be free from adult restraints and demands and
be able to experiment in play without risk of failure.
The sulky child forced to 'play' a game of picture
lotto by an adult is not really playing.   It has
also long been assumed that 'play is the work of
the child'.   Thus, through play the child is able
to practise old skills and develop new ones. By
providing children with stimulating toys and surroundings it was believed that they would instinct-
ively know how to play and, by playing, foster their
social and intellectual development.   Accordingly,
many teachers have been loath to 'interfere' in the
play of young children (recent research has shown
as little as 2% of the nursery teacher's time to be
spent actually playing with children), believing
that the opportunity to play is sufficient in itself
to encourage learning and emotional growth. However,
the results of studies in which children's behaviour
during play was observed have raised doubts about
the ability of all children to derive benefit from
purely self-initiated play.   For example, it has
been shown that socially disadvantaged pre-school
children do not demonstrate a range of imaginative
play nor do they participate in the variety of
activities that advantaged children do. Another
study demonstrated that working class children in
pre-school centres chose to spend 75% of their time
outdoors, thus failing to make use of the abundant
constructional, creative and fantasy material
provided for them inside.   It seems that left to

their own devices,with no adult participation,
guidance or interest, some children are either
unable or unwilling to use their opportunities for
play to their best advantage. If children are going
to develop intellectually, imaginatively or socially
through play they need the stimulus of a friendly
adult, not just as a provider of suitable materials,
but as an active participant, otherwise their play
may remain at a very low level and lack any kind of
progression.

Play and Difficult Behaviour

Children experiencing social or emotional difficulties are often the ones least able to help themselves
through play. Hyperactive children,for example,
are not going to benefit from their play experiences
if they do not stay in one place long enough to
explore the possibilities of the toys and materials
set out for their use.

> <u>William</u> is just such a child and is described
> by his teacher as being "like a wasp in a
> jam factory". He is boisterous and nearly
> always on the move, flitting from activity
> and rarely making use of the materials in an
> appropriate way. He can be destructive
> and is very wearing to both adults and
> children alike, as he disrupts group play
> continuously. Watching William is an
> exhausing activity in itself as an average
> two minutes taken from his teacher's notes
> will demonstrate. "William pushes his way
> into the house corner where he bangs the
> saucepans and kettle and throws them down.
> He runs off to the dressing up corner, grabs
> a cape and runs to an assistant to help
> him to put it on. He gallops around the
> nursery shouting 'Batman' and, as he passes
> an open cupboard,takes a swipe at the tins
> of powder paint. William runs into the
> cloakroom and jumps up and down on the wall
> bench. After being brought back into the
> playroom he returns to the house corner
> and pulls a doll's cot away from a child
> and jumps about in it!"

William comes from a materially very poor background and it could be that his behaviour is an
understandable over-reaction to what must seem to
him an overwhelming array of toys and activities.

His 'flitting' and disruptiveness are actually being exacerbated by his having free choice of such a wide range of toys.
    Similarly withdrawn or highly dependent children may not know <u>how</u> to play with other children and if they remain totally overwhelmed by large numbers of boisterous, active youngsters, will have a reduced chance of developing socially.

    <u>Richard</u> is an only child who is over-protected by his mother. Despite the fact that he is a well-developed and sturdy four-year-old he is sometimes brought to the nursery group in a pushchair, or is carried part of the way. At home he plays mainly on his own indoors and even though there are children of his age who live nearby his mother does not encourage him to mix. In the nursery group, Richard is rarely seen to speak or to play with another child. He has one or two favoured activities, such as sand and water play, but will only choose to play with them if there are no other children present. His teacher has never seen him join in any imaginative play activities, in the house corner for example, and has noticed that when other children try to join him in an activity he will often walk away.

    Obviously Richard has had little experience of other children and does not have the necessary social skills to either start or join in a game with any success. Without some guidance Richard's social development is going to remain at a very low level and his isolation may become self-perpetuating.
    Observations of children at play, carried out by Margaret Manning in Edinburgh (1978), have revealed that aggressive children indulge in friendly co-operative games rather infrequently. They are not often found playing bus drivers, shop keepers, doctors or any of the variations of Wendy House games of mummy and daddy, visiting, cleaning, cooking and so on. It should not be assumed, however, that aggressive children would not like to play such games and would not find them rewarding, as can be demonstrated by the following example of Manning's:

    <u>Alec</u> was charging in and out of the Wendy House, where he upset pots and pans, threw dolls around and disrupted the game that

was taking place. Surprisingly he eagerly
accepted the suggestion of the teacher
that he should play a game of mummies and
daddies with the girl who was 'at home'
and went inside saying, 'I'll be daddy'.
Unfortunately, the teacher then went off
to another part of the nursery leaving
the two children alone in the Wendy House.
There they sat for several minutes not
saying a word to one another and totally
unable to get the game going on their own.
Yet, Alec still wanted to play because
when the girl later 'went for a walk' with
two of her friends he followed them and
tried to join in, but without success.

Aggressive, disruptive children like Alec
often lack the necessary ability for initiating and
maintaining friendly domestic games, so that it may
be necessary for nursery staff to actually teach
such children how to play games like these. Staff
should not just suggest games but should take part
in them and actively keep them going when they are
in danger of foundering through lack of inventiveness or expertise on the children's part. How
different things might have been for Alec if his
teacher had stayed and involved herself in the game
she had suggested. Not only could she have set
the game in motion, but by staying for a while she
could have ensured that it did not peter out, either
by suggesting a story line or taking on a role
herself.

Play and Adult Participation

Some nursery staff have been reluctant to join in
chidren's play, arguing that as soon as an adult
participates the whole pattern of play changes;
the children feel dominated by the adult's presence
and either continually look to her for guidance or
withdraw entirely. This is an understandable
viewpoint, as the line between participation and
interference is finely drawn. However, it is
possible for adults to share in play without either
directing or dominating. Careful observation
and a knowledge of the individual children concerned
will enable you to judge when to become involved
and when to withdraw. The extent of your participation will be different with different children.
With a shy, retiring child, like Richard for instance,
you could play alongside him, making your own model

or sandcastle. In this way you are presenting
the child with several opportunities : he can carry
on playing whilst absorbing what you are doing; he
can imitate you; he can adapt your play and
incorporate it into his own, either then or later;
or he can share in your play or ask you to join in
his. Most importantly, by playing alongside the
child you show him that you value and enjoy sharing
his play and this could be an important step in
establishing a relationship with him.

In contrast, your involvement with highly
active children may be of a different kind altogether.
You may find you need to employ some of the techniques discussed in the section on Behaviour
Modification in order to get the children to sit
down and pay attention to toys, games or activities
for increasingly longer periods. Initially, they
will find these activities rewarding only if you
stay and play with them and praise them for their
efforts.

Whatever the children's difficulties, it is
important not to be discouraged if they appear to
ignore your presence or to reject your ideas and
suggestions. If you have not regularly joined
in children's play, it will take a while for them
to accept you in this new role and establish a
confident relationship with you as a partner in
their activities. Once accepted as a participant,
rather than as an onlooker or provider of materials,
you will be in an ideal position to initiate play,
help its development by your suggestions and maintain it through your continuing interest. More-
over, by involving yourself in play you are modifying
the picture some children may have of you as a
controlling and sometimes disapproving person. This
may be particularly true in the case of aggressive
or overactive children, who, because of their
behaviour, often attract a great deal of negative
attention from adults in the form of reprimands or
punishments. It is, therefore, important that
children with difficulties are not left to 'drift'
either because the nursery group is committed to a
'free play' philosophy or in the fond hope that they
will eventually settle in. Nor, on the other hand,
should they be coerced into play activities that
they are not ready for or find too stressful.
(Individual play activities will be discussed later.)

Using Play Activities with Children with Behaviour Difficulties.

The structuring of play activities to aid developmental progression is nothing new and has long been recognised as good nursery practice, but using play, games and toys as a focused way to help children with behaviour or emotional problems requires a slightly different way of looking at things.

As part of the assessment stage you should already have gathered a great deal of information about a particular child or children whose behaviour is causing concern. Some of this will have involved observing children at play and your notes should, therefore, give you some indication of the kind of toys they find interesting and also the complexity of their play - is it at a very basic level or are they inventive and imaginative in their use of toys? This initial observation is important, so that if you do decide to use play techniques you do not choose activities which will either be too difficult or will fail to hold the children's interest. At first you should aim for activities that are well within the children's capabilities so that they are guaranteed the satisfaction of success. Gruadually, you can make the activities more demanding, so that as well as helping to remediate problem behaviour, the play will aid the children's development in other areas too.

Before going on to describe specific play activities in detail it will be useful first to look at some of the general principles you should bear in mind when attempting to help a child with difficulties. Although we will discuss these principles for the four broad categories of behaviour we introduced in earlier chapters, it should be stressed again that the children you are working with may not fit neatly into these pigeon-holes. Children often display a mixture of several kinds of behaviour, but you are in the best position to decide which sorts of behaviour are being the biggest hindrance to the child and you will need to plan your action accordingly.

Aggressive, Anti-social, Destructive Children

Eric (aged 4) is an aggressive, anti-social, disobedient and demanding child. He is often rude and abusive when thwarted or frustrated, and has frequent temper tantrums.

He hits other children and finds it impossible to share toys, often over-reacting violently if his demands are not met. Although he likes to be the centre of attention, he shuns the physical contact offered by adults. He has good language and self-help skills and is an active child with good co-ordination.

Having a child like Eric in your group poses immediate problems, for you cannot allow his largely unprovoked aggression against other children to go unchecked. Inevitably when young children play together some conflicts and disagreements are to be expected, but if force becomes an established method of getting their own way, children like Eric risk social isolation, as other children will fear them and avoid their company. Eric needs to learn very quickly that kicking, hitting and biting are not acceptable behaviour and this is best achieved by removing him immediately from any such situation. This should be done in a matter of fact way, with the minimum of fuss and without accompanying comments such as "naughty boy" (see section on Behaviour Modification on "sit and watch"). It is not feasible or desirable to ban children like Eric from playing with other children as they need to learn from contact with others that there are effective, alternative methods of getting along which do not involve force. Until he has gained some measure of self-control Eric will need to have a much more structured day, with less free time than other children.

1. At first Eric should always be included as a member of a small supervised playgroup, where with guidance from a friendly adult he can begin to learn other ways of relating to his peers and can be immediately praised for any amicable behaviour. By keeping him constantly busy and in range of an adult, the number of opportunities he has for exhibiting his hostility are considerably reduced.

2. He should not be included in activities that ask too much of him too soon and which will lead to frustration or encourage destructive behaviour, e.g. group play with blocks or games involving long waits between turns.

3. He needs plenty of opportunity to
   let off steam in an acceptable way,
   e.g. large floor cushions are good
   for vigorous but safe bouncing.
4. Situations which have led to difficulties in the past should be
   avoided or better still altered in
   such a way as to defuse their potential
   for disagreements. For instance,
   if squabbles have occurred on several
   occasions because there are only two
   spades in the sand tray, the obvious
   solution is to provide enough spades
   for all the children who play there
   at any one time. This is easily
   done if the equipment involved is
   cheap and readily obtainable, but
   poses problems if the object in
   question is an expensive item such
   as a tricycle. However, the promise
   of five minutes uninterrupted play
   on the tricycle is a reward worth
   considering for good behaviour.
   Alternatively, the person on outside
   duty could arrange a rota of all those
   wishing to ride the coveted bike,
   perhaps using a cooking 'pinger'
   to time rides and signal when time
   is up.
5. In large groups, such as story time,
   he should be kept as near to the
   teacher as possible so that he can have
   an unobstructed view of what is going
   on and is less likely to hit another
   child for getting in his way.
6. Other adults must be kept fully in
   the picture about the strategies of
   management which are adopted with an
   aggressive child. It is important
   that all concerned are in agreement
   about how the child should be handled
   and stick to any decisions taken, as
   maintaining a consistent approach is
   a prerequisite for success.
7. Children such as Eric can be very
   upsetting, but it is important that
   adults around him do not resort to
   smacking him as he needs to learn
   that physical force is not the best
   way of handling things.

8. In the early stages aggressive children
   in a group should be given first 'go'
   at any activity they are involved in,
   whether it is stirring cake mixture or
   a game of lotto. Of course, they
   have to learn to delay gratification,
   to take their turn and wait patiently,
   but this should be a gradual process
   (see Section on Behaviour Modification).

Destructive Children

Usually a distinction is made between aggression and
destructiveness: an aggressive child generally
attacks other children without provocation whereas
a destructive child tends to break up equipment
and playthings. At an earlier developmental stage
children enjoy pushing over towers of bricks or
flattening sandcastles but normally they move on
quickly from this stage and building up takes
precedence over knocking down. The play of truly
destructive children consists almost entirely in
the pleasure of dismantling or destroying toys.
Why does this happen? It may be that from their
point of view they have exhausted the play possibilities of a particular game or toy. If they
are encouraged to explore other aspects of a toy
or given more challenging activities, the destructiveness may cease. At the other extreme,
frustration sometimes causes children to destroy
toys that are too difficult for them in much the
same way that older children (and adults!) may
upset a games board when they are losing. Yet
another possibility is that children who have been
reprimanded by the teacher or turned out of a game
may nurse resentment and vent their feelings,
not by directly attacking those responsible, but by
destroying constructions or hurling toys about.
You should guard against confusing destructiveness
with mere clumsiness as children are often unaware
of the need for care when handling fragile objects
and may not have attained the fine motor co-
ordination necessary to examine things without
breaking them. Curiosity and a wish to explore
the inner workings of things may also lead children to dismantle objects which as yet they are not
capable of putting back together again. This is
where your close observations of the circumstances
in which children show their destructiveness should
give you some indication of where the problem lies
and how you can best help.

Destructiveness brought about by frustration or boredom is most readily helped by ensuring that the child is guided towards games and toys that are of the right developmental level. For example, it is easy to see why a child who cannot complete a simple formboard has difficulty with a twenty-piece jigsaw and resorts to hammering the pieces together out of sheer frustration. An observant adult would encourage such children to try puzzles with which they would have a chance of success.

For children who enjoy dismantling objects, there are many take apart toys on the market, ranging from simple graded peg and ring people (Brio) to quite complicated trains and lorries connected by easily removable nuts and bolts. Diverting their interest into toys that can be legitimately taken apart may reduce the frequency of disasters occurring with more precious items.

Experience of handling animals, such as guinea pigs or rabbits (gerbils and hamsters are really too small and quick for nursery age children) can be valuable in demonstrating to clumsy children the need for care and a gentle touch.

Dealing with children who use destructiveness as a means of 'retaliation', either against their peers or you, can be difficult. A further reprimand or attempts to control the behaviour may lead to another bout of destructiveness elsewhere in the nursery. Trying to make children clear up the mess they have made or to apologise may be met with defiance. The more you demand, the more adamant a child may become and a situation is quickly reached where neither party can back down without loss of face. Solutions, such as diverting the child's aggression into more acceptable channels (e.g. hammering at the woodwork table) may work in the short term, but will probably have little lasting effect. It is more than likely that, when faced with a similar situation in the future, the child will again resort to destructive behaviour. Rather than discouraging or diverting the retaliatory destruction, your attempts to help would be better directed towards breaking the behavioural deadlocks these children find themselves in over and over again. Activities described in the section "Problem-Solving Approaches" might effect a lasting behaviour change than would benefit both the children and yourself. This section describes methods aimed at improving the child's social relationships with others, both nursery staff and children, thereby reducing the need for the child to indulge in destructive out-

bursts. Alternatively, you may like to consider
some of the play activities described later in this
section, which emphasise the quieter co-operative
aspects of pretend play and which may be applied
equally well to aggressive and withdrawn children
as well as those causing problems because of their
destructiveness.

Restless, Overactive Children

Earlier in this section we described <u>William</u>, a
highly overactive child, who was never still for a
moment and who needed constant adult attention if
he was not to cause chaos in his nursery group.

> <u>Nicola</u> (aged 4) has many characteristics
> in common with William although her rest-
> lessness is not nearly so extreme. She is
> nearly always on the go, rarely completing
> an activity before moving on to something
> else. Nicola comes from a caring home
> and although she is clean and tidy on
> arrival this rarely lasts long as she
> seems to attract mess of all kinds and is
> soon liberally spattered in paint, milk,
> clay etc. By the end of the session she
> is often without coat, cardigan, hair
> ribbons, shoes and socks as they have been
> taken off and dropped in whichever area
> she was passing through at the time. She
> tends to favour outdoor play, possibly
> because of the greater freedom of move-
> ment it allows her and does not show more
> than a fleeting interest in table-top
> activities.

Children such as Nicola and William have been
rather aptly described as being "all beginnings and
no endings". In William's case the multitude of
toys and activities available in the nursery group
actually worsened his behaviour and the 'flitting'
from one thing to another seemed to be related to
the number of new activities with which he had
suddenly been presented. Nicola, on the other
hand, if left to her own devices would spend a large
proportion of her time outdoors, racing around,
failing to take advantage of the other amenities.
Neither child is going to attain the habits of
concentration and attention so vital to later
learning if they never come to realise that quieter
activities, such as jigsaws, drawing, constructional

toys etc., can be rewarding too. What can be done
to help overactive children like this?

1. To begin with they need several short play
   sessions during which they have the
   exclusive attention of an adult, who will
   immediately praise every sign of co-operation and attention, however fleeting these
   may be at first. It is a mistake to
   attempt too much too soon and the children should be allowed to move off after
   a short period to do something else.
   Gradually, over a period of weeks, the
   demands upon their concentration can be
   increased, but they should be encouraged
   to achieve and value results even if
   initially this only means completing a
   simple inset tray.

2. Ideally, all distractions should be
   deliberately reduced in these sessions,
   either by using a screened-off corner
   or a table facing a wall with nothing in
   view but the toy or activity in hand.

3. What may be needed to hold the attention
   of a distractible child is a toy that
   gives big results for little effort,
   such as jack-in-the-box or pop-up cone
   tree. Since these children are also
   attracted by novelty another way of
   gaining their co-operation in the first
   place may be by providing a toy or game
   not normally available in the nursery
   group. Provided that presentation is
   carefully thought out and repeated
   attempts are made with toys and activities
   of the right developmental level, the child
   should begin to take part in longer and
   longer play sequences.

Shy/Withdrawn Children

It is all too easy to overlook shy withdrawn children such as Richard in the bustle of a nursery
session, as they do not make the same demands upon
your attention as an aggressive or restless child
does. If, after a suitable settling-in period,
a child you have been observing remains isolated
from others, then you should intervene as the child
needs help in overcoming these fears before the
withdrawal becomes self-perpetuating. Your attempts
to integrate a shy child more fully into nursery

life will have to be carefully timed and structured very gradually, beginning with activities in pairs perhaps before any involvement in larger groups.

1. From your observations try to gauge whether the child has shown any interest in a particular toy or activity that will serve as a useful starting point. You may find the child is hovering near a favoured activity, and a wistful expression or a glancing eye movement may indicate that you are on the right track.

2. In the beginning you may have difficulty in getting any response but do not try to force the child's involvement with you as this may make the situation worse. If a child shrinks from physical contact, stares blankly into space when spoken to, or refuses to take an outstretched hand, persist quietly and gently with your efforts until you get some response, however small, that you can praise. Your first attempts may not be highly success-ful but do not withdraw in frustration as this will only reinforce the child's isolation and make it more difficult to establish contact when you next try.

3. Face-to-face confrontations can be very threatening for shy children, and so it may be better to place yourself beside them and avoid staring directly at them when you speak. Puppets, either the usual glove variety or a hand-and-arm puppet like Emu, can be useful props. Children may respond to a puppet, perhaps only waving to it or shaking its hand at first, even though they will not communicate directly with you. If you use a puppet be sure you give children a chance to respond by leaving some gaps in the con-versation. They may not be talking only because they cannot get a word in edgeways.

4. Try to encourage the child in turn-taking activities as it is sometimes easier to produce a physical response rather than a spoken one. You could, for example, take it in turns to:

(a) blow bubbles for bursting;

(b) roll marbles down a run;

   (c) build towers of bricks and knock
       them down;

   (d) keep a water wheel turning by
       pouring water.

   You can devise many more reciprocal games
   of this kind using the toys you have
   available.
5. Look critically at the layout of your room
   and the kind of materials and activities
   you provide to see if they can be modified
   to increase the likelihood of co-operation
   and social play occurring between children.
   For example, you could put out floor
   jigsaws for groups of children to complete,
   or provide very large sheets of paper for
   group painting or collage sessions. Try
   letting several children make one large
   junk model on the floor rather than
   individual ones at a table. With a little
   thought and ingenuity you can easily con-
   trive more situations to foster social play
   amongst children in your group.

Immature/Dependent Children
Anxiety and a certain amount of 'clinging' behaviour
are to be expected when young children are left
by their mothers for the first time. Sometimes,
however, the problem continues and you may find you
are being followed around by a child who has the
persistence of a terrier.

   Jonathan (aged 3½) is a small, sickly-looking
   child. His allround development was at such
   low level that the health visitor arranged
   for an educational home visitor to provide
   tuition and stimulation prior to his enrolment
   in the nursery. On arrival he cries and
   frequently clings to an adult for assurance.
   He cannot attend to his own needs and his
   inability to communicate adequately makes
   it difficult for other children to include
   him in their activities. On some days he
   wanders aimlessly around the room, oblivious
   to all that is happening around him, and is
   unresponsive to commands and questions.

   To lessen dependent children's reliance upon you
and promote their self-confidence and initiative

requires similar tactics to those employed with shy
children.

1. Try to include dependent children in small
   groups of children younger than themselves,
   preferably involved in a messy activity
   which requires two hands (such as clay,
   water, or sand) making it easier for you
   to slip away.
2. Often such children are physically timid
   and possibly clumsy, having had restricted
   opportunities to indulge in the normal
   childhood pursuits of climbing, swinging
   or rough and tumble play. Increasing
   physical confidence may have a beneficial
   effect that spills over into other areas
   of a child's functioning. You could
   begin by encouraging the child to jump
   off the lowest part of the climbing frame,
   to run about with you outside: to push
   the swing etc. Gradually increase your
   demands, encouraging more daring feats,
   such as jumping down from a higher part of
   the climbing frame, and at the same time
   reducing the amount of help you give so
   that eventually they will manage independently.
3. Sometimes dependent children are lacking
   in self-help skills, perhaps because
   everything in the way of dressing and washing has been done for them by over-
   solicitous parents. Task analysis
   (pp.163-174) is a good way of teaching
   children to manage these important skills
   for themselves, thereby lessening their
   dependence on you. Another alternative
   you could consider is making a big rag doll,
   with removable clothes, which incorporates
   all the common fastenings (e.g. press
   studs, zips, laces, buttons, hooks and
   eyes etc.) for the child to practise on.

In the following pages we are going to examine
in some detail the kinds of play which have an
important role in fostering the social and emotional
development of children. The emphasis is placed
largely upon ways of encouraging imaginative and
social play because these provide such a rich source
of social learning opportunities for children
experiencing difficulties with their behaviour. For
the sake of clarity, imaginative and co-operative
play will be discussed separately, although the

distinction is rather artificial as there is
obviously a great deal of overlap between these
categories and also with other areas of play.

II. Imaginative Play

All nursery staff are aware of the value and functions
of imaginative play in early childhood but it is
worthwhile to look at the way such play can help
children with behaviour difficulties.

1. Imaginative Play Helps to Promote Thought and Language.

Communicating with shy children, such as Richard,
can be a problem, as they will often not respond to
direct approaches made by adults or children. Using
puppets, however, can be a useful ploy in getting
withdrawn children to talk as most children are
fascinated by puppets and will chatter quite happily
to them.

   Because imaginative play is based on plots and
themes, it requires the unfolding of longer sequences
of activity than other sorts of play and helps
children to develop the ability to organise and plan
ahead. This aspect of imaginative play has particular relevance for overactive children, like Nicola
and William, who engage in continuing restless
behaviour, requiring little or no reflective thought.
Recent research has shown that helping and encouraging overactive children to take part in domestic
and fantasy play increases their concentration and
reduces their restlessness. In marked contrast
to the kind of rough and tumble play they previously
favoured, they become absorbed for longer periods
in make-believe play and are able to resist distractions and interruptions from their immediate
surroundings. This proved to be the case with
Nicola, whose teacher involved her in regular role-
playing games over a period of several weeks. Every
afternoon Nicola joined a group of about six children
in the 'quiet area' and for ten minutes they were
led by an adult in a variety of imaginative games.
These included acting out small scenes from everyday life, such as a trip to the shops in town or a
day at the sea-side, as well as more adventurous
themes involving Red Indians or jungle animals.
Nicola greatly enjoyed these sessions and joined in
with gusto. Although she still favoured outside
activities, she was beginning to play for longer
periods in the Home Corner and was most attentive
during story time, where previously she had been

very disruptive.

2. Imaginative Play Helps Children to Understand Others.

By adopting roles in imaginative play, children learn to put themselves in another's place and they get some idea of what it feels like to 'be' mummy, daddy or baby. Through such experiences they gain understanding of the role in question and its attendant responsibilities as well as of the re-lationships of people to each other. They are also acquiring skill in looking at situations from different points of view, for sometimes they are the 'baddies' and sometimes the 'goodies'. It is possible that children who have learned to see the other child's point of view through make-believe are less likely to be physically aggressive or vicious in their behaviour. Another of the hidden assets emerging from these games, and which is linked to role play, is the increase in sharing and taking turns which you will find. This is not an easy skill for a small child to learn and aggressive children often fail to master it.

Role play also offers the withdrawn child the opportunity of trying out a new, more assertive role (perhaps that of 'Batman' or 'teacher' for example) within the safety of the Wendy House or den. Domineering, aggressive children also learn to accommodate to the demands of the game and to the ebb and flow of the mood of a small group, for with-out some co-operation the game cannot continue.

3. Imaginative Play Offers the Chance of Practising New Skills

By imitating adults and adopting their roles, child-ren can practise skills they will need later on. These can be of a practical nature such as dressing, washing and cleaning etc.and, perhaps more import-antly, also social skills such as holding a convers-ation, sharing, concern for others, leadership and co-operation. Often, children with behaviour problems are totally lacking in some of these basic skills, the aggressive child like Eric using force to get his own way or the shy child, such as Richard, being unable to start and continue a con-versation. Through imaginative play children can learn from adults and children alternative and more appropriate ways of responding.

4. Imaginative Play Helps Children Come to Terms with their Anxieties

During play children are free to act out, at their own pace, situations which may have worried or disturbed them, thereby lessening their potential for upsetting them on subsequent occasions. Make-believe can act as a safety valve for children as they can play out in an acceptable way some of the violent impulses they may feel. Children can be angry towards their dolls or imaginary characters, and screaming or hitting can all be part of the game without any harm being done, as no real people are involved.

Unobtrusive observation of this kind may furnish you with insight into the problems of home or school that are worrying children and which may have some bearing on their current behaviour. Take for instance the case of a child who is feeling very jealous of a new baby in the family. You may notice games in the nursery in which imaginary crying babies or dolls are always scolded or spanked or suffer dreadful punishments. Not only does this suggest that the child wants more attention but it opens the way for introducing more pretend play that will help the child to cope with the role of big brother or sister. Play that offers the child possible ways of sharing in looking after the baby will help in regaining lost self-esteem and in handling the understandable annoyance at the new-comer more constructively.

The Role of the Adult in Encouraging Make-believe Play

Observation. Watching children playing make-believe games is an art in itself, as you have to take care to be unobtrusive and blend into the background. For nursery staff it can be an especially difficult task, as with many children and a high noise level, it is hard to keep track of a particular child, especially when there may be many other demands upon your time and attention. It is, however, a very valuable exercise to set aside five or ten minutes to watch children weaving through the group in free play.

There are several points you should look out for and make note of:

1. does the child you are watching eagerly

join in imaginative play or instead hang about at the edge of the group looking on but not participating?

2. does the child initiate make-believe games or latch on to an established group?
3. does the child always insist on the dominant role, or can a minor role be accepted if insisted upon by playmates?
4. does the child offer to swop roles with other children, taking turns to be the leading light?
5. does the child find a corner and develop solitary play situations?
6. does the child spend most of the time in wild, chasing games of soldiers, Star Wars, Batman etc., with little story line or development?

At this stage it is probably best not to try to introduce a solitary child into a group or to interfere when a rumbustious child is seemingly spoiling the game for others. When you have observed for a while you will quickly begin to pick up play themes, recurring speech patterns, signs of fear or hesitancy and the level of plot complexity. Then you will be in a better position to intervene usefully by offering help and alternative game suggestions.

Set out in Table 5.1 is a simplified guide to the stages of imaginative play, which may be of help when observing children. It should be stressed that imaginative play develops gradually and does not suddenly jump from one stage to the next. You may find when observing children that they incorporate elements from several stages, but with practice you will be able to judge at which level the majority of play takes place.

Table 5.1   Stages of Imaginative Play

First level	Pushes car along (no other actions associated with driving a car). Pretends to feed self, to be asleep, to get washed etc.

Second Level	Imitates a single action, e.g. dusting; ironing; steering; digging. Simple pretend play, e.g. puts doll to bed (maybe upside down), uses box as car.
Third Level	Sequences pretend play - prolonged make-believe involving several 'events' in order, e.g. feeds doll, undresses it, washes doll, puts it to bed. Involved in make-believe play with imaginary characters and imaginary objects, e.g. can pretend to drink from imaginary cup or drive an imaginary car.
Fourth Level	Dresses up and adopts a role, e.g. bridge, doctor, policeman. Uses 'play' voice and appropriate actions. Play is on a particular theme, involves several children and could extend over a period of days.

Participation. The child's world of make-believe is often viewed as a 'secret domain' which should be free from adult participation or interference. It is often said that adult involvement alters the situation, inhibiting rather than promoting children's imagination. Despite the fact that there is a great deal to be said for children being free to develop play as their own imagination dictates, this opportunity on its own may be insufficient for children with behaviour problems. As mentioned earlier, some children are unable to sustain imaginative sequences, particularly those of the quiet, domestic variety, either because they quickly run out of ideas or because they lack the social skills necessary for maintaining a co-operative activity. This may be because these childre have not been encouraged in make-believe before joining the nursery group; perhaps their parents may not have realised the value of such play or may not have had the time to encourage it. Some children have not had the opportunity to watch older brothers and sisters playing and, therefore, have lacked a model to copy. Your participation in the play situation may enable you to introduce elements of imaginative play which may be missing and act as a model that can subsequently be copied.

Planning Activities to Stimulate Imaginative Play. From your observations you should have discovered whether or not the children you have been watching are making the most of their play opportunities. You may find, for instance, that the withdrawn child indulges only in solitary make-believe or that the imaginative play of a hyperactive child, like William, consists almost entirely of running around in a cape shouting, "Batman!" If on the basis of your observations you decide to intervene, you will need to plan carefully in advance what you hope to achieve and how this can best be done within the framework of your particular group. Some suggestions will be offered as to how you can incorporate these activities into your normal routine, but there can be no hard and fast rules about this, as nursery groups will differ in both organisation and in the number of adults available. Many of the activities suggested will be familiar to you and you may feel that you are already doing most of them, but it is intended that you should use them in a much more structured and systematic way than is usually the case, focussing on the deficiencies or difficulties children may be facing in their play.

Group Size and Composition. Most of the activities are designed for small groups of five or six children working with an adult for 20-30 minutes per session. In a group of this size there are sufficient children to ensure plenty of interaction but not so many that some children never get a chance to participate. This number should not be too overwhelming for quieter children and allows them the chance to remain on the periphery of the action without causing undue concern, as even if they do not become involved they may be absorbing a great deal and this will be reflected in later play.

Richard is an example of a little boy who perfectly illustrates this point. He was, as you may remember, a shy child who chose mainly solitary activities and had rarely been observed to speak to or play with another child. For several weeks his

teacher included him in a small group of
four year olds who met for twenty minutes
each day and took part in a variety of
role playing games and activities. Richard
did not join in at all but sat unspeaking
and watched the games intently. During
all this time his teacher continued to
observe Richard in free play sessions and
found that a remarkable change was taking
place. He was becoming much more outward going, to the extent that one member
of staff had to reprimand him for being
giddy and noisy. He began to challenge
other boys for the use of the nursery's
only bicycle and was seen in the playground
taking charge of a small group of children,
leading them around in a line chanting
and singing a song. For the first time
he joined in playing imaginative games
with other children in the domestic corner
and was overhead making up a story whilst
playing with the doll's house.

This example shows that even shy children have
the capacity for make-believe but may need some form
of encouragement or model to follow before they can
easily become involved. Richard not only found
himself playmates but was trying out new words and
increasing his vocabulary, as well as becoming more
assertive and self-confident.
    Try to ensure that all the children in the group
are at about the same level of play and do not
include very young children who may not be ready for
group play and may be disruptive as a consequence.
Similarly, gathering together in one group all the
children you consider to be having difficulties
could be a recipe for disaster. You will have to
use your judgement and try out various combinations
of children until you achieve fairly balanced
groupings.

Suitable settings. Ideally, the activities should
take place in a quiet area screened off from the
main body of the room. Some nursery groups have
separate story or quiet rooms which could be used;
otherwise you could improvise by re-arranging large
items of furniture to create a private space free
from distractions. This is especially important
for overactive children, whose concentration may be
easily lost if they can see interesting activities

elsewhere in the room.

Organisation. Some nursery groups may be lucky
enough to have a high ratio of adults to children
so that it is relatively easy for one adult to work
undisturbed with a small group for part of the
session. If you are working with only one other
person, small group work can pose problems. However, if all the children come together for story
time or singing then this could be your opportunity
to take your group off elsewhere for twenty
minutes or so, leaving the other adult in charge
of the remainder. You could also consider, if you
do not do so already, inviting mothers as helpers
to either the morning or afternoon sessions. If
they come in on a regular basis then you can use
the times when there are extra adults around to
work with your groups.

Again, some nursery groups have a rota system
whereby every adult is responsible for particular
activities in different areas of the nursery each
week (e.g. outside play, messy activities such as
sand, water, clay or a collage and model building
area). Perhaps in this case, one adult could
oversee two adjacent areas, freeing someone else
to take over the play sessions with a small group.
Adding the play sessions to the weekly rota would
also give each adult a chance to plan activities
for the week ahead rather than it being the responsibility of one person. This system has the added
advantage that all the personnel would be involved
at some stage and would be fully aware of the
problems and progress of individual children.

In nursery groups where each adult is responsible
for a particular group of children with whom she
is expected to complete some daily activity, then it
should not be difficult to introduce group play
sessions at these regular 'get togethers', providing,
of course, that the numbers in the groups are not
too large.

Suggested Activities for Imaginative Play Sessions
Overleaf is a list of activities for you to try
out in your play sessions. Although by no means
comprehensive, the list of games will act as a
starting point and, no doubt, as you progress they
will be transformed and elaborated upon by the
children taking part.

1. <u>Developing Awareness of Feelings</u>
One of the difficult skills that children must learn
as they grow up involves understanding the messages
people send to each other without words. Facial
expressions, body positions and gestures all convey
messages about the way people feel. Children
discover these clues to others' emotions slowly
and learning what facial expressions signal is
perhaps the easiest part of the process to begin
with. You can help children develop sensitivity
to another's feelings by increasing their awareness
of the facial and bodily expressions of those around
them through games and activities. Poorly adjusted
children may not be aware of the effect of their
behaviour on others, and games which increase their
awareness of other children's feelings will aid
their emotional and social development.

<u>Faces Game</u>. For this game you will need a large
mirror, pictures cut out of magazines showing
different facial expressions and stories illustrating some of the different moods children experience
(see booklist at end of section). The idea is to
demonstrate different moods to children through
your own facial expression and have them guess
what you are feeling. You could show happiness,
sadness, anger, surprise or disgust, talking about
each of them as you go along. See if the children
can pick out examples of each type of face from
the pictures you have collected. Let them imitate
your expressions and watch themselves in the mirror
as they do so. Ask questions and give examples of
the different faces people use on different occasions,
e.g. "What kind of face do you have when its
raining and you cannot go out to play? Show me a
'sad face'" or "Ooh, some of your dinner fell off the
plate and made a mess on your dress! Show me
a 'disgusted face'. Now clean it all up and show
me a 'happy face'". Once you have led the way the
children may make up their own stories and suggest
the faces to go with them. Read stories that
demonstrate different emotions and ask the children
to show you how the characters felt (e.g. how did
Baby Bear feel when he came home and found his
chair broken? Show me a sad face).
By watching you pretend you are sad or happy
or angry, and by imitating your facial expression
and looking at their own in the mirror, children
will begin to learn to identify the expressions of
others around.

2. Role-Playing Games

The idea of these games is to encourage children to try out a variety of roles and thus extend the repertoire available to them in make-believe play. Being able to adopt appropriate roles in pretend play opens the door to additional ways of making contact with other children and of learning further roles along the way. A child who quickly grasps what is involved in a game of 'spacemen' or 'school' is able to move smoothly into a small group and be accepted into the game, unlike the little boy, Alec, who wanted to be 'daddy' but did not know how to go about it.

(a) Who am I?

In this game you mime the activity of someone at work for the children to guess. Keep the mimes simple at first and ensure they are concerned with a familiar person or event, e.g. a policeman controlling traffic, a bus conductor, a road mender, a milkman, a postman. The child who guesses correctly mimes the next person for the group to guess. Initially you may have to offer suggestions and even the mime, encouraging the child to copy your actions.

(b) What am I doing?

This is a similar game but this time you mime an action the children will be familiar with from everyday activities for them to guess. The child who guesses correctly mimes the next action, e.g. eating, washing up, driving a car, knitting, sewing etc.

(c) Bag of Hats

Children seem attracted to hats of all kinds and often will happily assume a new identity with the addition of the correct headgear for the occasion. Collect as many hats as you can, e.g. for a nurse, king or queen, fireman, policemen, cowboy, sailor, soldier, a bride, a bridesmaid, a spacemen, a motor cyclist, a witch or wizard, a magician; and for home roles, a lady's hat and a man's hat or cap. Put all the hats in a large bag (a black plastic refuse bag would be ideal) and let

the children pull out one at a time. When
they put on the hat help them to act out
the character as suggested in the examples
below:

<u>Nurse's hat</u> - have the children pretend to
be ill. Ask the nurse to look at their
tongues, feel their pulse, take temperatures
etc. The nurse can pretend to administer
medicine to make them better.
<u>Fireman's hat</u> - all pretend to smell the
smoke - dial 999 for the fire brigade and
make loud siren noises as the fire engine
arrives. Help the fireman to put up
his ladder, unroll his hosepipe, rescue
the family and put out the fire with
plenty of swooshing noises for the water.

(d) <u>Acting-out Stories</u>
Most children in a nursery group will have
joined in with actions to favourite rhymes
and songs such as 'Incy Wincy Spider'
and 'Row row row your boat' and so it
should be a relatively easy step to acting
out simple stories with several characters.
A familiar tale is much easier for children
who are playing a role for the first time,
as they are less self-conscious if the story
is part of their world (good examples are
the Three Billy Goats Gruff, Goldilocks
and the Three Bears, the Three Little Pigs).
Be sure to read or tell the stories aloud
several times first and afterwards
encourage the children to remember the
correct sequence of the plot by discussing
the reasons behind some of the events in
the story. For instance, "Why did the
Billy Goats cross the bridge?" or "Why did
little Bear start to cry?" or "What happened
next?" etc.
At first the whole group can go through
the actions of the story together, e.g. all
standing up and looking big and strong when
Father Bear is mentioned or making themselves
small and using a tiny voice for Baby Bear.
Later the children can be assigned individual roles and act out the appropriate part
as you tell the story.
Only a minimum of props are required.
In the 'Three Billy Goats Gruff', for
example, a small table will serve as a bridge

for the troll to hide under, whilst the goats walk across the top. Do not be tempted to use costumes as they distract children from the story, and in the limited time available may cause more trouble than they are worth.

Once the children have gained confidence by acting out familiar stories they will find it easier to draw on their own powers of inventiveness and you can then move on to acting out familiar or recent events that have happened in their lives, such as a birthday party, a visit to the hairdresser or a trip to the seaside.

(e) **Puppets**

Some children feel less inhibited about acting a story or singing a song if they can do it through a puppet rather than by themselves. If this is the case, it may be better to introduce puppets in an earlier play session before attempting to act out fairy stories.

Puppets can be easily made from old socks, mittens or old rubber balls on sticks. You may be lucky enough to have a puppet theatre or a three-sided screen that doubles as a shop or a theatre. If not, a large box, with the bottom folded inwards, standing on a table, will do just as well. Drape a piece of material over the back of the box, so that the puppeteers are not seen by the audience.

The children can make the puppets sing, enact nursery rhymes or even act out simple stories, as suggested above.

(f) **Play themes using small scale toys**

For these sessions you will need a collection of small scale toys such as cars, lorries, trains, boats, miniature dolls such as Play People, together with plasticene or playdoh, lego, wooden blocks and shapes.

The idea is to act out small plots or themes (based, if possible, on the children's interests) in which the miniature people are made to talk and engage in make-believe roles and the play materials are used imaginatively as props.

Have a clear idea of the theme you intend to use, beginning with simple everyday occurrences, such as a shopping trip to town, and in later sessions move on to more exciting plots such as pirates, witches or rocket trips to the moon.

For a game of pirates, for example, you could use a large sheet of blue paper for the sea, plasticene for islands and sharks, lego or wooden blocks for boats and play people for the pirates. The ships can sail along with the pirates keeping a look out for a treasure island. Suggest adventures they could have on the way : a man overboard, sharks coming, a storm, rescue at sea and so on. Finally, they reach the island and dig up the treasure. Encourage each child to help in the construction of the boats, islands and sharks and to adopt a role and talk as though he were a character in the story you are unfolding. They can also be shown how to simulate the sound of waves and wind and teach them 'pirate' phrases such as "Yo ho ho and a bottle of rum" and "Shiver me timbers".

Small scale play themes such as pirates can easily be transformed into large scale versions by the provision of suitable props for the children to use, such as eye patches, headscarves, gold earrings, cardboard swords and moustaches.

By carefully planning activities you should be able to encourage skills and help the children learn to play with their peers and to work through some of the feelings or rivalry and jealousy that are common in this age group. But this can only happen if you do not overwhelm them by making the games another duty or task to be mastered. Be careful not to dominate the game or organise the play too highly so that it turns into a chore or a drill. You need to be able to recognise the moments when you may be pushing too hard and when a quick change of direction can make all the difference in helping a child to use to the full what you are offering in your play sessions together. Play may be the main 'business' of childhood, but if it is not fun it is not really play.

III. Social Play
We will now turn our attention to activities aimed

at promoting social play, i.e. activities based on
interaction between two or more children.   It is
only at the beginning of a child's fourth year that
co-operative play begins to emerge and even then it
rarely involves more than two children who may not
stay together for very long.   Only among the older
four and five year-olds does group play become
increasingly common, involving up to six children
playing together for much longer periods.
        There is some evidence (Sylva et al., 1980)
which suggests that the most natural and fruitful
grouping to encourage amongst pre-school children
is the pair.   Observations in playgroups and
nurseries revealed that not only did play between
two children enhance social interaction, but that
the highest proportion of challenging and complex
play occurred while the children were in pairs.
They concluded that nursery staff should encourage
children to play in pairs as this might foster
interpersonal skills and improve the intellectual
level of their play.
        It is worthwhile considering some of the many
reasons why social play is particularly important
for children in this age group who are experiencing
difficulties.

1. Shy children may isolate themselves from
   other children by deliberately choosing
   solitary activities such as painting at
   an easel or completing an inset tray.
   Thrusting them prematurely into a group
   of children may totally overwhelm them
   and only increase their isolation.
   A less stressful way of easing them
   into nursery life may be to engineer
   play activities for them that follow
   the normal stages of development of
   social play.   Thus the first step
   would be to encourage them to build a
   block castle or draw on a large sheet of
   paper with one other child.   Each need
   only be concerned with his/her bit of it
   but working together with another child
   greatly increases the chances of them
   co-operating to produce the finished
   article, particularly if you suggest
   a few different types of buildings they
   could make or an idea of a picture to
   draw.   Once a child is used to the idea
   of playing alongside another child you
   can try introducing activities that really

do require co-operation such as simple picture dominoes or lotto or other basic board games. By providing rewarding alternatives to solitary play you may find the child manages the transition into group play much more easily than would otherwise be the case.

Remember Jonathan, the withdrawn, immature and dependent little boy whose problems were compounded by his poor language skills? On entry to the nursery his play was at a very low level. He would suck and chew toys baby fashion and would throw a tantrum if other children tried to join in with his play. After a period of observation his teacher planned a programme of activities for Jonathan designed to take him through some of the earliest stages of play in an attempt to improve his level of social development. To build up a trusting relationship with him she began by playing some of the games mothers play with small children whilst simultaneously trying to encourage his speech. Gradually, over a period of two terms, the games became more demanding and other children were introduced into the sessions. To begin with, one other child stood and watched and later he sat down and was included in the activity. By the end of the school year Jonathan was able to participate quite happily in a game of picture lotto with a group of children, chatting both to them and to his teacher.

2. Children who are boisterous and aggressive may be rejected by all but a few like-minded children because of the wild rough and tumble games they favour. Aggressive children are often very selfish, wanting their own way, rarely considering another child's point of view and backing up their demands by force. To some extent all young children are selfish, but generally as they grow older they learn to adapt and find more socially acceptable ways of resolving situations than by hostility. Social play can be a valuable tool in helping aggressive children to share and take turns, which in the long run makes them easier to get on with. You could, for

instance, teach such children simple board games so that they are bound by a clear cut set of rules and turn-taking is essential for the game to continue. Once they have mastered the rules, on the poacher turned gamekeeper principle you could then suggest that, since they are so good at the game, they should teach another child how to play. This will boost their self-esteem and allow them to show off their prowess in an acceptable way rather than proving themselves by boasting and physical domination. Even though they seem unlikely candidates, aggressive children often prove to be surprisingly good instructors of tasks or feats at which they are adept.

3. Many resless overactive children spend most of their day in physical pursuits, running, climbing and swinging and often have difficulty in adjusting to school later on because they find it difficult to sit still and concentrate for more than a few minutes at a time. Some of the table-top activities suggested further on would be useful in introducing children to the quieter sedentary occupations that will be expected of them later. Initially you may have to play the games or do the activities with them, so that they are praised sufficiently for their efforts and will then come to find the activity rewarding in itself.

William, for instance, was given ten minutes of exclusive attention everyday by an adult in the peace and quiet of the Head's office with a toy, book or game of his choosing. His concentration during these periods was much greater than his teacher had originally thought he was capable of sustaining, and it began to spill over into the rest of his day. Having once experienced the satis-faction of completing a jigsaw with the help and praise of an adult, he began to try others on his own and eventually would persevere even with quite difficult ones.

Fostering Social Play

In a sense all play can be 'social' play. Many imaginative play activities, for example, are particularly suited to getting children to play together. To begin with, however, it is a good idea to direct children towards activities which really do need two children and are not capable of being played by a child on his own. You are, in effect, 'forcing' the children to play together as the activity can only continue if both take part. Ideally, the first games should not involve one child waiting for a turn while the other plays, and neither should you have to stay and direct operations. One other point to bear in mind is that the children should be able to cope with the action or actions that the activity demands. Children who are frustrated by a difficult physical element in a game will stop playing.

Set out below are a few suggestions for both energetic and table-top games, chosen because of their intrinsically social nature. This is not meant to be a comprehensive list and it is likely that you will have many ideas of your own which will extend these basic suggestions or add to them. It is also a good idea to take a close look at all your games and equipment and evaluate them in terms of their potential for increasing co-operative play. For instance, many of the normally solitary activities such as drawing, painting, modelling in clay or plasticene etc., can easily be adapted for two by providing larger sheets of paper or bigger boards. A little thought about the activities provided and the layout of your room can greatly increase the likelihood of co-operative play developing and thriving in your group.

Energetic Activities

Push carts and tyres on castors. Toys like this, where one child pushes whilst the other rides, are greatly enjoyed by children and the activity can be extended by introducing an imaginative element, e.g. pretending it is a bus or a train.

Rocking boats. A much safer, if more expensive, version of the old fashioned see-saw. Rockers, whether of metal or wood, lend themselves to all kinds of fantasy play and children have to co-operate to produce the rocking motion.

Ball games. Simple throwing, catching and kicking games between two children are as much social play as they are good outlets for surplus energy. Very young children may need to practise throwing and

kicking with you first, to ensure they have
sufficient skill to maintain a game with another
child without becoming frustrated. Large foam
balls (made by Combex) are ideally suited to a young
child's first attempts at throwing and catching, as
they do not hurt if they accidentally hit a child
in the face.

Table-top Activities

Apart from games with rules, which will be described
separately, most table-top activities do not usually
require two children. However, you should encourage
children to play together in other activities, even
ones which they could play by themselves.

Drawing. Give a pair of children a large sheet of
paper they can both draw on without getting in each
other's way. Suggest a particular scene for them
to draw themselves, each child being responsible
for a different part, or draw an outline yourself
for them to colour in. Perhaps you could make
this joint activity rather special by allowing
them to use felt tip markers (if these are not
normally available) or a special set of new, un-
broken crayons.

Large jigsaws. Large table or floor jigsaws, which
can be worked on by two or more children, could be
made available as well as the more usual small inset
variety.

Games with Rules

Even young children can master the rules of simple
board games, which once learned greatly increase
the range of social activities available to them.
Admittedly, at first you will have to spend some
time explaining the rules and acting as referee,
but as the children's ability to play correctly
increases, you should be able to leave them to it.
    Games for two are best to begin with, as the
more children taking part, the longer each will have
to wait for a turn with accompanying impatience.
They should have a minimum of rules and for this
reason a home-made game may be preferable to a
commercially produced one, as even a simple game
such as 'Snakes and Ladders' has too many rules
for a beginner to grasp all at once.

A basic game for beginners.   You need two strips
of card, each divided into about 10 squares, and a
die marked with three red and three green spots.
The children take turns in throwing the die, but only
move forward one space when the green spot is upper-
most.   The first child to reach the end of a strip
is the winner.

The game has only ten squares, so that it does
not go on long enough for the children to lose
interest.   Having the squares in a straight line
makes it easier for children to see and understand
the rule of moving from start to finish.   Replacing
the die numbers with spots allows children to get
used to throwing the die without necessarily being
able to count.

The game can be made more interesting by using
toy cars instead of counters with a picture of a
garage at the end of the strip for them to 'drive'
into; having plastic frogs hopping to a pond; plastic
spiders climbing drainpipes; mice going up a grand-
father clock etc.

Once the basic idea of the game and rules are
understood, you can make more complicated versions
by having a longer course; varying the shape of the
course by adding bends and loops; having only one
course that children race along together; using a
die with dots, perhaps only 1 and 2 dots to start
with; introducing hazards such as ladders that
take the counters back several spaces, etc.

Other Games

You probably already have simple dominoes (either
the picture, shape or touch varieties), lotto games
and Pelmanism, but it is worth looking at other
more complicated games such as ludo, to see
whether or not you can make a simpler version yourself.   If you are stuck for ideas it may be useful
to scan the pages of Educational Supplies catalogues
for inspiration.

Obviously it would be impossible to cover all
the various kinds of play activities which could be
used constructively to help children overcome the
emotional and behavioural difficulties they may be
experiencing in the nursery group.   However, it is
hoped that you will find the suggested games and
activities useful when planning a programme for an
individual child.

Included at the end of this section is an
annotated list of several books which contain many
more ideas for play activities than can be included

Special Help in the Classroom

here. Also appended is a list of children's books
which may be useful starting points for imaginative
play.

BIBLIOGRAPHY

Freyburg, J. (1973) Increasing imaginative play in
    urban disadvantaged children through systematic
    training in J.L. Singer (Ed.) The Child's World
    of Make Believe: experimental studies of
    imaginative play. New York : Academic Press.
Garvey, D. (1977) Play.London : Fontana/Open Books.
Gould, R. (1972) Child Studies through Fantasy.
    London : Quadrangle Books.
Jeffree, D.M., McConkey, R. and Hewson, S. (1977)
    Let Me Play. London : Souvenir Press.
Manning, K. and Sharp, A. (1977) Structuring Play in
    the Early Years at School. London : Ward Lock
    Educational.
Manning, M. (1978) Exploratory study on the manage-
    ment and treatment of difficult children in a
    nursery school (personal communication).
Marshall, H. and Hahn, S. (1967) Experimental
    modification of dramatic play. Journal of
    Personality and Social Psychology, 5, 119-122.
Saltz, E.,Dixon, D. and Johnson, J. (1977) Training
    disadvantaged pre-schoolers in various fantasy
    activities : effects on cognitive functioning
    and impulse control. Child Development, 48,
    367-380.
Singer, D.G. and Singer, J.L. (1977) Partners in Play.
    New York : Harper and Row.
Smilansky, S. (1968) The effects of sociodramatic
    play in disadvantage pre-school children.
    New York : Wiley.
Sylva, K., Roy, C. and Painter, M. (1980) Child-
    watching at playgroup and nursery school.
    London : Grant McIntyre.

FURTHER READING

Jeffree, D.M., McConkey, R. and Hewson, S. (1977)
    Let Me Play.London : Souvenir Press.
    Written for parents, teachers, nursery assist-
    ants and playgroup leaders of handicapped
    children. Contains a programme of games
    devised to encourage motor and sensory skills,
    intellect, imagination and social confidence.

It was developed through the Parental Involvement Project of the Hester Adrian Research Centre at the University of Manchester.

Manning, K. and Sharp, A. (1977) <u>Structuring Play in the Early Years at School.</u> London : Ward Lock Educational. Based on the work of six hundred teachers who took part in the Schools Council Project on the Structuring of Play in the Infant and First School. It describes ways in which teachers can structure play by the provision of materials and their own involvement. Examples of play situations that teachers can adapt for use in their own classroom are included.

Riddick, B. (1982) <u>Toys and Play for the Handicapped Child.</u> London : Croom Helm. As well as describing the developmental needs of babies through to 5-year-olds, also provides a 'consumer's guide' to choosing and buying toys.

Singer, D.G., and Singer, J.L. (1977) <u>Partners in Play : a step-by-step guide to imaginative play in children.</u> This book sets out the basic principles of fantasy play, and presents in a step-by-step format, explicit games to stimulate the various senses and encourage make-believe for the 2-5 age group. Included are indoor and outdoor games and activities suitable for the solitary child or groups.

(2) BEHAVIOUR MODIFICATION

<u>INTRODUCTION</u>
Mark is an overactive, uncontrolled and rather awkward little boy. He rushes around the nursery at high speed, bumping into furniture, knocking over a half-assembled tower and then disrupts the activities of another group of children playing quietly in the Wendy House. Despite strenuous efforts and repeated requests by the nursery staff to slow down and join in with the others for a reasonable length of time, he continues to be a very disruptive influence in the nursery. The staff feel that he is basically unhappy about not joining in with the other children and that he rushes around a lot in order to gain attention from them and from the staff. They believe that he <u>can</u> be helped but are at a loss to know where to start and

what to do to help him.

Those who believe in behaviour modification techniques would suggest a course of action to help Mark along the following lines.

Firstly, Mark's behaviour needs to be carefully observed over a period of time, with sample observations being taken each morning for a few minutes in each hour. The aim is to try to find out when he seems more active than usual and what conditions seem to trigger off this overactivity. His quieter moments will also be noted and the circumstances in which he slows down, perhaps when he comes across a favourite toy or has contact with a particular friend. On the basis of these observations, collected over a series of days or weeks, the conditions which seem to make Mark's behaviour better or worse can be discovered. The observations will also show Mark's normal behaviour level, and will act as a 'baseline' on which a programme of retraining or intervention can be built, making the most of the situations where his behaviour is nearest to acceptability. Some suggestions follow as to what you could do if you had a child like Mark in your class.

First of all, you must decide what it is you want Mark to do. This is the goal towards which you are aiming and the programme you devise is intended to encourage Mark towards the behaviour you would like to see - for example, sitting in his seat for a reasonable period of time. How would you set about it?

Restrain Mark in a firm but gentle way and make him sit down at a table. Keep him there for a few minutes and then give him a reward, perhaps a smile and a hug, and then allow him to run about for a few minutes (a further reward). A little later in the morning restrain him again and reward him in a similar fashion. You may go on like this for several days.

When Mark shows a tendency to approach a chair, reward him with a wave and a smile, or give physical prompts (i.e. point at a chair and tell him to sit down). In the early days of the programme he should be rewarded each time he slows down and approaches a table or chair in a controlled way. What you are doing is building up his good behaviour-establishing a number of good responses that will result in his becoming more controlled and more able to join in with the other children. Naturally, you give him a lot of praise and attention if he sits down.

If Mark does anything constructive, like helping in a game involving children, <u>reward</u> him. He may be merely approaching other children in a controlled fashion and picking up a toy that has fallen on the floor. Reward him <u>strongly</u> - give lavish praise, even though this may appear inappropriate for such a trivial act. In terms of Mark's behaviour, it is not trivial, it is a very big step forward and possibly the beginnings of a major improvement that will be maintained.

Mark's behaviour must be monitored carefully (i.e. observations of his behaviour must be continued on a daily basis and his record kept up to date) so that you will have an objective statement of any change (for better or worse) in his behaviour. If at the end of the programme his behaviour has not improved as much as you had hoped, you will have to try again, perhaps modifying the programme somewhat. With a good deal of persistence and skill on your part, Mark's behaviour should improve and, though progress may be painfully slow at first, a change will almost certainly be achieved.

<u>To summarise the approach that you have adopted with Mark</u>:

Question: What did you do for Mark?
Answer: You <u>SATIM</u> down!

You helped him become more controlled and able to sit down and concentrate and enjoy games with the other children by applying the following procedures to his problem behaviours:-

S ystematically observing
A ssessing and analysing
T argetting (i.e. setting a goal for him)
I ntervening and systematically training
M onitoring, reassessing and changing the
                      intervention.

The approach is largely based on the assumption that most of our behaviour (whether this is 'good', 'bad' or inappropriate) is <u>learned.</u> Thus the degree to which a child joins in the activities in the nursery group will be the result of the success or failure of the social learning experienced in the home, nursery and elsewhere. The essence of the behaviour modification approach is put succinctly by Vance Hall (1977), ".... behaviour modification, as the name implies, is concerned with changing behaviour in desirable directions, that is, increasing the strength of appropriate behaviours and decreasing the strength of those that are inappropriate".

Behaviour modification is, therefore, a very 'common-sense' approach. It deals with the realities of the child's behaviour as you observe it and aims to devise a sensible course of action to help the child, within the confines of what can be done in the classroom or group. It places great emphasis on the importance of the real-life situation. In essence it says, "Here is the child, this is how he or she usually behaves and this is what we will attempt to do to help this child". It recognises the paramount importance of parental influence - much work has been done in training parents as behaviour modifiers - and aims to help the child deal with real-life problems in a better way. Nursery staff, if they decide to adopt this approach, will be concentrating upon the child's present behaviour in the nursery environment and will be seeking to arrange conditions in such a way that the child's problem behaviour can be controlled and modified for the better.

Time and Staff Involvement

Very often, the use of behaviour modification will merely involve giving a little more structure to the activities that are carried out normally in the nursery. In fact, the techniques will be more readily understood if you try to relate them to your daily nursery activity. For example, you may wish to encourage a shy child to involve herself more in playing constructively in the Wendy House with a group of other children. The changes that you make might be merely to concentrate more attention on this one child by prompting and rewarding her actions in a more systematic way than you do with the other children in the group. Again, if you have an aide, or if more than one teacher is working in the room, you can arrange for individual attention to be given to the child in question either by yourself or by someone else who fully understands what you are aiming to do.

Outline of the Rest of this Section

It is not possible here to give a comprehensive review of behaviour modification. What we have tried to do is to select those procedures that seem to be most appropriate for helping young children in a nursery setting.

The rest of the section is divided up as follows:-

Part I   discusses the basic principles which underlie behaviour modification

Part II   deals with methods of observation, assessment and measurement

Part III   examines methods of encouraging or increasing appropriate behaviour

Part IV   looks at methods of discouraging or decreasing inappropriate behaviour

Part V   describes some applications of behaviour modification techniques to typical problem behaviour

Part VI   outlines the specialised technique of TASK ANALYSIS

Do not be put off by the apparent length of the section as a whole. What we suggest you do in your initial reading is to quickly review Parts I, II, III and IV. Then read Part V fairly thoroughly as this will give you a good idea of how the method is put into practice. At a later stage in your reading you will want to read all the parts more thoroughly but remember that you are not expected to plough laboriously through it from first to last. Part VI on task analysis can be treated largely as a separate entity, though many of the basic principles described in Part I will be relevant to it.

PART I

BASIC PRINCIPLES

1. Reinforcement
The idea of reinforcement may be stated simply as follows:- if behaviour is immediately rewarded, then it is more likely to be repeated. For instance, if you smile at your next door neighbour in the morning on the way to work and she smiles back, you are much more likely to smile at her again the

next morning than if she had frowned and looked away. Put in another way, the fact that she smiled back at you <u>reinforced</u> your act of smiling at her.

Reinforcers (rewards) have been classified in a number of ways, but for the practical purposes of applying behaviour modification techniques they may be thought of as <u>tangible</u> (or <u>material</u>) rewards such as food, drinks or tokens and <u>social</u> rewards such as praise, a hug or other signs of approval. Often reinforcers are presented together; thus good behaviour might be rewarded by giving a child a sweet and a hug and saying clearly what it is that is being rewarded. In broad terms, reinforcers will determine future behaviour. Both children and adults will tend to repeat behaviours that they feel have brought them a reward, and they will tend not to repeat behaviours that are not rewarded.

Some basic principles of reinforcement are given below, but a word of caution might be given at this juncture. Though these principles have been tried and tested and found, on the whole, to be true in controlled experimental situations, the chances of obtaining success in applying them in 'real-life' will depend a great deal on your skill in observing the child's behaviour, analysing this carefully and designing an appropriate plan to intervene and help the child. Thus much depends on your own intuitive skill and experience with young children. The following principles will only succeed if you can begin to work out their appropriate application in the particular setting that you are in and with a particular child's behaviour problem in mind (see also Sarason et al., 1972).

(i) <u>Reward Appropriate Behaviour</u>
Ensure that you only reward the behaviour that you want to increase. If you give children rewards for the sake of keeping them quiet (e.g. sucking a sweet does prevent children from crying out and tends to keep them preoccupied with the pleasant taste), you may be inadvertently establishing bad behaviour. Thus, if the child threw a temper tantrum prior to being given the sweet, there will probably be another temper tantrum because this brings the very pleasant reward of a sweet. An appropriate behaviour to reinforce might be sitting quietly and looking at a toy; this can be rewarded with a smile of approval and perhaps some verbal points.

(ii) <u>Reward Appropriate Behaviour Immediately</u>
This is very important. The reward should be given immediately after the good behaviour has occurred so that the child does not produce another piece of behaviour before receiving the reward. That is to say, the good behaviour alone must be rewarded. If a reward is delayed until the end of a piece of activity and you decide to reward the child because of good behaviour 'on the whole', you will in fact be rewarding both the good and the bad behaviour that occurred during that activity.

(iii) <u>In the Early Stages of Changing Behaviour, Reward the Good Behaviour Each Time it Occurs</u>
When the process of learning good behaviour is in its early stages, a reward should be given <u>every time</u> the good behaviour occurs. If rewards are given inconsistently, the child will become confused about what is being rewarded and what is not. Take advantage of encouraging an appropriate piece of behaviour each time it occurs at the beginning of the programme.

(iv) <u>In the Later Stages of Changing Behaviour, when the Good Behaviour Begins to Occur Frequently, give a Reward on Fewer Occasions</u>
Put in another way, reward the good behaviour now and again once it begins to occur at a satisfactorily high level. It would appear from learning theory that once a 'good' behaviour has reached a certain level it is sufficient for the child to know that a reward will be coming sooner or later, and giving a reward each time will devalue it. Commonsense tells us that a child who has received twenty smarties during a session will find the twenty-first smartie less attractive than the first few - though this does, of course, depend on the particular child's capacity for smarties.

(v) <u>Tangible and Special Rewards when Applied Together will Often be More Reinforcing than if One of these Alone is Given</u>
The aim of carrying out a behaviour modification programme is to obtain appropriate behaviour for its own sake. That is, the well-adjusted behaviour is seen as being rewarding in its own right and the reward is not allowed to become an end in itself. It is the social approval of the child's classmates and the adults with whom there is interaction that should be the ultimate rewarding factor.

With this in mind, it is useful to pair tangible rewards with social reinforcers when this is possible. In practice in the nursery setting it may be difficult or inappropriate to supply some tangible reward. Thus, it may appear unfair to other children if one child alone is given a sweet or drink whilst the rest go without. In that case you might use token rewards such as stars and points, in combination with social reinforcement. There is a wide variety of possible rewards, ranging from things the child can eat or play with to opportunities to help the teacher or take part in a favourite activity. The important thing is to find out what the child would like, as only then is the reward truly rewarding.

How do we decide on an appropriate reinforcer? Remember these four methods:-

(a) ask the child what he or she really likes;

(b) ask the parents or friends of the child what he or she likes;

(c) do a preference check (try out many rewards before arriving at a choice);

(d) apply the Premack Principle; where no appropriate rewards can be decided upon, use part of the child's behaviour that occurs frequently to reinforce another less frequently occurring behaviour (thus overactive children may be taught to sit attentively for a short period of time if they are allowed on occasion to rush around - the "rushing around" acting as a reward in this instance).

Summary : Positive Reinforcement

Positive reinforcement of a behaviour means that the reinforcer (reward) given after the behaviour has occurred is pleasant for the child, so that the behaviour will tend to occur again. By applying positive reinforcement to good behaviour, you increase the probability of that behaviour occuring again. Thus, by smiling and saying "Good boy, you are paying attention so well", you will encourage the child to repeat the good behaviour of sitting and attending. Remember the basic principles of reinforcement: reinforce when the desired behaviour occurs, and each time it occurs at first; give the

reinforcement <u>immediately after</u> the desired behaviour
then gradually tail off giving the reinforcement
once the behaviour occurs frequently and appears
to be well established.

2. Extinction and Punishment

(i) Extinction

Extinction means removing the conditions that maintain or increase the likelihood that certain
behaviour will occur.   In other words, it means
withholding a reward which has been given on
previous occasions so that the behaviour which
the reward has been helping to maintain will tend
to die out (i.e. be extinguished).   To extend
the example given previously, if your next door
neighbour ceases to smile back at you each morning,
you will tend not to smile at her on subsequent
mornings.   That is, your response of smiling will
be extinguished.

Ignoring bad behaviour may not be a good
example of extinction.   Thus, for the sake of peace
and quiet, we may ignore a temper tantrum or
aggressive display by a child in the hope that this
bad behaviour will simply go away if we pay no
attention to it.   However, we may find that the
behaviour is so intolerable on the following day
that it simply cannot be ignored.   So the removal
of attention is inconsistent and the behaviour will
not be extinguished because it is still, on occasion,
bringing the child the reward of gaining attention
sooner or later.   Thus, if the removal of attention
is to be applied to a problem behaviour, do it
<u>consistently</u>.   If you want to extinguish a certain
behaviour, you must make sure that it is never
rewarded when it occurs.   A good idea may be to
reward other behaviour which stops the child
carrying out the undesirable behaviour. (These
points are discussed further in Part IV of this
section pp.149-153.)

(ii) Punishment

This is, perhaps, the method most often used in an
attempt to change or modify children's behaviour.
It is used in one form or another by almost all
parents and teachers at some stage.   Punishment
can obviously be used to control immediately the
problem behaviour, but the effect of punishment would
appear to be to suppress the behaviour problem for
the time being (e.g. until the punisher leaves the

room), not to change it fundamentally over time.
To extinguish the behaviour might be more satisfactory.

PART II

METHODS OF ASSESSMENT AND MEASUREMENT

In behaviour modification, measurement is important.
It involves counting the number of times a certain
type of behaviour occurs and recording how long it
lasts on each occasion. We will describe some
convenient methods of collecting and recording
observations of a child's behaviour in as simple
and straightforward a way as possible, but because
behaviour is so complicated, it may take you a
little time to get used to measuring it. What you
have to do is to define, count, record and chart
the behaviour. These steps will now be discussed
in detail.

1. <u>Defining and Counting Problem Behaviour</u>
In order to <u>define</u> behaviour objectively it must be
broken down into units that are specific and
observable. A child could be described as
'aggressive' or 'naughty', or his/her behaviour
could be said to be 'disturbing others', but none
of these descriptions tells us accurately what the
child actually does or what the consequences of
his/her behaviour are. They are merely labels which
describe in a very general way what may be a wide
variety of different kinds of behaviour. Listed
below are a number of examples of poorly defined
behaviour and opposite is given a clearer and more
specific description of what the observer really
meant. The definitions given on the right hand
side can be more readily recognised and counted.

	<u>Poorly Defined</u>	<u>Clearly Defined</u>
(a)	Poor attitude	Refuses to join in group activities such as playing in the Wendy House or ball games unless given the dominant role. Refuses to allow other children to take their turn as leader of a group activity.

Poorly Defined	Clearly Defined
(b) Immature	Clings to adults a lot, frequently whines and asks to be cuddled. Tries to climb up on adult's lap and seeks comfort, unlike most other children of a similar age.
(c) Is cheeky and insulting	Talks back to staff when not appropriate, e.g. says 'why should I' when instructed to sit down, or refers to characteristics of others.
(d) Cannot concentrate	Flits from activity to activity all the time, and cannot settle down to play quietly and constructively for more than a minute or two at a time.

By following the clear definition, it becomes possible to count the number of occurrences of this type of behaviour. For example, you may decide to count separately the number of occasions of clinging (C), whining (W) and demanding (D) that occur during the whole or part of the session. A record chart can then be drawn up with different categories for each type of behaviour, as shown on the following page.

You can design your own record charts or follow the examples given in several of the references at the end of this section (e.g. Walker and Shea, 1976). Again, you must decide beforehand exactly what kinds of behaviour will be denoted by the code letters. In this particular instance they could have been as follows:-

C - clinging to adults' clothing or body as they pass by; trying to grasp hand or arm of adults to draw their attention etc.

W - whining: speaking to adults or other children in a self-pitying way; making complaining noises, grizzling

Behaviour Record Chart

Frequency of Clinging, Whining and Demanding

Observer's Name . . . .   Date . . . .

	MONDAY			TUESDAY			WEDNESDAY			THURSDAY			FRIDAY		
	C	W	D	C	W	D	C	W	D	C	W	D	C	W	D

Observation
Interval
(e.g. whole of
morning session
or 10 a.m. to
11 a.m. etc.)

Total number of
occurrences

Child's Name (or code) . . . .

D - demanding comfort and attention; a
direct appeal to adults to be allowed
to sit on their lap or close to them;
asking to be cuddled or comforted.

The particular codes and the number of different
categories that you adopt is a matter for you to
decide. It may be convenient to have just one
category - where the behaviour is a very specific
one - or you may select two or more types of
behaviour to concentrate your attention upon.
Essentially, you will want to collect as much information as is necessary for you to plan a sensible
course of action to change the behaviour in question.

2. Recording Different Aspects of Behaviour

(a) Frequency
Here, the observer keeps a tally of the number of
times a specific behaviour occurs over a certain
period of time (per hour, morning, day or week).
The nursery staff could have a pencil and pad always
to hand. They can then keep a record of how often
a child gets up, talks out or hits another child.
An alternative would be to have a simple digit
counter such as a pocket calculator or other device
which could be used to keep a record of the particular behaviour you have decided beforehand to
observe. The behaviour record chart described
above is one example of how to count the frequency
with which a selected behaviour occurs.

(b) Duration
This simply involves recording how long a particular
behaviour lasts and may be achieved by the use of
a stopwatch or by the use of a wristwatch with a
seconds hand. Very often a simple frequency count
will not provide sufficient information about a
behaviour. For instance, a child may cry or whine
for quite lengthy periods at a time, and we need
to know how long these periods are. A drawback
to duration recording is that it requires the
nursery teacher to concentrate her attention on
the one child for the necessary length of time, and
she may simply be too busy to do this. When there
is more than one adult in the room, of course, this
difficulty can be avoided.

(c) <u>Type of Recording</u>

(i) <u>Continuous</u>
As the name implies, a continuous record of the
child's behaviour could be kept (i.e. you watch all
the time) but this is virtually impossible to
achieve in practice.   Extensive recording of
behaviour might be possible if there were teams of
observers available,but we are faced with a situation where there will normally be only a nursery
teacher and aide or playgroup leader and helper to
share out the observation between them, whilst
trying to carry out all sorts of other jobs.   One way
out of this difficulty is to take sample recordings
of the problem behaviour.

(ii) <u>Time-sample recording</u>
     <u>Sample Recording</u>
In this situation the observer watches the child for
a certain interval of time every so often e.g. the
nursery teacher will keep an eye on a particular
child for five minutes at the end of each half-hour
throughout the whole session, and will note down
whether a particular behaviour occurs, and how often.
In this way a record can be built up of how often
a particular type of behaviour occurs during that
session.

     <u>Fixed-interval Recording</u>
Here, the observer notes down at the end of a fixed
interval of time say, every 2 minutes for half an
hour at a time, what the child is doing.   The
nursery teacher might want to obtain a record of
how much time a child spends 'on-task', for example,
when painting or drawing.

Minute	2	4	6	8	10	12	14	16	18	20
Behaviour	+	+	−	−	+	−	−	−	−	+

   A record sheet like that above allows the
observer to record the behaviour of the child at
two-minute intervals for a period of twenty minutes.
At exactly two-minute intervals the observer looks
at the child and awards a '+' if the child is
actually doing the task or a '-' if not.   What
goes on during the two-minute period is ignored.

(d)   When to Record

(i) Any problem behaviour should be observed as much as possible, but when time is limited you may have to observe at set times only or for short intervals at random during the whole session. If a problem behaviour occurs infrequently but is very severe you might be limited to observing it just when it occurs and describing the situation that gives rise to it, i.e. where it happens, others present, what actions seem to trigger it off, how long it lasts, how you usually try to cope with it and so on. If a problem behaviour occurs very frequently, then observing it for short periods during the session, as described above, may give a good estimate of its seriousness. Try to work out a timetable for watching that will give a number of observations as representative as possible of the problem be-haviour.

(ii) Before an intervention is planned, you will need to obtain a 'baseline' of the behaviour that you hope to change. The baseline is the record of how often the problem behaviour occurs before you begin to try to change it. The baseline will help you to compare the behaviour before, during and after the intervention. It is difficult to give any definite guidance as to how long a real-istic baseline period should be. It will vary with the type of behaviour that is being observed as well as practical considerations such as the time available for observation. If a behaviour occurs fairly frequently, e.g. at least half a dozen times in any one observation period, then a good estimate of the usual level of occurrence should be obtained after a week or ten days.
       On the other hand, if the behaviour only occurs fairly infrequently but is nevertheless causing concern, a much longer period of observation might be needed. For example, a child may be wet only once or twice a week. You should also try to assess the intensity or seriousness of difficult behaviour as well as how often it occurs (frequency) and how long it lasts (duration). If a child behaves so badly as to cause injury to another, then you might decide that no baseline is necessary and begin the intervention right away.

(iii) Observation should be continued during and following an intervention programme. This will enable you to monitor how the intervention is progressing, that is, assess whether it is having an effect on the problem behaviour. This raises the question of how long an intervention programme should be persevered with before it is abandoned or changed. Clearly, if a particular programme has not altered the behaviour in any way after several weeks, then it should be abandoned and the whole problem reviewed afresh. If, however, the intervention is having some success, but only to a limited extent, you may wish to change the approach based on new information that has come to light or on an intuition on your part that a change of procedure might lead to greater success. As you try out programmes, you will begin to see when and how they could be improved.

3. Graphing

(a) It will be very valuable for you to graph the information that you have recorded for the child. This will give you a visual representation of the situation, and will show clearly the changes, if any, that you have brought about by your programme. The general form of the graph could be as shown in Figure 5.1(a)

Behaviour
(specifically
defined)

Time
(minutes,hours,days)

FIGURE 5.1 (a)

(b)   Figure 5.1(b) gives a hypothetical graph for
a child's time 'out of seat' for the baseline period
and during the intervention.

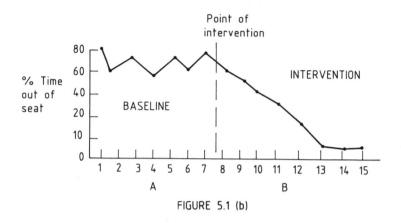

FIGURE 5.1 (b)

This graph shows that during the baseline
period (A) of seven days the child spent approximate-
ly 60 to 80% of time out of seat but that level
dropped dramatically to stabilize at about 10%
during the following eight days (B) when intervention
was taking place.
       Further examples of how to graph your informat-
ion will be found in Part V and in the texts referred
to at the end of this section.

Summary of Procedure

       1.   Define the problem behaviour clearly and
            objectively
       2.   Observe current behaviour and obtain a
            baseline
       3.   Graph the information
       4.   Plan the programme of intervention (i.e.
            decide what you are going to reward)
       5.   Introduce the programme and monitor the
            behaviour by continuing to graph what
            happens

PART III.   METHODS OF ENCOURAGING OR INCREASING
CERTAIN BEHAVIOUR

1.   Positive Reinforcement
This procedure has already been discussed (pp.132-136)
and simply involves rewarding appropriate behaviour
after it has occurred.   Commonly used rewards or
positive reinforcers are material rewards such as
food or drink, and social rewards such as praise,
a hug or a smile.   The principles of reinforcement
outlined in Part I should be borne in mind when
applying positive reinforcement.   Staff should
decide on the particular kind of reward to use,
e.g. ten minutes of free play activiy following some
good behaviour, and how to schedule this reward
(i.e. decide beforehand how often the child will be
allowed this free play activity).   A positive
reinforcement programme might be used to build up
appropriate behaviour such as obeying the teacher's
instructions or joining in the nursery activities
with the other children.

2.   Differential Reinforcement
It has been found that it is relatively easy for an
adult to increase or decrease behaviour that children are already showing.   Thus staff might decide
to increase the behaviour of a child when he or she
is playing quietly and cooperatively and decrease the
child's aggressive tendencies or overactivity.   They
could do this by paying a lot of attention to the
child when he or she is actually producing the
desirable social-play behaviour - by smiling and
saying 'very good' etc. - and ignoring the child
when overactive or demanding of attention.   In this
way the occurrence of appropriate behaviour is
increased and that of the inappropriate behaviour
decreased by 'differential reinforcement'.   There
are many studies which show the value of this method.
It is used every day by teachers and other nursery
staff, but for behaviour modification it needs to
be rather more systematic than is usually the case.

3.   Shaping, Prompting and Fading

Shaping
Shaping means systematically rewarding approximations
of the desired behaviour until gradually the proper
desired behaviour is achieved and then firmly
established.   It is used to develop behaviour which
the child is seemingly unable to learn or has
difficulty in learning.   Rewards are given as the

145

child's behaviour more and more nearly approximates to what you want him to do.

The steps in shaping behaviour are usually:

(i)   select the behaviour you want the child to achieve;

(ii)   obtain baseline information (i.e. what the child is now doing which is closest to what you want done);

(iii)   select reinforcers (rewards);

(iv)   reward successive approximations of the desired behaviour each time they occur until the child achieves the desired behaviour;

(v)   reinforce the newly established behaviour each time it occurs;

(vi)   maintain the level of the new behaviour by rewarding it now and again.

Shaping has been used, for example, to develop a child's speech where there is difficulty in this area. Typically, an adult would sit with a child and point to an object such as a spoon or knife and ask the child to say what it was. Responses might approximate the correct word such as "'poon" or "'oon", and each better approximation is rewarded by giving the child a sweet or drink and a smile or hug.

Shaping might also be used to change social or play behaviour. Thus a child who has difficulty in joining in ball games with other children might be helped by shaping any good play patterns shown. For instance, a child may have rather poor co-ordination, and tend to dash around in a random fashion during a ball game played by children in a circle. The unco-ordinated child could be helped by the staff encouraging him to stand with the others, giving clear directions when and where to run and rewarding with praise each time the correct behaviour is shown. By doing this successively with each aspect of the game, the child's behaviour can be shaped into an appropriate pattern for the play activity.

Prompting and Fading
When children are slow to produce something near to

the desired behaviour, thay may be prompted by the teacher to do so. Thus, in the verbal shaping procedure described above, the teacher might supply a prompt by pointing at the spoon, saying 'spoo ..' and allowing the child to join in to finish the word off.

In the example of shaping play behaviour, the teacher might help children by pointing to the spot they are supposed to run to and saying, 'Go on, run over there'. Further physical prompts might involve guiding the children's throwing action or guiding them through other actions involved in the game.

Fading refers to the gradual phasing out of the verbal or physical prompts given by the teacher to the child. Thus, the teacher might begin to point to the spoon and not give a verbal prompt. In the example of the ball game, the teacher might stand back and give fewer verbal instructions to the child, thus allowing him to carry on on his own.

4. Modelling or Imitation
One of the most frequently used methods of encouraging new behaviour is that of modelling. The child's attention is directed to appropriate behaviour in adults, other children or the group, and he is encouraged to copy this behaviour or model his behaviour on theirs. In this way, the child will:

(i)   acquire new behaviour;

(ii) unlearn some of the inappropriate behaviour previously shown;

(iii) be encouraged to go on and develop further appropriate behaviour.

Before you try to encourage modelling, you should consider whether:

(a)   the child is sufficiently mature to be able to understand what he is imitating and why this is desirable;

(b)   the child will be rewarded for imitating desirable behaviour or whether this will be done 'for its own sake'. (In this case it might be wise to reward the child in the initial stages, but to gradually fade out the reward);

Special Help in the Classroom

(c)   the model really is a 'good' one. Thus,
      a child may imitate a lot of another
      child's behaviour, but only parts of the
      latter's behaviour may be desirable i.e.
      guard against a child imitating undesirable
      as well as desirable behaviour.

   Again, staff should remember that in all their
actions and attitudes they are acting as models for
the children. Thus, it is not a good thing for
adults to express anger or irritation however badly
behaved a child may be, since this emotional
behaviour may well be copied by the children. If
children think it appropriate to express anger by
shouting (or physically attacking others), they
may be basing their actions on the teacher's behaviour

Summary : The   Importance of Feedback
If you decide to employ any of the approaches
described above, it is important that children
should know why rewards are being given and how
their behaviour is improving or deteriorating.
That is to say, you must comment on their behaviour
thus providing feedback for the child or the nursery
group so that they will get some indication of how
they are progressing and for what they are being
rewarded or not rewarded.
   This leads us to another important idea about
learning. Generalisation is the process by which
a response or a piece of behaviour that is rewarded
or reinforced in the presence of one stimulus will
occur when another different but related stimulus
is presented. Generalisation is a useful process
since it cuts out the need to learn the same
behaviour again each time a new stimulus or situation
that requires the same response occurs. An example
of generalisation is when a child learns originally
to drink from a bowl or plastic cup and this later
and very quickly leads to drinking from a cup or
glass tumbler. It can be encouraged by drawing the
child's attention to the similarity between the new
activity and what he can already do.
   Inappropriate generalisation may be avoided
by teaching a response or behaviour consistently
in the setting for which that behaviour is appropriate.
Teaching a child to use the toilet may be brought
about by helping in the initial stages with clothes
and other necessary actions in the toilet itself
rather than in another room and subsequently allowing
the child to go to the toilet.

148

Ways of encouraging or increasing behaviour
have been described in general terms. How they are
actually implemented will depend on the child, the
nursery environment and your skills and preferences
in applying the techniques suggested. Remember that
you must plan carefully in advance how much time
you can spend in trying out any method with a child
and always select rewards that are suitable for that
particular child. An outline of the steps involved
in the behaviour change process will be provided
in summary form at the end (p. 163), but we will now
go on to consider methods of discouraging or decreasing behaviour that you do not want.

PART IV. METHODS OF DISCOURAGING OR DECREASING
UNDESIRED BEHAVIOUR

In this part we will expand on methods that could
be used by nursery staff to decrease behaviour that
is unacceptable or disrupting. Examples of such
behaviour are extreme overactivity (a child rushing
around in an unco-ordinated and seemingly mean-
ingless fashion), incessant whining and clinging
behaviour, frequent crying, aggression (hitting or
bullying other children) and so on.

1. Encouraging Incompatible Behaviour
One way to combat disruptive behaviour is to reward
incompatible behaviour. That is to say, a
behaviour that makes it impossible or difficult
to indulge in the negative, unacceptable behaviour
is strengthened. Thus, a teacher may reward a
child for sitting quietly by smiling and showing
approval, but withdraw this rewarding attention
when the child gets up and rushes around. Encouraging incompatible behaviour is a positive method of
decreasing unacceptable behaviour and does not
involve any punishment of the child.

2. Extinction
Another procedure that could be used to cut down
undesirable behaviour is to withhold any reward
given to the inappropriate act. Thus, a teacher
may have paid attention to children each time they
whined or started to cry so that the attention
became reinforcing. By ignoring children when they
begin to whine and attending to them when they are
not whining, the teacher may be able to extinguish
the whining. Again, temper tantrums are often

brought about by the child wishing to gain attention, and withdrawal of that attention during the tantrum will often lead to the extinction of that behaviour.
There are some difficulties involved in the use of extinction with children in a nursery classroom or group. One of these is that a teacher cannot ignore a child when he or she is genuinely distressed and in need of reassurance. It must fall on the nursery staff to judge whether a child's behaviour shows that he or she is genuinely in need of comfort.
A second difficulty is that the rest of a group may provide rewards for children's extreme behaviour by giving them attention (laughing and talking to them) so that some reinforcement is still being given for the undesirable act. Adults might combat this by asking the others to help by not giving the children in question such attention.
Finally, nursery staff should be aware that the severity of temper tantrums or of bad behaviour will often increase when attention is first withdrawn. When beginning the process of withdrawing attention, therefore, staff should not weaken and give in to an increased display of bad temper or emotion, but persist until the behaviour settles down or clearly needs some other method of coping with it.

3. Restraining
Clearly, there are times when children will have to be restrained physically by the nursery staff. If one child attacks another with a toy or in some other way, the child will have to be immediately restrained before any serious physical injury can result to the other child. When restraining children to prevent harmful behaviour you should bear the following in mind:

(i)   only use restraint when strictly necessary and only just enough to stop an attack;

(ii) explain as far as possible to children why they are being restrained.

Often it will be effective merely to use verbal restraint (e.g. wagging a finger at a child and saying, 'You must not do that') so it is essential that children should be able to understand what it is that they are doing wrong. Very young children are often unable to do this, but there are ways of helping the child to achieve more insight (see section on 'Problem-Solving Approaches' pp.177-202).

Restraint can also be used to begin to change
behaviour as well as just to prevent its occurrence.
When used along with an insistence that children
should 'sit and watch' (see below), restraining
should encourage calm and controlled behaviour. That
is, the adult ceases to restrain children only when
they have calmed down and are sitting watching
others at play.

4. 'Sit and Watch'

Young children who are slow to develop acceptable
patterns of play can often cause considerable
disruption in the nursery. Nursery staff are sometimes advised to redirect or distract children who
are misbehaving. This might involve the teacher
telling a child, "No, don't throw the toys about
like that. Come over here and play with this toy
instead". This approach can be very demanding of
the staff's time, however, and may often be inadequate
in dealing with severe disruptions.

The technique of 'sit and watch' was developed
by Porterfield et al. (1976) to combat just such
disruptive behaviour. 'Sit and watch' involves the
adults following the steps outlined below:

1. the nursery staff explain briefly to the
   child (we shall call her Jenny) the
   behaviour that is inappropriate and why
   it is inappropriate e.g. "No, don't
   snatch the toys from the other children,
   ask them if you can borrow the toy or
   ask me if you can have it";

2. Jenny is then moved to the edge of the
   play area,without close company or play
   materials. The nursery staff then
   instruct her to sit and watch the other
   children at play, e.g. "Sit and watch
   how the other children ask for the toys
   that they want";

3. when the staff are satisfied that Jenny
   has observed the other children at play
   for a brief period (usually less than
   one minute), they ask her if she is
   ready to rejoin the play activity, e.g.
   "Do you know how to ask for a toy now?"
   If the response is positive the child is
   allowed to rejoin the game. If the
   child says 'no' or makes no response
   she is told to sit in the same place

and watch the play activity for a little
longer. This is repeated until a positive
response is given by the child that she
understands how she should play with the
other children;

4. when Jenny returns to the play activity
the nursery staff give her praise and
positive attention for playing appropriately,
e.g. when she asks for a toy, the staff
might say, "Very good, you asked for the
toy that time".

Nursery staff should give some comfort to
children who are upset or crying whilst they are
sitting and watching the other children at play. If
they continue to be very upset during this period,
however, the staff might take them to a 'rest area'
(e.g. a chair at the far end of the nursery which
is screened off from the play area) and say, "Have
a little rest here before you go back to watch
the other children playing". When children have
calmed down sufficiently (usually after a few
minutes), they may return to their spot to sit and
watch the play activity, and the procedure described
above is followed once more.

5. Reducing Anxiety
A child who shows fear or anxiety at the approach
of an adult might be helped by the staff planning
a series of gradual approaches to the child to
overcome this feeling. The staff might sit down
well away from the child and smile and wave reassuringly, later they might beckon the child or
move slightly nearer at a slow and relaxed pace,
later still they might walk up quietly to the child
and stroke an arm reassuringly. By gradually
increasing the directness of approach, the nursery
staff would hope to reach the point where they could
walk directly up to the child and even give a
reassuring hug without being afraid of frightening
the child. This method of overcoming fear is
known as 'systematic desensitisation'.

Summary : Which Procedure to Use?
All of the procedures outlined above have, at one
time or another, been used as a means of discouraging problem behaviour in young children, with
varying degrees of success. More than one of the
procedures might be used together with a particular

child or several different procedures tried one after the other if little success is achieved with the first method tried. A great deal will depend, once again, on the skill of the nursery staff in using the various approaches consistently and realise istically, i.e. they must be applied properly and be manageable in terms of time and commitment. It would be helpful if you were to read some of the numerous case studies showing the application of those methods which appear in the books mentioned at the end of this section. We will now go on to look at how some typical problem behaviour that might be encountered in the nursery could be coped with using some of the behaviour modification methods.

PART V. TYPICAL PROBLEMS

In the previous parts of this section we have described the underlying principles, ways of assessment and some of the methods of behaviour modification. These should form the basis of your plan of action.

It is possible that you may need outside help in coping with problem children but often you will be in the best position to help them as you have much more contact with them than anyone from outside the nursery group. Nursery staff soon acquire an intimate knowledge of children's problems and what their likes and dislikes are. Enlist the help of your colleagues whenever possible to aid in gathering basic information about children's behaviour and perhaps to help with carrying out any intervention planned. Once the problem behaviour has been defined and described and the baseline information obtained, you will have to decide which approach to try out with the child. It would be sensible to start off by trying to modify relatively simple problems, using very basic techniques such as positive reinforcement or extinction, until you are sufficiently practised and feel able to cope with comparatively difficult procedures.

What approach should you use? This will depend on several factors, including the type and severity of the problem, and the time and resources available to you.

As outlined in Chapter 2, most of the problem behaviour encountered in the nursery group will fall under the following four main categories:

(i)   shy/withdrawn/timid

(ii)   immature/dependent

(iii)   restless/overactive

(iv)   aggressive/anti-social/destructive

However, it is not sufficient merely to label
a child as belonging to one of the above categories.
You must state precisely what behaviour makes you
conclude that a child is having problems and define
the difficulty in as much detail as possible. Thus
shy, withdrawn children may be described as being
very reluctant to approach or talk to adults or
other children, to spend a good deal of time (say
how much)on their own, and to shun joining in
general activities with others. There may be
specific times or situations when this behaviour is
worse than usual, e.g. the child may dislike mixing
with a large group of children playing outside in
the yard, but be reasonably willing to play with
one another child in a quiet part of the nursery.
The same procedure holds good for the other three
categories - describe specifically and clearly what
behaviours are being exhibited and how severe they
are.
A child may show behaviour that falls into two
or more of the above categories. Thus, a child
may be very restless and overactive and also have
a tendency to be aggressive and destructive. You
should describe the observed behaviour in detail and
not worry too much about which category it falls
into in the main. You have then to decide which
particular aspect of the behaviour you are going
to tackle first.
We will now go on to give some examples of the
action that might be taken to help.

(i) WITHDRAWAL AND ISOLATION

The Problem
       Anna is a very timid and shy little girl. Out-
       side she is more often than not to be found
       standing alone in the yard when most other
       children are playing noisily and happily
       together. In the nursery she seems to seek
       out the quieter spots and rarely talks to or
       approaches another child. She is not fearful
       of the staff and will approach them from time

to time but not as much as the other children do.

(a) Behavioural Method Used

The nursery staff decided to try out a behaviour modification approach to help Anna become less isolated and to help her interact more freely with the other children.

(b) Definition of Behaviour

If Anna was not interacting with at least one child on the occasions when she was being observed, the staff recorded an instance of isolated behaviour. If Anna was with a member of staff, there had to be at least one other child present for it to count as social behaviour. Social interaction was defined as talking to or playing with another child, not merely being close to one.

(c) Measurement of Behaviour

The staff used a time-sampling procedure to measure Anna's isolated behaviour throughout the nursery day. Observations of her behaviour were made on average every twenty minutes during the nursery day. About fifteen observations per day were made, therefore. Observations were carried out for ten days to give a baseline of Anna's isolated behaviour. The information obtained was graphed (p.156).

(d) Procedures and results

The staff decided to use a simple positive reinforcement procedure (p.145). Thus every time Anna approached another child, talked or began to play with children, she was praised by the teacher who would smile and say, 'Well done, Anna. I'm glad to see you are joining in with the others'. (The reward would be varied, e.g. giving a hug or allowing Anna a favoured activity.) Reward was only given when Anna indulged in some form of social interaction or other. In a situation where there was very little initiation of the desired behaviour by the child, the staff might decide to use prompts. Thus, Anna could be taken by the hand and guided to where a group of children were playing and helped to join in by the teacher demonstrating how to play the game. As soon as Anna began to approach play situations spontaneously, the prompts were to be gradually faded out.

After fifteen days of this procedure, the graph the staff had drawn up (Figure 5.2) throughout the intervention programme showed that the frequency of Anna's isolated play had decreased dramatically following the introduction of the programme.

FIGURE 5.2   THE FREQUENCY OF ANNA'S ISOLATED PLAY

Figure 5.2 shows that the percentage of time Anna spent playing in isolation, after an immediate increase, decreased on average from about 70% to 10% following the introduction of the positive re-inforcement procedure.

(e)   Stopping the Programme
The nursery staff decided to discontinue the pro-gramme at this point, since the amount of time that Anna spent playing on her own was less than that of several other children in the nursery and was well within the range of what would be considered to be normal.   After three weeks they carried out a further ten days observation (a post-intervention check) and found that Anna still only spent about 20% of the time playing on her own, so no further special action was considered necessary.

(ii)   IMMATURE, DEPENDENT BEHAVIOUR

The Problem
Malcolm is three and a half years old but seems more backward than the other children of the same age.   He frequently whines and cries and seeks comfort from the nursery staff who find that they have difficulty in carrying on

156

with their work because of his clinging behaviour. The staff propose trying to modify Malcolm's whining and clinging behaviour.

(a) Behavioural Method Used

The nursery staff decided to use an extinction procedure (p.149) to try to stop Malcolm's whining and clinging behaviour. They noted that as soon as one of the staff gave him some attention, his whining would stop and he would cling to the adult for comfort. Extinction would consist of withdrawing this attention and comfort.

(b) Definition of Behaviour and Measurement

The staff collected baseline information about Malcolm's whining and clinging behaviour using a time-sampling procedure over a period of eight days. Observations were made at various intervals but on average about every 15 minutes. Eighteen observations per day were made. Whining was defined as any verbalisation that was complaining and delivered in a tremulous, emotional manner. Clinging was defined as approaching an adult and seeking attention by pulling at clothes or limbs or attempting to climb on the adult's lap. The information was graphed.

(c) Procedure and Results

The staff decided on the following procedure. Each time Malcolm whined he would be ignored by the staff, who would normally have asked him what the trouble was and probably approached him. If Malcolm came to them, they would gently but firmly refuse him physical contact and perhaps move away from him. They decided to try out this procedure for a period of fourteen days.

Figure 5.3(a)and(b) shows the effect that this procedure had on Malcolm's behaviour.

(a) Malcolm's whining behaviour

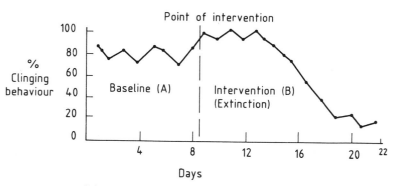

(b) Malcolm's clinging behaviour

FIGURE 5.3

The graphs show that the programme had little effect on Malcolm's whining and clinging during the first few days. In fact, it seemed to increase the frequency of the behaviour but after about eight days the extinction procedure began to take effect, and the frequency of both unacceptable behaviours declined to quite a low level.

(iii)   RESTLESS, OVERACTIVE BEHAVIOUR

The Problem

Lucy is a very restless, fidgety and generally overactive little girl. She rushes about the nursery in a random fashion disturbing other children who are playing quietly. She cannot keep still for a minute, and staff are constantly checking her and attempting to keep her quiet by involving her in some play activity, but sooner or later she leaves that activity and dashes to another part of the nursery.

(a)   Definiton and Measurement of Behaviour

The nursery staff decided to try a behaviour modification procedure involving elements of restraining (p.150) and differential reinforcement (p.145).

The staff used the percentage of time that Lucy spent in constructive play activity, whether on her own or with other children, as a measure of Lucy's appropriate behaviour. Observations of Lucy's behaviour were made at fixed intervals, every half-hour during the nursery day. Twelve observations per day were recorded over a period of 10 days. This baseline information was graphed.

(b)   Procedures and Results

Restraining. At certain times during the nursery day (every hour), Lucy was restrained by a member of the nursery staff at a table where a game was laid out. Restraining involved one of the staff sitting or squatting by Lucy and making sure that she did not dash away from the table. Each time she attempted to do so, the adult would put an arm around her, gently prevent her from going and attempt to bring her attention back to the game. After about five minutes Lucy was allowed to run about as she pleased for a few minutes.

Differential reinforcement. At other times, the staff would reward Lucy with praise, a hug, and occasionally a sweet when she was sitting quietly or playing in a relatively controlled way. That is, any behaviour shown by her that was incompatible with rushing around the nursery was rewarded.

Staff continued to observe and record Lucy's behaviour and noted every half hour whether she was taking part in constructive play or was behaving in a controlled manner. The graph was continually added to. After twelve days of applying these

procedures, they were withdrawn and a further six
days (second baseline) of Lucy's behaviour were
observed.   After this second baseline period,
the procedures were reintroduced and observations
of Lucy's behaviour again collected as before.
     Figure 5.4 illustrates graphically the
information collected on Lucy's behaviour.   It shows
that the percentage of time spent in constructive
play or controlled activity increased as a result
of the action taken by the nursery staff.   When
the intervention was stopped, however, Lucy's
constructive activity soon declined again.   Upon
reintroduction of the procedures, however, Lucy
once more began to spend more time involved in
constructive activity and less time in uncontrolled
random activity.

FIGURE 5.4   LUCY'S CONSTRUCTIVE ACTIVITY BEFORE AND
AFTER INTERVENTION

(c)   Stopping the Programme
Over the following weeks, the staff made more baseline observations and re-introduced the intervention
on two further occasions before they were satisfied
that Lucy's behaviour had settled down at a point
where she spent some two-thirds of her time being
reasonably controlled.   This was felt to be the
best that could be achieved at this stage and
certainly represented a marked improvement over her
previous behaviour.

(iv)   AGGRESSIVE, ANTI-SOCIAL, DESTRUCTIVE BEHAVIOUR

The Problem
   Frank is difficult to cope with in the nursery.
   He uses little speech and resorts to pushing
   and shoving when he wants to join in an
   activity. He snatches toys and equipment from
   others, only to throw his prize down and rush
   off. He has no respect for the other
   children's activities, and , because of his
   behaviour and the fact that he is a big boy,
   some of the more timid children are afraid of
   him. Children who try to stand up to him
   come off badly and finish up in tears usually.

(a) Behavioural Method Used
The staff decided to try a blend of differential
reinforcement and shaping. They had noticed that
water play attracted Frank, although his participation frequently ended with the soaking of other
children and the flooding of the surrounding area.
The staff decided to reinforce Frank's acceptable
water play and use it to improve his communication
and his interaction with others.

(b)   Procedure and Results
Careful records were kept over a number of days of
Frank's behaviour at the water tray. He was
observed by a member of staff each time he went
there and, as trouble was not long in breaking out,
the whole episode was recorded each time. Records
showed that his behaviour deteriorated according to
the number of children present and the equipment
available. Frank seldom used his hands to splash
with but would throw or pour water from various
containers. Graphing was carried out to show the
length of time Frank spent at the water tray before
he either rushed off or began to throw water about.
As staff always had to keep an eye on him, gathering
information was no problem.
   The intervention programme consisted of a
member of staff inviting Frank to come to the water
tray when the other children were involved elsewhere.
Most of the equipment had been unobtrusively removed.
The adult played in the water with her hands, talking
to Frank about the feel of the water, its appearance
and other related topics (rain, seaside, bath etc.).
Frank proved to have things to say in these
circumstances, although he had difficulties in
expressing himself clearly. He was helped without
being nagged and new vocabulary was gradually

introduced.   Play moved on to using a colander and
objects that sink in water or absorb water.   The
length of time Frank spent at the water tray
lengthened considerably - and, as a bonus, the water
stayed longer in the tray.   The sessions were still,
of course, brief (between 1 and 10 minutes).   One
other child was then encouraged to join the member
of staff and Frank and, although Frank did not
welcome the intrusion to begin with, he began to
realise that another pair of hands and other ideas
added to the game.   The adult showed by her
behaviour how the other child could be brought in
and how equipment could be shared.   When more
children were added to the group, there was a
tendency for Frank to become aggressive again, but
he was encouraged to show them what he could do
with the apparatus and was found to be urging others
not to spill the water.

(c)   Stopping the Programme
The work in the water tray was only a very small
beginning and there was a great deal still to be
done to help Frank.   It had, however, shown that

1.   he could continue to play for longer than
     the staff had thought possible;
2.   he could use spoken language when he
     wanted to, thus giving staff the
     opportunity to shape his speech and
     extend it;
3.   he could interact positively with other
     children.

The intervention programme was considered to
be successful as far as it went.   However, a
positive reinforcement programme was now required
to establish the behaviour (i.e. rewarding the
acceptable behaviour) and then to maintain it in the
absence of the members of staff.   The programme,
therefore, had to be adapted and continued.
In this part we have given some brief descriptions of the procedures involved in some
hypothetical cases of behaviour problems.   To get
a better grasp of how the behaviour modification
approach can be used, you should look at some of the
case studies described in the reference books given
at the end of this section.   These will contain
more detail of what behaviour modifiers actually do
and will serve as guidelines for you when you plan
your own programmes.   A summary of the steps
involved in behaviour modification is given overleaf.

Summary of the Steps Involved in the Behaviour
Change Process

1. Define the problem and select a target:-

    (a) state clearly and objectively what
        the problem behaviour is;

    (b) select a target or level that you
        wish that behaviour to reach; you
        should be able to see the behaviour
        and count it

2. Use objective measurement techniques

    The process of measurement involves:-

    (a) defining

    (b) counting

    (c) recording

    (d) graphing

3. What to do about the behaviour

    You can either:

    (a) leave it alone (i.e. you wish the
        behaviour to be maintained at its
        present level)

    (b) increase it (i.e. teach new behaviour
        or develop infrequent behaviour)

    (c) decrease it (i.e. eliminate or
        reduce the level of the behaviour)

4. Continuously monitor the behaviour

    Keep records of the behaviour before,
    during and following and intervention.

PART VI.   TASK ANALYSIS

1. Introduction
In essence, task analysis is concerned with breaking
down a complex piece of behaviour into recognisable

smaller pieces of behaviour. The 'task' may be the act of putting on an overcoat to play outside or washing one's hands after a messy activity. In the latter instance the task might be broken down into the discrete steps of approaching the sink, putting in the plug, turning on the tap, grasping the soap, soaping and scouring hands, rinsing and drying hands, removing plug and rinsing out the sink after use. With a behaviour problem such as extreme overactivity a relevant task might be getting the child to sit attentively at a desk or table in order to play with a puzzle or join in a group activity. Here the task (of sitting down attentively) might be broken down into approaching the table, pulling back the chair, positioning the body immediately above the chair, grasping the table for support and finally easing down into a sitting position with eyes focused on the puzzle.

This process of breaking down the task into seemingly trivial steps may seem at first sight to be complicating the learning process unnecessarily but we hope to show later on that there are sometimes good reasons for doing so. The important thing to remember is that you are trying to establish a 'good' piece of behaviour (the task), and that for a particular child the learning of the task may have to be broken down into simple steps that can be systematically linked together into a coherent whole. The process of linking these simpler bits of behaviour together has been fairly widely researched by teachers and therapists concerned with mentally retarded or handicapped children and has been called 'chaining'. We will discuss some of the ideas and examine some of the problems involved in the chaining of responses below, but to re-emphasise the basic point - in task analysis we aim to analyse a fairly complex piece of behaviour into smaller component parts in order to institute a systematic training programme to enable the child to learn the complex behaviour.

2. Chaining
Chaining as a method of teaching a skill involves writing down in a series all the steps involved in attaining the end or target behaviour. Thus the steps can be seen as a series of objectives to be reached by the child. Basically there are two kinds of chaining : forward chaining and backward chaining.

Forward Chaining involves breaking down the task into a series of steps, the first of which must

be attained before proceeding to the third, and so
on until the target is reached.

Example 1
Removing a sock using FORWARD chaining

A. Sock moved down to ankle
B. A + sock pulled over heel
C. A + B + sock pushed down to toes
D. A + B + C + removes sock from toes

To use this method,the child would first be encouraged to carry out step A and rewarded for doing it.
When A is established, B is tackled in addition,
also using reward.   And so on.

Backward Chaining involves starting at the end
and working backwords so to speak.   Thus, the task
could be analysed as follows:

Example 2
Removing sock using BACKWARD chaining

Begin with the sock already pulled down to
the toes, then the sequence becomes:
A. Removes sock from toes
B. Removes sock from toes and heel
C. Removes sock from toes, heel and ankle
D. Removes sock completely

Chaining is most usefully employed where steps
can be put in an unvarying and fairly close time
sequence.   Thus, long delays between one or two
steps in a task would make chaining a less appropriate method to use.
Hemsley and Carr (1980) say that there are no
clear-cut research findings to show whether forward
or backward chaining is the more reliable or
efficient method, but that, on the whole, backward
chaining is the more dependable method.   The reason
given for this is that starting with the almost
completed task is a more rewarding situation for the
child.
In the early years at school a number of
important skills can be learned by chaining, including tying laces, using scissors, throwing and
catching a ball.   In their turn, these become part
of more complex activities, such as printing and
writing, and playing ball games.   As Gagné (1976)
puts it, " .....chains of motor responses become
the components of motor skills, often as 'part-

skills'. The latter are combined into organised
motor performances which learning and continued
practice invest with characteristics of smoothness
and precise timing".

The Essentials of Task Analysis

Gardner and Tweddle (1978) suggest that there may be
three levels of complexity in task analysis.

1. First Order task analysis involves a
   simple transfer of learning from one
   objective to the next.
2. Second Order task analysis uses a
   particular teaching method (e.g.
   chaining, shaping and fading).
3. Third Order task analysis includes
   prompting procedures.

   Examples of these three levels are given
below.

(i) FIRST ORDER TASK ANALYSIS

The important factor here is that the task is broken
down into several steps, and each step is an objective which has to be attained before the child
proceeds to the next one. That is to say, a
sequence of objectives is drawn up, as in the
following illustration concerned with learning to
kick a ball.

Programme 1

A. Kicks stationary ball with preferred foot
B. Kicks slow rolling ball with preferred foot
C. Kicks fast rolling ball with preferred foot

   The rationale here is that the learning of A
will make it easier to learn B, i.e. there is a
transfer of learning from A to B to C.

(ii) SECOND ORDER TASK ANALYSIS

Here, the way in which the task is analyzed is
governed closely by the nature of the method used to
teach the task. Shaping (p. 145) as a technique
has been found to be particulary useful for this
level of task analysis. An example given by Gardner
and Tweddle of learning to thread a needle involves

grading the teaching materials in order to shape
the child's activity.

Programme 2 : Threading a Needle

A. Threads needle with $\frac{1}{2}$" diameter hole with
    thin string
B. Threads needle with $\frac{1}{4}$" diameter hole with
    thin string
C. Threads needle with $\frac{1}{4}$" diameter hole with
    thick sewing cotton
D. Threads darning needle with thick sewing
    cotton
E. Threads darning needle with thin sewing
    cotton
F. Threads sewing needle with thin sewing
    cotton

Using such a programme would involve some
preparation of materials but it may well ensure that
the child learns the required skill (threading a
sewing needle) more rapidly and with less frustration
than might otherwise be the case.

(iii) THIRD ORDER TASK ANALYSIS

This type of task analysis uses physical prompts to
help the child acquire the skill.   Though prompting
can be used at the second order level as well, it is
used to a greater extent at this level.   Thus, when
a child fails to learn a task at the first or
second levels, it might be necessary to introduce
a programme where a lot of physical prompting is
given, as in programme 3 below.

Programme 3 : Removing a Sock (using physical prompt)

A. Removes sock <u>from toe</u> when told to with
    physical prompt (i.e. teacher takes child's
    hand and guides it through the action of
    removing sock)
B. Removes sock from toe when told to with
    gestural prompt (i.e. teacher imitates the
    necessary action)
C. Remove sock from toe when told to with
    gestural prompt (i.e. teacher points at
    the sock while saying, 'Take off your sock')
D. Removes sock from toe when told to <u>without</u>
    prompting.

The sequence is then repeated to remove sock from toe and heel and so on.

A point to watch when using prompts is to ensure that not too many prompts are given i.e. use only as many physical or gestural prompts as are necessary and gradually reduce these (fade them out).

3. Some Applications of Task Analysis to Typical Problems

Case 1. Overcoming shyness and isolation and teaching ball skills

Jimmy is a shy and isolated child who is often to be seen sitting or standing on his own when most of the other children are joining in games and noisily enjoying themselves. Even when Jimmy joins in the fun, he is so awkward and clumsy that he more often than not spoils the game for the other children. The nursery staff decided that they would approach his problems in two stages:

1. by teaching Jimmy to approach others and join in games more readily, thus overcoming his shyness, and
2. by teaching Jimmy some basic skills necessary to enable him to join in ball games.

The following programmes were devised.

Stage 1 : Overcoming shyness and isolation
The staff used a shaping procedure to increase gradually Jimmy's approach to and contact with other children. Each time Jimmy glanced at or took a tentative step towards the other children, the staff would reward him by saying, 'Good boy, go and join in', or smiling and waving him on. When Jimmy went for long periods without giving even these first steps, the staff would approach him and gently guide him (i.e. prompt) towards the other children and perhaps say, 'Come on Jimmy, let's see you join in the fun with the others'. As soon as Jimmy showed a fairly consistent tendency to approach others, the staff gradually faded out the physical promptings but continued to give him verbal praise and encouragement when he displayed this behaviour.

Stage 2 : Teaching Ball Skills using 1st, 2nd and 3rd order task analysis
Overlapping with Stage 1, as soon as Jimmy showed

168

more and more tendency to approach the other children, the staff devised the following programme to teach Jimmy the elements of throwing a ball.

Throwing

First Order Task Analysis
A. Throws large ball underarm using both hands to adult.
B. Throws bean bag underarm using preferred hand to adult.
C. Throws small ball underarm using preferred hand to adult

Second Order Task Analysis (using shaping)
A. (1. Throws large ball underarm with both hands (any direction)
((2. Throws large ball underarm with both hands into large basket nearby
((3. Throws large ball underarm with both hands to adult close by

B. (1. Throws bean bag underarm with preferred hand (in any direction)
((2. Throws bean bag underarm with preferred hand into basket nearby
((3. Throws bean bag underarm with preferred hand to adult close by

C. (1. Throws small ball underarm with preferred hand (in any direction)
((2. Throws small ball underarm with preferred hand into large basket
((3. Throws small ball underarm with preferred hand to adult close by

Third Order Task Analysis
A1 ((a) Throws large ball underarm (any direction) with both hands with physical prompt (i.e. stands behind child and physically guides his arms through the action of throwing the ball)
(
((b) Throws large ball underarm (any direction) with both hands with gestural prompt (i.e adult imitates the action of throwing the ball)
(
((c) Throws large ball underarm (any direction) with both hands when asked to without prompting

```
((a)Throws large ball underarm into large basket
(    nearby with both hands with physical prompt
(    (i.e. adult stands behind child and points
(    him at the basket and physically guides his
(    arms through the action of throwing the
(    ball)
(
A2 ((b)Throws large ball underarm into large basket
(    nearby with both hands with gestural prompt
(    (i.e. adult imitates the action of throwing
(    the ball into the basket)
(
((c)Throws large ball underarm into large basket
(    nearby with both hands when asked to without
(    prompting

A3      and so on ......
```

The third order task procedures (i.e. the same procedures as for the second order but incorporating physical prompts, gestures and verbal commands) are then repeated for each of the other steps in the process. Because Jimmy was so poor at throwing, the third order task procedures were felt to be most appropriate for him and the programme began with them.

Stage 3 : Maintaining Skills
Over several weeks of training Jimmy's behaviour was observed at intervals; any tendency to withdraw from contact with the other children or to give up trying to throw was countered by introducing an appropriate training session.

Case 2. Teaching Attention and Cooperation and Developing Coordinated Movement in an Overactive Child
Sally is a very restless and overactive little girl. She seldom sits still for more than a minute and cannot concentrate or pay attention to any one activity for very long, despite the efforts of the staff. She seems to have boundless energy and enthusiasm, but she expresses herself in a totally unco-ordinated way by rushing around the nursery, bumping into furniture and other children or crawling aimlessly over the floor or apparatus.

The nursery staff decided to try to teach Sally how to pay attention, be more cooperative and develop more smoothness and coordination in her movements.

A.   Teaching Attention and Cooperation

Sally is asked:

1. (a) 'Come over here' and is physically guided
       to a chair

   (b) 'Come over here' and is gestured towards
       a chair

   (c) 'Come over here' without any physical or
       gestured guidance from the staff

When 1(c) has been successfuly achieved, the
staff proceed to the next stage.

Sally is asked:

2. (a) 'Come over here and sit down' and is
       physically guided to the chair and gently
       made to sit down

   (b) 'Come over here and sit down' and is
       gestured towards the chair and motioned
       to sit down

   (c) 'Come over here and sit down' without
       any physical guidance or gestures

Each step is practised, obviously, until the
child has achieved it, before going on to the next
step.
     As soon as 2(c) has been successfully carried
out, the staff proceed to the third stage.

Sally is asked:

3. (a) 'Come over here, sit down and watch me
       for a while', and is guided to the chair,
       encouraged to sit down and persuaded to
       watch the staff member completing a task
       (e.g. doing a simple drawing). Any
       attempt to get up and dash away is
       countered by gently restraining her

   (b) 'Come over here, sit down and watch me
       for a while', and is made to do so by
       the use of gestures rather than physical
       guidance or restraint

   (c) 'Come over here, sit down and watch me

> for a while', without any physical
> guidance or gestures being used

Again, each step may have to be repeated several
times before the staff are satisfied that they can
proceed to the next one.

At the same time as teaching the later stages
of developing attention and cooperation, the staff
try to encourage Sally to move in a more controlled
and coordinated way and to avoid rushing, falling
and bumping into people and objects.

B. Developing Controlled and Coordinated Movement
The staff devised the following series of activities
for Sally. Again, physical guidance and gestures
were used for the initial steps before Sally perform-
ed the activities on her own with only verbal
instructions from the staff.

1. Walks along a simple obstacle course
    which requires her to go under, over
    and between suitable obstacles (e.g.
    desks, chairs or benches)

    Step (a) with physical guidance
    Step (b) with gestures
    Step (c) verbal instructions only

2. Walks up and down stairs

    Step (a) with physical guidance
    Step (b) with gestures
    Step (c) with verbal instructions only

3. Climbs up and down a small step ladder

    (Steps (a), (b) and (c))

4. Runs along an obstacle course

    (Steps (a), (b) and (c))

5. Hops along obstacle course, first on right
    foot and then on left foot

    (Steps (a), (b) and (c) as appropriate)

6. Jumps forward ten times, both feet together,
    then backward ten times, both feet together

(Steps (a), (b) and (c) as appropriate)

7. Jumps over a skipping rope held stationary one foot above the floor

   (Steps (a), (b) and (c))

8. Jumps over skipping rope rotated slowly by helpers

   (Steps (a), (b) and (c))

9. Skips on her own using rope

   (Steps (a), (b) and (c) as appropriate)

Summary : Points to Bear in Mind

The use of procedures such as chaining and shaping in a teaching programme may be a new departure for you, and you should remember that certain basic elements must be present before these procedures can be effective.   Some of these basic elements are listed below.   The child must have:

1. the verbal and general ability to understand the task;
2. the physical attributes necessary to do the task;
3. the motivation to learn, and the alertness necessary to perform the task;
4. rewards for any improvement, however slight;
5. adequate rest periods between intensive training sessions;
6. a variety of materials to make learning more interesting;
7. both tangible and social rewards at appropriate times;
8. adequate opportunity to practise the skill;
9. the realisation that learning a new skill is rewarding in itself;
10. a good model that can be imitated;
11. sympathy and understanding when having difficulty with parts of the task;
12. enjoyment and happiness whilst learning.

Task analysis and its associated techniques have been widely applied in a variety of settings over the last few years and there are a number of good

training manuals and books available for the interested reader. It is recommended that you read at
least one or two of the references given at the
end.

Conclusion

It is good advice to suggest that if you are thinking
of using any behaviour modification methods in your
nursery group, you might be wise to discuss your
intended programme with an educational psychologist
if this is possible. Talking things over can help
to clarify matters in your own mind as well as
opening out other possibilities.
    There may be a problem of time in some cases.
It would be inadvisable to spend too much time
concentrating on one individual to the detriment
of the other children. You may have to adapt your
programme once you have worked out how much time
you can justifiably spend on the child with the
problem. In some instances this may be no more than
a few minutes each day. However, even a few
minute's' application of a well thought-out intervention programme may produce dramatic changes in
that child's behaviour over several weeks.
    Some of the methods described in this section
may be difficult to apply in your particular setting
or with a particular child. You will have to use
your experience and judgement to pick out what is
practical and what is not, but do not do this
'out of hand' without a thorough analysis of the
situation. Many of these methods really do work,
but only if they are used properly.
    The other children in the nursery might well
be used to help their classmates to become better
adjusted. The children will be of particular help
when a technique is embedded in a play-situation
which will often have to involve other children in
order to structure a game (e.g. chaining the
teaching of ball skills).
    It is important to keep parents as fully inform-
ed as possible about what you are doing. Consult
the parents at all stages, gain their agreement and
try to involve them in the assessment and intervention that you will be carrying out.
    A further point that may bother you is whether
it is ethical to apply what may seem to be highly
manipulative techniques to a child's behaviour.
The answer to this is that behaviour modification
must always be humanely and thoughfully used. Any

174

procedure that might indirectly exacerbate a child's problem should be considered unsuitable. In reality most of the techniques are not 'manipulative' in a derogatory sense but merely constitute a systematic way of teaching a new behaviour pattern that will make the child a good deal happier in the long term.
Finally, many of the procedures of behaviour modifcation (e.g. rewarding good behaviour)are very 'common-sense' notions, and often those attending a course on the application of these techniques pass the remark, "...well, we do all that already, anyway". Without wishing to appear too defensive, we say that, in fact, this is not usually the case! Yes, it is true that many of the ideas underlying behaviour modification are familiar in everyday life and are rooted strongly in 'common-sense' (and this is to be welcomed since it probably means that many of these ideas are closely related to the fundamental laws of behaviour), but it is the <u>systematic, structured and consistent</u> manner in which these ideas are applied that makes behaviour modification a distincitive new approach to the treatment of behaviour problems in young children.

REFERENCES

BEHAVIOUR MODIFICATION

Hall, Vance : In Axelrod, S. (1977) <u>Behaviour Modification for the Classroom Teacher.</u> New York : McGraw Hill.
Porterfield, J.K., Herbert-Jackson, E. and Risley, T.R. (1976) Contingent Observation : an effective and acceptable procedure for reducing disruptive behaviour of young children in a group setting. <u>Journal of Applied Behaviour Analysis,</u> 9, 55-64.
Sarason, I.G., Glazer, E.M., and Fargo, G.A. (1972) <u>Reinforcing Productive Classroom Behaviour.</u> New York : Behavioural Publications, Inc.
Walker, J.E. and Shea, T.M. (1976) <u>Behaviour Modification : a practical approach for educators.</u> St. Louis : C.V. Mosby.

<u>Recommended Books (good outlines of applications of Behaviour Modification)</u>
Axelrod, S. (1977) <u>Behaviour Modification for the Classroom Teacher.</u> New York : McGraw Hill.

Herbert, M. (1978) Conduct Disorders of Childhood
    and Adolescence. New York : Wiley.
Vargas, J.S. (1977) Behavioural Psychology for
    Teachers. New York : Harper and Row.
Walker, J.E. and Shea, T.M. (1976) Behaviour
    Modification : a practical approach for
    educators. St. Louis : C.V. Mosby.

FURTHER READING

Blackham, G.T. and Silberman, A. (1975) Modification
    of Child and Adolescent Behaviour. Belmont :
    Wadsworth.
Cambrill, E.D. (1977) Behaviour Modification : Hand-
    book of Assessment Intervention and Evaluation.
    Washington : Jossey-Bass.
Hersen, M. and Barlow, D.H. (1976) Single-Case
    Experimental Designs. New York : Pergamon.
O'Leary, K.D. and Wilson, G.T. (1975) Behaviour
    Therapy : Application and Outcome. New Jersey :
    Prentice-Hall.
Willis, J. and Giles, D. (eds) (1976) Great
    Experiments in Behaviour Modification.
    Indianapolis : Hackett.

REFERENCES

TASK ANALYSIS

Gagné, R.M. (1977) The Conditions of Learning
    (3rd Edition) New York : Holt, Rinehart and
    Winston.
Gardner, J. and Tweddle, D.A. (1978) Some Guidelines
    for Sequencing Objectives. Training document,
    available from School Psychological Service,
    Walsall.
Hemsley, R. and Carr, J. (1980), and Tsoi, M. and
    Yule, W. (1980) - Chapters in Yule, W. and Carr,
    J. (eds.), Behaviour Modification for the
    Mentally Handicapped. London : Croom Helm;
    Baltimore : University Park Press.

FURTHER READING

Ainscow, M. and Tweddle, D.A. (1979) Preventing
    Classroom Failure : An Objectives Approach.
    Chichester : Wiley.
Burland, J.R., Brown, T.W. and Mendham, R.P. (1977)

Steps to Self Sufficiency : a training manual
developed at Chelfham Mill School, Devon,
and available on request.

(3) PROBLEM-SOLVING APPROACHES

Introduction

Philip (aged 4½) is a very active, lively
boy who likes to be the centre of attention.
He demands his own way frequently and if
he is thwarted or frustrated he is abusive
to staff and children alike and often hits
out in temper. Philip sometimes takes it
upon himself to 'punish' other children
for what he sees as misbehaviour on their
part, usually picking upon younger, weaker
children. His teacher, Mrs. G., frequently
finds herself intervening in problem
situations which have been provoked by
Philip's behaviour, either pacifying children in tears or sorting out squabbles and
fights. Philip always manages to come up
with some justification for his behaviour.

It often seems to be the case that children,
like Philip, whose behaviour is a cause for concern
repeatedly find themselves in the same kind of
situations and always meet their difficulties in
the same way with the same disastrous results. For
example, if Philip wants to play with a trike that
another child is riding, he has been known to try
and push the child off and forcibly wrest the trike
from him or her. The other child then either
retaliates or becomes upset and Mrs. G. is called
upon once again to act as arbiter or comforter.
Behaviour such as pushing, grabbing and hitting are
very common in three-year-olds, but generally, as
children develop they learn to adapt their behaviour
and try other ploys to get their own way, such as
offering to share or to give a toy in return. Some
children, however, get stuck in a 'rut' and like
Philip their only means of 'solving' a problem may
be to use force because they cannot readily adopt
new strategies for resolving their difficulties.
Like Philip's teacher when faced with unacceptable behaviour you may find yourself saying,
"Stop it, Philip, you must not hit (push, grab, kick

177

etc.). David, wait until he has finishing riding the
trike and then you can have a turn." We often
make demands upon children to stop hitting, kicking
or whatever "because I say so" perhaps adding the
rider "you might hurt him" or "you will have to
learn to share and take turns". But, in all
probability, when in similar circumstances the child
will do the same thing again. All Philip learned
from Mrs. G's interventions was that she was not
very pleased with him. Although she intended to
help, her actions were not successful in achieving
lasting positive changes in his behaviour. This
was largely because her direct commands and comments
on what he 'ought' to do in his position gave him
little help in sorting out the situation for himself because all the thinking had been done for him.

As an alternative to imposing external solutions
on Philip's problems Mrs. G. sometimes adopted the
role of arbitrator, helping to sort out the argument
and explaining why a particular behaviour was not
acceptable. Although this was an improvement on
the 'because I say so' approach this method had only
limited success. Typically, if Philip had worked
himself into a temper and was upset, a lengthy
explanation of the rights and wrongs of the matter
washed over him and he understood very little of
what his teacher said and failed to grasp the underlying principles of her reasoning. This is not to
say that she should not have offered such explanations, but it may have been better to delay them until
tempers had cooled and the children involved were
in a more receptive frame of mind. At least, in
her role as arbitrator Mrs. G. gave Philip a chance
to explain himself and his grievances and become
involved in working towards an acceptable solution,
but even so she felt that this approach, although
an improvement on the 'because I say so' method,
was doing little to change Philip's behaviour for
the better.

What Does the Problem-solving Approach Offer?
The problem-solving approach has a great deal in
common with the arbitration method outlined above.
However, in this approach the adult's role is rather
different. Instead of suggesting the most acceptable
answer to a problem or explaining why particular
actions meet with disapproval, the adult acts as
a guide in encouraging the children to think up
their own ideas of resolving the situation to everyone's satisfaction. The adult helps the children
to think about alternative courses of action for

themselves, to look ahead to possible outcomes and on this basis to choose the best solution. This does not involve teaching children specific solutions to specific problems but rather assisting them to think up their own options and their consequences, i.e. teaching children how to think, not what to think. The implicit philosophy on which the method is based is that if one wishes to change the behaviour of children one must influence the thinking which controls the behaviour. As demonstrated by Philip, merely prohibiting a behaviour does not prevent its re-occurrence, largely because the thought processes, which produced the behaviour in the first place, remain unaltered. The problem-solving approach, if used effectively, aims to develop flexible thinking and demonstrates to children that there is more than one way of solving a personal problem to their own and everyone else's satisfaction.

Perhaps this can best be illustrated by showing how Mrs. G. could have used problem-solving to sort out Philip's dispute over the tricycle.

Philip, you may remember, had wanted to ride on the trike which David was pedalling around the playground. He ran over to David and tried to push him off but David retaliated by kicking Philip,and both children end in tears. Mrs. G. comes over to sort things out.

Mrs. G. : Philip, what happened when you tried to push David off the bike?

Philip   : He kicked me.

Mrs. G. : How did you feel when he did that?

Philip   : It hurt, he made me cry.

Mrs. G. : I know you wanted to ride the trike and pushing was one way of getting it, but can you think of another way?

Philip   : I could hit him.

Mrs. G. : Yes, you could hit him, but what might happen if you do?

Philip   : He'd hit me back.

Mrs. G. : He might, so hitting isn't such a

good idea because he might make you
cry again.   Can you think of a
different way?

Philip   :   I could ask him.

Mrs. G.   :   Yes you could.   Why not ask David
and see what he says?

(She calls him over)

Philip   :   Can I have a ride on the bike
please?

David   :   No!   (Philip begins to get cross
again)

Mrs. G.   :   Oh dear, he said no.   Well, Philip,
I know you're upset now but I bet
if you think really hard you'll
find a different idea.   You've
tried asking, what else could you
do?

Philip   :   (After several seconds)   Can we
take turns?   I'll have a little go
and then you have it back?

David   :   All right.

Mrs. G.   :   Good boy Philip, you thought of a
different way all by yourself.
Do you feel better now?

David   and Philip   :   Yes.

In this situation Mrs. G. did not simply put a
stop to the kicking and pushing, nor did she tell
them to stay away from each other or even direct
them by suggesting other activities.   Instead
she brought both children together and guided Philip
in thinking through the problem for himself.   She
did not tell him what to say or what to think;   she
merely used the circumstances to direct him towards
a successful outcome to the problem.   This is
important, since it is much more likely that Philip
will act upon a conclusion if he has worked it out
for himself than if he is given a ready-made solution
by an adult.   It should also be noted that Mrs. G.
did not reject Philip's negative suggestion out of
hand but encouraged him to judge its merits in the

same way as more acceptable ideas.

Which Children will Benefit from this Approach?

Although so far we have only looked at an
example of an aggressive child, the approach can be
used equally well with any children who are having
difficulties in adjusting to the nursery group.
Withdrawn children, for example, may not know how
to join in a group game because of their very limited
social skills, and simply thrusting them into a
group activity and hoping for the best may leave them
floundering. The problem-solving approach used in
conjunction with some of the play activities
(see pp. 92-128) offers opportunities for you to
help withdrawn children become more adaptive and
socially outgoing.

The problem-solving approach aims to develop
logical thinking, but it should be stressed that
you should not expect too much rational behaviour
on the part of very young children. Learning to
think logically takes time (even adults do not
always act on the basis of reason) and you should
be prepared to accept and encourage partial
responses and partial understanding of the concepts
involved.

To work successfully, this approach requires
a child to be competent in certain language skills
and also capable of grasping the concepts involved
in logical thinking (e.g. Why did I fall off my
bike? I fell off my bike because I was going too
fast). For this reason it may not be the most
suitable method to use with very young children
or children who are slow developers, particulary if
their language is immature. With these qualificat-
ions in mind, we suggest that the problem-solving
approach gives nursery staff a framework for teaching
children the skills necessary to deal with social
difficulties.

Using the Problem-solving Approach in the Nursery Group

The problem-solving approach has two main
components, both of which should run concurrently
if maximum benefit is to be gained.

1. Group Activities

In order to develop the language and cognitive skills
necessary for successful problem-solving, children
need experience of practising these skills within
the security of a small group. The group sessions
involve a variety of activities and games which will

be outlined in detail later on in this section. They
are specifically designed to enhance children's
awareness of the effects of their behaviour on others
and to help in understanding that problems can have
a number of different solutions. The basic
principles of this approach are derived from a
nursery programme developed by George Spivack and
Myrna Shure. There are three stages of activities.

    A.   developing basic language skills;
    B.   developing an awareness of others;
    C.   using the skills from the first two
          stages to solve hypothetical problems.

2. Adopting the Problem-solving Style
Although you are teaching the skills and techniques
by means of group activities, if they are to be
effective in positively changing a child's behaviour,
you will have to ensure that what has been learned
in the group generalises to the remainder of the
child's day. Once you are familiar with the basic
principles of the approach you should be able to
incorporate them into your daily routine. Thus
when problems arise between children, you should
be on hand to prompt them in working out a solution.
A consistent application of the techniques in guiding
children through the real life difficulties they
encounter during the day will lead to their more
successful handling of similar situations in the
future.
    The remainder of this chapter is devoted to
practical guidelines for implementing both parts
of the problem-solving approach in your nursery
group.

1. GROUP ACTIVITIES

Organisation
The games and activities of stages A, B and C(see
above) are designed for group sessions with 6 - 8
children for ten to fifteen minutes a day. Suggestions concerning the settings, composition and
organisation of small groups are to be found in the
section "Play Activities" (pp. 113-115) although
it is worth mentioning several points in particular
here. All the activities require the children's
participation, so it is best to try and achieve a
balanced group of responding and non-responding
children, as the former are a great help to the
latter. Have the quiet children sit in the middle

of the group near the front, so that you can encourage
them to whisper in your ear if they are too inhibited
to respond in front of the others.   Similarly, if
you have disruptive children in your group you may
consider having them sitting next to you in order
to maintain their attention more easily.   It is
probably unwise to gather all the children you
consider to be having problems into one group.   Later
on you will find suggestions on handling the kinds
of difficult behaviour you may encounter in the
group sessions (pp. 195-197).

Sequencing of Activities

The activities of each stage, and the stages themselves, are based on a step-by-step progression so
that success in the later games is dependent on a
good understanding of the earlier ones.   For this
reason it is important that the activities are
introduced in the sequence suggested, although you
may need to spend several sessions on some of the
topics, and on revision, if it is apparent that
the children have not mastered a particular concept.
For this reason, many of the activities include
suggestions to extend the game, for example, by
introducing a different set of pictures, and you
can probably think up some more variations yourself.

Materials for Each of the Stages

Most of the materials needed for the activities are
those normally available in nursery groups and are
listed below.

Stages A and B (Language and Awareness Games)

Several sets of large pictures, preferably coloured,
mounted on card and covered in clear plastic.   You
should try to collect a set of each of the following:

        pets
        food (fruit, sweets, vegetables)
        faces (children who are smiling, laughing,
              crying, afraid, angry etc.)
        action pictures (children who are running
              jumping, eating, skipping etc.)
        toys (for boys and girls)
        forms of transportation

        The faces and action sets should include
pictures of different children doing the same thing.
        Also required are a hand mirror, a glove puppet,
two small collections of objects (e.g. hats, paint-
brushes, cars, dolls) and an apple or an orange.

Stage C (Problem-solving)
In this stage you can, if you wish, use pictures
of children at play to illustrate the hypothetical
problems you will be presenting to the group. These
may be more difficult to obtain but there are several
possible sources you could consider:-

    (a)   old educational supplies catalogues which
              include pictures of children playing
              with toys and equipment (e.g. Community
              Playthings, Abbatt toys, Galt Early Stages);

    (b)   the early books of the 'Dominoes' or
              'Through the Rainbow' reading schemes,
              which contain coloured photographs of
              children playing;

    (c)   the school library service will often
              provide, on request, a box of dis-
              carded picture books suitable for
              cutting up.

Stage A : Developing Basic Language Skills
The activities described in this section introduce
the basic vocabulary upon which the problem-solving
approach is based. Some children may be sufficiently competent in their use and comprehension of
language to by-pass this initial stage. If,
however, you are at all uncertain about your children's abilities, it is best to take them through the
programme from the very beginning, as success in
the later activities is dependent on these early
skills. The goal of all these activities is to
teach children to use language as a tool to solve
personal problems. Thus absolute grammatical
accuracy is not required, provided that a child
has grasped the particular concept involved, e.g.
"I've not got no cars" is just as acceptable as
"I haven't any cars" as long as the child understands
the concept of negation.

(a)   'Is' and 'Is Not'
Children have to be familiar with the concept of
negation if they are to decide not to do something
in favour of something else, e.g. "I'll not hit
him, I'll ask him to share."
    Begin the activity by pointing to individuals
in the group and saying, for example, "Tracey is
a girl, Gareth is a boy, James is a boy etc."
Go around all the children in the group and reinforce
the idea by having them tap their knees if you point
to a girl and raise their hands if you point

to a boy.   Next introduce the work 'not' by pointing out that Tracey <u>is</u> a girl, she is <u>not</u> a boy and
repeat with the other children.   Let the group have
fun with the word 'not' by naming silly things they
are not, e.g. "Gareth is <u>not</u> an elephant, Gareth is
<u>not</u> a dustbin etc."   To maintain interest give the
children objects (e.g. hats and cars), and ask who
is and who is not holding a car/hat.   To encourage
them to take notice of others ask individual
children what another child is holding, e.g."Robert,
is Jane holding a car?" or "Lisa, point to someone
who is <u>not</u> holding a hat, etc."   The game can be
extended by using pictures from the faces and action
sets.   The children can point to someone who <u>is</u>
smiling and someone who is <u>not</u> smiling, a child
who <u>is</u> running and one who <u>is</u> <u>not</u> running etc.

(b)   <u>'Or'</u>
If children are to learn to think of alternative
solutions to a problem they must be able to use the
word 'or' correctly, e.g. "I can hit him <u>or</u> I can
ask him to share <u>or</u> I can swop cars with him".

    Introduce 'or' by asking questions such as:

    "Am I pointing to Richard <u>or</u> am I pointing
    to Susan?"
    "Is Peter standing up <u>or</u> is Peter siting down?"
    "Am I holding a pencil <u>or</u> am I holding a book?"

    Reinforce the words learned in the previous
game in the answers you model:

    "Good Mark, I'm holding a pencil, I'm <u>not</u>
    holding a book."
    "Peter is <u>not</u> standing up he is sitting down."

    Use pictures from the food and pet set and ask:

    "Is this a cat <u>or</u> is this a dog?"
    "Is this an apple <u>or</u> is this a banana?" etc.

    Go around the group asking individual children
a variety of questions using 'or'.

(c)   <u>'Same' and 'Different'</u>
These words are important in naming new and different
alternatives and in being able to discriminate
between them when solving problems.   They also have
a part to play in demonstrating individual preferences, for instance, <u>different</u> children like

different things; some children like playing with
dolls and some do not; not everybody likes the same
thing.
     In this activity try to keep the focus on
children and the things they do. A good way of
introducing the words is by performing various
movements (waving, patting your head, standing up,
nodding your head etc.,) and first of all having
the group do the same thing as you and then asking
them to do a different action from yours. Each
child can take turns to come out and perform an
action, the group first copying the action and then
doing a different action. In this way the children
are not only thinking about the words 'same' and
'different' but are also given the opportunity to
think about what other children are doing.
     The game can be extended by using pictures from
the action set and letting the children make pairs
of pictures sometimes illustrating the same action
and sometimes two different actions. Make sure
you reinforce the words by continuously monitoring
what the children are doing (e.g. "Yes Richard, you
have chosen two boys doing the same thing. This
boy is running and this boy is running") and also
by questions (e.g. "Are these girls doing the same
thing?").

(d) 'Happy', 'Sad' and 'Angry'
As part of this approach involves demonstrating to
children how their behaviour can affect other children's feelings, by making them upset, angry or
happy, they need to know the various adjectives used
to describe emotions, as well as the ways these
feelings are expressed.
     Use pictures from the faces set to demonstrate
expressions such as laughing, crying, smiling etc.,
and talk about the relationship between facial
expressions and emotions, e.g. we smile when we are
happy and cry when we are sad etc. Demonstrate
a range of facial expressions yourself and see if
the children can identify your emotions from your
face. Encourage the children to make the same
faces as you and let them see themselves in a mirror.
Ask questions and give examples of the different
faces people use on different occasions, e.g.
"What kind of face do you have when someone gives
you a birthday present? Show me a 'happy' face".
"How would you feel if you lost your mummy in the
middle of town when you were out shopping? Show me
a 'sad' face", etc. Once you are certain that the
children have mastered the basic vocabularly move

on to the next stage.

Stage B : Developing an Awareness of Others

(a) How Can we Tell?

Attending to another child's feelings and preferences
is an important element in developing children's
abilities to solve personal problems successfully.
Understanding words such as 'happy','sad' and 'angry'
help children to learn that different people feel
differently, that feelings change and that it is
possible to find these things out by watching,
listening and asking.
The first activity demonstrates to children
that watching is one way to find out how someone
feels. Show the children a picture of a smiling boy
and ask, 'How can we tell if he is happy or sad?'
Point out that we can tell he is happy because we
can see him smiling. Repeat with pictures of sad
and angry children, emphasising that we can tell
how they feel because we can see with our eyes
whether they are frowning, crying, laughing etc.
Listening is another way of finding out how
people feel. Show this by covering your face
with a book and laughing loudly. Ask the children whether you are happy or sad and how they can
tell? Emphasise that they can tell not because
they can see you with their eyes but because they
can hear you with their ears. Cover your face again
but this time cry and repeat as for laughing. Let
the children take turns to cover their faces and
laugh or cry. The rest of the group have to guess
how they are feeling.
See if the children can think of another way
to find out whether someone is happy or sad. If
no one replies, tell them that the third way is to
ask. Go around the group asking the children how
they feel and encourage them to ask one another.

(b) Individual Preferences

The aim here is to show children that not everybody
chooses the same thing, as young children frequently
assume that others would choose what they choose
and this can lead to faulty conclusions. These
games offer guidance on how fo find out what other
children like and the children take an active role
in doing the asking. Throughout, the point is made
that different people like different things and this
is perfectly all right.

Choosing Game. Use pictures from the food or pets

set and present them to the children in pairs, e.g.
cat and dog, ice cream and crisps, chips and
biscuits etc.   Let children in the group say which
of the two they would prefer.   Point out that not
all the children choose the same thing, some prefer
cats and others dogs.   Repeat with several pairs
of animals/food asking all the children in the group
individually.   Encourage the children to say what
they think others would choose, e.g. "Brian, what do
you think Alan would choose, a cat or a dog?"   When
Brian has guessed let him see if he was right by
asking Alan himself what he would really like.
Repeat this with other children, making it clear
that asking is an important way of finding out what
others like.

Do you Like?   To reinforce the idea that not
everybody likes the same thing let the children ask
each other questions about what they like, e.g.
"Kevin, do you like sweets?   Do you like cars?
Do you like dolls?"   Allow the children to get
carried away with the phrase "do you like?" and
ask other children as many questions as they can
think of.

(c)   Why - Because Game
If children are to understand how their behaviour
affects others then they need to know something
about causality.   Children who realise, for
instance, that the reason why their playmates hit
them is because they hit first, will be more aware
of the consequences of hitting and a better judge
of the usefulness of this tactic next time around.
        This game aims to establish the connection
between 'why' and 'because' and for it you will need
a glove puppet.   Have the puppet introduce itself
and explain that it has come to play a game with
the children.   To begin, the puppet makes a statement, such as "I'm tired" or "I'm hungry", and the
children are prompted to ask "Why?".   The puppet
replies "Because I went to bed late" or "I didn't
have any breakfast", etc.   If you play the game
with the puppet first, the group will more easily
grasp what is required of them.   After several
such statements and questions, the game changes
and the children are encouraged to think of reasons
for the statements themselves.   E.g. the puppet
says "My friend Jean won't come out to play today.
Does anybody know why Jean won't play out?   Perhaps
she won't because ......"   At this point the children have to think of as many different reasons as

they can. For instance, she is not feeling well,
it's raining, her mummy won't let her,etc. Repeat
back to the children all the reasons they come up
with for each statement. Carry on until the children run out of reasons and then have the puppet make
a new statement and repeat the game again. The
game can continue with the children making statements
and the puppet asking 'Why?'.

Thinking of alternatives in this way is good
practice for later when the children have to think
of alternative consequences and solutions to problems.

(d) Fairness

Fairness is an important concept in learning to take
into consideration the rights of other children and
in being sensitive to their feelings. Included in
these activities is the notion that sometimes being
fair means having to wait.

Divide up an orange or an apple, explaining
that there is one piece for everyone in the group,
but they are not to eat them straight away. Point
out that it is _fair_ for everyone to have one piece,
but if someone takes two then it is _not_ fair as
someone will have to go without and this will make
them unhappy or angry. Demonstrate by handing
round the apple/orange so that the adult has two
pieces and someone else none at all, and show how
this can be put right so that everyone has a fair
share. Go on to give other examples of what is
fair and what is not fair, such as two children
wanting to look at the same book or play with the
same toy. Encourage the children to say what would
be the fair thing to do under the circumstances.

To illustrate that being fair sometimes entails
waiting, you can make up a little story about a
trip to the seaside. Make a pretend car out of
chairs or boxes that will seat only half the children in the group. Explain that there is only room
for some of the children so that you will have to
make two journeys, some going on the first trip
and some on the second. Choose half the group and
pretend to set off with them to the seaside, going
through the motions of driving and paddling in the
sea before pretending to return. Ask the group
who should go on the second trip,explaining that it
would _not_ be fair for some children to go twice.
Name some of the children who went on the first trip
and some who did not and ask whether it would be fair
for them to go on the second journey. Make a
second trip with the children who were not chosen
the first time. Fairness is not an easy concept

for children of this age to grasp and even though
some children will understand the idea they will
still find it difficult to put into practice.

Stage C ; Problem-solving
The aim of these group sessions is to enable
children to think of alternative solutions to hypothetical problems and to encourage them to appreciate
the consequences of their actions.   The activities
in this section are divided into three parts:

   (a)   alternative solutions;

   (b)   alternative consequences;

   (c)   pairing solutions and possible consequences.

   It should be stressed that, in working through
a problem, the children should be guided to think
of their own solutions and consequences.   Never
tell the group what you consider to be the best
solution but allow them to work this out for themselves with your help.

How to Organise these Group Sessions
Children of this age cannot be expected to understand hypothetical problems without some assistance
from props or visual aids.   You may find that the
group will solve problems more readily if you choose
two of them to 'act out' examples of problem situations.   This need not be anything very elaborate;
you could, for example, choose one child to sit and
look at a book and ask a second child to snatch it
from her.   Having watched an actual demonstration
of a problem the group may then be able to talk
about how the first child might feel, what might
happen next and so on.   By using role play in this
way to illustrate typical problems, children may
find it easier to relate the hypothetical problems
to situations in real life.
   Alternatively, you may want to use pictures
and photographs to illustrate difficult situations.
These pictures do not need to depict an obvious
problem as you can utilise any pictures of children
playing and define the problem verbally when you
show it to the group.   For example, a picture of
two children eating biscuits could form the basis
of a story in which one child snatches a biscuit
from the other.   You can then talk about the story
in the light of what is fair and what might happen

as a consequence.   Inventing a problem situation
from a picture is not difficult and although
suggestions will be given you can, if you wish, make
up a variety of problems which are typical of your
nursery group.

(a)   Alternative Solutions
The aim here is to use the basic word concepts
learned earlier to guide the children towards
thinking in terms of alternatives.   In each session
the children are either shown a picture depicting
a common problem or act out a problem and then are
asked to think of as many different ways as possible
of solving the problem.

A typical example might be a situation involving
two boys playing with a box of bricks.   Tell the
children that David and Gareth have both been playing with the bricks, but now that it is time to put
them away Gareth does not want to help.   The problem
is how can David get Gareth to help him clear away?
The story is discussed in terms of what is fair and
what is not fair and the group is told that the
idea of the game is to think of lots of different
ways for David to get Gareth to help him.   Each
solution offered is repeated to the group and they
are urged to think of what else David can do to get
Gareth's co-operation.   When ideas of what to do
are no longer offered, the children are asked what
David can say to Gareth and the solutions are
enumerated once again.

At this stage children will often suggest a
variation of the same solution rather than a
different one.   The most common variations are:
giving something (give him a sweet, give him your
car);   telling someone (tell his daddy or his mummy,
tell the teacher); hurting (hit him, kick him, bite
him).   Let the children do this for a while and
then classify their statements so that they learn
to distinguish between mere variations and solutions
that are categorically different.   For instance,
"Giving Gareth a car or a sweet or a crisp are all
'giving something'.   Can anyone think of an idea
that is different from giving something?"

Again, if 'giving something' is suggested as a
solution, you should point out to the group that
not all children like the same things.   Before
offering to give a sweet or a toy they would first
have to find out if the other child wants or likes
what is being offered by asking.   Sometimes children appear to give seemingly irrelevant solutions
to the problem ('cry' or 'be good' for example), in

which case you will have to question the children
as to why they think this is a good idea by asking
them to tell you more about it.

It is important to accept <u>all</u> the children's
ideas at this point without making any value judge-
ments, so that 'hit him' is just as relevant as
saying 'please' and should be included in the list
of solutions offered.   Later on, both forceful
and non-forceful solutions will be looked at in the
light of their consequences.

Listed below are some suggestions of problem
situations which you can use in these sessions.
They can be illustrated either by pictures or by
children 'acting out' the situations you describe
for them.   As mentioned earlier you may make up
your own little stories if you wish.

> (i)   A boy wants his friend to help with
>   clearing away the toys.
>
> (ii)   A child wants another to sit down and
>   stop blocking the view of the picture
>   book being read to them by an adult.
>
> (iii) A child wants to ride on a bike (swing,
>   scooter, cart, rocking horse etc.) that
>   another child is already playing with.
>
> (iv)   A child wants another child to play
>   with in the Wendy House.

(b)   Alternative Consequences

In the next few sessions the children are presented
with similar problems and again asked for solutions,
but here your aim is to teach them to think in
terms of the consequences of particular solutions.
Through questioning (e.g. "What might happen next
if you hit her?"),the children are encouraged to
think for themselves, weigh the pros and cons of
an action and then decide whether or not their
idea was a good one.   This is perhaps best illustrated by the following example:

> Either show the group a picture of two
> children standing by a rabbit hutch and tell
> them that the boy wants the girl to let him
> feed the rabbits or act out a similar sit-
> uation using two children from the group. As
> in previous sessions, encourage the children
> to think of alternative solutions to the
> problem.   Take one of the proffered solutions,

such as "push her out of the way", and ask
the children what might happen next if this
course of action was followed.   Encourage
the children to think of as many different
consequences as they can.   If they run out
of ideas prompt them with further questions
such as:

> "What might the girl <u>do</u> if the boy
> pushes her?"
> "What might the girl <u>say</u> if the boy
> pushes her?"
> "How might the girl <u>feel</u> if the boy
> pushes her?"
> "Will she be sad, happy or angy?"

Reiterate to the children all the alternatives
they have thought of so far.   When it becomes
apparent that no further suggestions are
forthcoming, ask the group if they think pushing is or is not a good idea and why.   Then
take one solution at a time and elicit all
the consequences you can before going on to a
different solution.   Try to choose forceful
as well as non-forceful solutions for the
children to evaluate at each session.   You
may find it useful to record the solutions
and consequences so that you can refer to
them if need be.

Set out below are a number of problems which
you might like to use in the sessions on alternative
consequences.   Remember to elicit a number of
different solutions before examining them individually in terms of their consequences.

    (i)   A boy wants a girl to let him feed the
          animals.

    (ii)   A girl wants a boy to stop knocking
          down her building brick houses.

  (iii)   A boy on the slide wants a girl at the
          bottom to get off so that he can slide
          down.

    (iv)   A girl wants to be a nurse but someone
          else is already dressed up in the
          nurse's outfit.

(c) <u>Pairing Solutions and Consequences</u>
In these activities the children are given a problem, have to think of a solution and then think immediately of its consequence. Ultimately, it is hoped that the children will learn to think of solutions, evaluate them, and then decide which alternative is the most appropriate before taking action.

As in parts 'a' and 'b' explain the problem to the group and ask for solutions in the usual way. When one solution has been suggested ask immediately what might happen next as a consequence. You can use any of the following questions to elicit consequences:

> "What might happen next if ....?"
> "What might B <u>do</u> if A ....?"
> "What might B <u>say</u> if A ....?"
> "What might B <u>feel</u> if A ....?"

Ask only for one consequence per solution and then move onto a second solution and a second consequence, perhaps asking individual children for pairs of solution and consequence. Continue pairing solutions and consequences in this way until no new ones are offered. Occasionally follow up by asking a child if a particular solution is a good one and why.

Here are a few more suggestions for problem situations:

(i) A boy wants another child to stop scribbling on his picture.

(ii) A girl wants another child to stop chasing her.

(iii) A boy would like to play a game of lotto but all his friends are outside in the playground or in the Wendy House.

(iv) A girl on a bike wants a girl on a scooter to get out of her way.

Before going on to Part II which describes the informal use of the principles and techniques of the problem-solving approach throughout the day, some reference should be made to handling difficult behaviours which may occur in the group sessions.

Managing Difficult Behaviour in the Group Sessions
The Child who will not Respond
Since most of the activities require a response from
the children in the group you will soon be aware of
any child who is not participating. There may be
many reasons why children do not respond : they may
be too shy or hesitant to speak in front of even
a small group; they may prefer not to think about
what is going on and are not listening; perhaps
they are unsure of what is happening and hesitate
to join in; or they may be temporarily upset and
not in the mood to play games.

Children who consistently do not respond, and
sit in the group day after day merely as onlookers,
can sometimes be coaxed out of their passivity if
you approach them warmly and with extreme patience.
You could try phrasing the questions to them in
such a way that they can respond with a nod or a
shake of the head. Often a physical response may
be easier for them than a verbal one. Similarly,
in some of the games involving individual preferences,
it is feasible to have shy children point to the
object they would prefer, as even pointing is better
than no participation at all. Any sign of a
response, however minimal, should be praised but if,
after gentle prodding, the child will not even
respond with a nod of the head the matter should be
dropped for a while. Too much pushing may upset
the child and too much time taken with one child
may cause the rest of the group to become restless
and lose interest.

Shy children should not be further isolated by
being allowed to sit at the back apart from the rest
of the group. Have them sit near to you so that
they can be encouraged to whisper in your ear when
a verbal response is called for. Once shy children
have been prompted to make a physical response, the
next stage is often to parrot the responses of
others in the group. They should be praised for
this as such participation can be a stepping stone
to thinking for themselves. Only after they have
been allowed to parrot for several days should you
ask them to think of a different idea of their own.
Given simple choices, the opportunity to respond
minimally at the beginning, and praise for even
tentative signs of involvement, the shy child may
blossom.

Sometimes children who normally join in may be
temporarily upset or in an obstinate mood and refuse
to participate. If this is the case, a useful way

of gaining their attention is to engage the rest of
the group in thinking about what they are doing and
treating such behaviour as a problem to be solved.
You could say, "Is Judith feeling happy or is she
feeling sad?   Yes, she is feeling sad.   Judith,
why are you feeling sad?"   If the child does not
respond, the rest of the group can be brought in -
"Can anyone guess why Judith is feeling sad?   Perhaps
it is because ....?" or "Can anyone think of a
way to help Judith feel happy again?"   Often if
children are only wanting attention then they can be
supplied with it legitimately by using the techniques
of this approach to 'solve' their problem.

Disruptive Behaviour
You may find you have a child in the group who cannot
sit still, goes backwards and forwards from one side
of the room to the other, fidgets with any object
nearby and is generally a disruptive influence in
the group.   Obviously, it is best to position such
children away from toys, bookshelves and distracting
objects and to separate two such children who may
happen to be friends.
    If a child walks away from the group it is often
more effective to ignore this than distract the
others by calling the child back.   Sometimes children
like this will come back when they hear something
that interests them.   If they continue to be a
nuisance you can call upon them for ideas or have
them come to the front to be the leader.   Another
useful technique is to focus attention on the
disruptive child by saying, for example, "George
is doing something <u>different</u>.   He is playing a
different game.   What is George doing?"   Such
attention is perfectly acceptable and far more
effective than threatening that they will have to
leave the group if they do not behave.   Where the
motive for disruptive behaviour is attention seeking,
as with the obstinate child, they can learn through
the games and activities that there are more efficient
and satisfying ways of being noticed.   Generally,
such disruptive behaviour should not become contagious
as children in the group receive plenty of attention
whenever they respond and, as noted earlier, even
when they do not.

Dominating Behaviour
Some children have long drawn-out stories to tell,
or as soon as you ask a question they are the first
to shout out an answer, oblivious to the fact that
other children have not had a chance to participate.

Without meaning to, such a child can easily dominate
the whole group with the result that the others lose
interest and become restless.

You will have to handle dominant children with
care, for if you stop them or discourage them they
may also lose interest and become disruptive. An
effective ploy is to let them tell their story on
the understanding that afterwards it will be someone
else's turn, perhaps allowing them to nominate the
next child. Again, focussing on dominant children
by allowing them to be leaders for some of the time
can be helpful. The key to managing this kind of
behaviour is to be firm but friendly, allowing
such children to be the centre of attention within
acceptable limits.

'Silly' Behaviour
Occasionally a child will respond with irrelevant or
opposite answers, will laugh or make faces or funny
gestures. If you are reasonably certain that the
child understands the question being asked and is
merely being silly to attract attention, then it is
best to say, "Oh, you're just teasing me", and
ignore any further outbursts. If a child carries
on being silly and parrots another child just to be
annoying, continue to ignore the behaviour and only
give attention and praise for normal responses.
Especially in the later games children may be silly
because they have nothing to contribute. Try to
focus their attention on the game, rather than
reinforcing their silly behaviour, as only by
developing their thinking skills, so that they have
more to offer, will their silliness diminish.

2.   ADOPTING THE PROBLEM-SOLVING STYLE

The games and activities are designed to increase
a child's chances of success in dealing with real
life problems but you will have to try and ensure
that the skills learned in the group do generalise
to the remainder of the child's day. Now that you
are familiar with the basic principles of the approach, you should be able to incorporate them into
conversations over difficulties which arise between
children in the nursery and prompt them to work out
a solution for themselves. By consistently applying
the techniques of guiding children through problems
as they arise during the day you will be helping
them to handle similar situations with more success
in the future.

Outlined below are some examples of problems that commonly arise between young children and how the problem-solving style can be used to bring about a successful resolution.

Hitting and Grabbing
Hitting, grabbing, pushing and kicking can be started by a child but are often a response to having been attacked or mistreated in some way.   Examples of both situations will be given.

Example 1
David was seen, by a member of staff, to push John off a scooter and she goes over to investigate.

Adult: David, why did you push John off the
         scooter?
David: I want a go on it.
Adult: What might happen if you push like that?
David: He might fight.
Adult: So is pushing a good idea?
David: (defiantly) Yes!
Adult: Why?
David: He won't let me have a go.
Adult: Pushing is one way to get the scooter,
         but can you think of a different way
         to get him to give you a turn?
David: (Shouts to John) Can I have it when
         you're done?
         John nods his head.

Although this conversation was carefully guided by the adult she did not tell David what to do, but helped him to think through the problem and arrive at his own solution.   When it was obvious that David was more interested in getting the scooter than the fact that John might fight, she accepted that 'pushing' was one way of getting what he wanted, but rather than condemn this tactic outright she prompted him to think of an alternative.

Example 2
A member of staff sees Susan hit Joanne, who then retaliates.

Adult: Joanne, why did you hit Susan?
Joanne: She hit me first.
Adult: Susan, why did you hit Joanne?
Susan: (Pouts and refuses to answer)

Adult:	What did Joanne do when you hit her?
Susan:	(Still sulking)
Adult:	Did she go away or did she hit back? (a child is much more likely to answer if given a choice of two simple statements than if questioned directly)
Susan:	Hit back.
Adult:	Susan, how do you feel now? Are you happy or sad?
Susan:	Sad.
Adult:	How do you feel, Joanne?
Joanne:	Sad.
Adult:	Well, you don't feel happy Susan, and neither does Joanne. Can one of you think of a way to make you feel happy again?
Joanne:	Play house with Susan.
Adult:	Why is that a good idea?
Joanne:	We'll be friends.
Adult:	You'd better ask Susan if she wants to play with you.
Joanne:	Do you want to play?
Susan:	Yes. (both children go off, chanting "We're friends", into the Wendy House)

In this situation the teacher does not simply remonstrate with the children about their behaviour but brings both together and guides them through thinking about the conflict themselves. Rather than make an issue out of who hit first she tries to restore positive feelings by using the problem-solving style. Direct questioning may meet with little response if the children are upset (as in this case), whereas the techniques of offering two alternative answers will often prove successful.

Example 3
Sometimes the problems that have been dealt with in the group sessions may actually arise in the nursery, and the strategies used then can be brought into play.
During story time Tracey cannot see because Andrew is kneeling up and she pushes him out of the way.

Adult:	Tracey, pushing is one way to get Andrew to sit down but what might happen if you push him?
Tracey:	He might push me back, but I can't see!
Adult:	Can you think of a different way to get him to sit down?

```
Tracey:   (Crossly) No!
Adult:    Do you remember the picture I
          showed you of children at story time?
          One of those children wanted someone
          to sit down.
Tracey:   Yes.
Adult:    We thought of lots of things the boy
          could do.   Can you remember one of
          them?
Tracey:   (To Andrew) Please sit down.
Andrew:   (Sits down)
Adult:    There you are, that was a different
          idea and Andrew sat down.
```

It sometimes happens that a disagreement between two children gets out of hand before anyone notices, and you are faced with either two weeping or two angry children.   If both of them are too emotional to respond it often helps to bring over a third child (or several) and encourage them to offer ideas and try out ways of making the unhappy pair feel better. Sometimes children respond to another child more readily than to an adult.

There may also be times when children will not respond at all to your attempts at involving them in the kind of problem-solving dialogues described so far.   If this is the case you must decide whether to pursue the questioning or to drop it, as in the following illustration:

> Jane was hitting Sarah because Sarah wanted to share her plasticine.   Jane grabbed all the plasticine and shouted, "You go away.   I'm making a model on my own and I'm not playing with you!"   The adult decided not to use the problem-solving approach for two reasons: Jane usually did share her possessions, and there are times when a child should have the right to play alone; and Jane was far too emotional to think clearly anyway.   In this instance the adult simply interested Sarah in doing something else and left Jane to play on her own.

Avoiding Potential Problems and Accidents

As well as resolving actual difficulties, the problem-solving style can be used to avoid problems and

accidents.   Typical incidents when such techniques
can be applied are, for example, a child standing
in front of a moving swing, running around wildly
inside, using scissors dangerously, or jumping off
the top of a climbing frame without looking to see
who was underneath.   Rather than saying, "Don't do
that" or "If you do that you'll hurt yourself" you
can encourage the children to think of the consequences of their actions for themselves.
     You can use the following dialogue in all
potentially hazardous situations:

        Adult: Is ...... a good idea?
        Child: ....
        Adult: How might you feel if you (fall, hurt
                yourself, land on Steven, etc.)?
        Child   ....
        Adult: Can you think of a different (place
                to stand, way to use scissors, way
                to jump)?

     Unless children have to be physically stopped
because danger is imminent, they should be guided
in thinking about the situation just as in handling
problem behaviour.   You help children to focus
on the presence of a danger by means of its
consequences.
     A point which must be emphasised, when using
the problem-solving style in real life, is that you
should follow through each episode to ensure that
the solutions arrived at are in fact carried out.
If, for example, two children agree to share a book
rather than squabbling over it, you should stay
long enough to make sure they do.   Although young
children are usually responsive to the guidance
given, initially they may be unable to carry through
solutions of their own.

Conclusion
It is hoped that by using the techniques outlined
above you will be able to improve the personal
adjustment of children in your care by developing
their ability to see a human problem, their
appreciation of different ways of handling it and
their sensitivity to the potential consequences of
what they do.
     Remember not to expect too much too soon, as a
young child will not turn into a logical, reasonable
being overnight.   However, practice in the group
sessions and a consistent application of the

problem-solving approach in the nursery group should help in laying the foundations of more logical thought processes.

REFERENCE

Spivack, G. and Shure, M.B. (1974) <u>Social Adjustment of Young Children</u>. San Fransisco : Jossey-Bass.

Chapter 6

MAKING A PLAN OF ACTION

In this section we will try to offer you some guidelines to help you plan a programme of action to help
a child with difficulties.   You will need to:

1. collate all the available information about
   the child;
2. make further observations or obtain
   additional information if necessary;
3. examine the resources, support and time
   available.
4. draw up a plan of action;
5. write down a detailed plan;
6. try some pilot runs if appropriate;
7. implement the programme;
8. monitor progress;
9. decide when to stop the programme or
   take further action.

We will look at each of these points in turn
and then describe in detail some case studies which
were carried out by nursery staff in different
schools, using a pilot version of this handbook.

1.   Collating the Information
Assuming that the initial assessment and information
gathering stage has been completed, this
information should be summarised in Section I of the
record booklet.   Thus you should have details of

(i)   the Behaviour Checklist (Schedule 1)
(ii)   the Behaviour Assessment Schedule
        (Schedule 2)
(iii)   the General Assessment Schedule
        (Schedule 3)
(iv)   Talking to Parents (Schedule 4)
(v)   Help from Others (Schedule 5)

Making a Plan of Action

A good starting point would be to read and thoroughly
familiarise yourself with the details of Section I
of the record book, and then go through all the
assessment schedules in turn to obtain a general
overview.   Look also at <u>all</u> the notes you have made
since the beginning - whether these are in rough
form or not - in case you have missed some small
point that could be of significance.   Very often,
details may not appear to be important until you
have reviewed the whole problem.
        Having thoroughly immersed yourself in the
available information, take some time off to allow
the whole thing to be digested, and then quickly
review it again.   It would be very useful if you
could then discuss possible courses of action with
your colleagues, who should be kept in touch with
the whole procedure.   Ensure that your colleagues
have also seen the material and are familiar with
it.   You will then have a basis for discussion
which could well lead to your gaining fresh perspect-
ives on the problem and some concrete suggestions
for tackling the difficulties.

2.   <u>Making further Observations and Obtaining more</u>
<u>Information</u>
When you have digested the information and discussed
it all with your colleagues, you may decide that
you need to know more about how the child behaves
in certain situations, or that there is a need for
observations of a particular activity which may be
highly relevant to the problem.   For example, a
child may have a much wider repertoire of behaviour
than you had originally thought.   Remember the
example of <u>James</u> (p. 33).   His teacher, Mrs. S.,
after a period of observing him closely found
that, ..." contrary to her immediate impressions
he did, in fact, show interest in a wide variety
of activities and was observed participating in
almost the entire range provided by the nursery!
His social contacts were much broader than at first
thought."
        We recommend in the Behaviour Assessment
Schedule (2) that you observe the child closely
for at least a week, but you may wish to extend that
period in order to cover further situations or to
look at more specific aspects of the problem behaviour
in question.   In the case of behaviour modification,
a period of specialised observation to obtain a
baseline of certain behaviour is essential.   So if
you are contemplating using a behaviour modification
approach, you should ensure that you have sufficient

information on which to base this extended observation. Is the behaviour sufficiently clearly defined? Have you covered adequately the most important situations in which the behaviour is likely to arise? Will the method of observing adopted be suitable to obtain a representative sample of the problem behaviour? These and other questions that occur to you should be considered carefully before you embark on further observation. Again, having examined all your notes, you may decide that you do not have sufficient information about the family or that you are unclear about how an outside agency is involved. You should try to decide now whether or not it is necessary for you to know more. If you conclude that you need more information, then now is the time to try to get it. For instance, you might have felt too inhibited on a previous occasion to ask the parents about a child's attitude to his brother or sister, but having observed that a lot of his behaviour shows evidence of being over-competitive and domineering, you might wish to find out if he behaves similarly at home. This could have an important bearing on how you plan the programme; for example, whether you include a routine specifically designed to counteract 'jealous' behaviour and provide insight for the child into how to deal reasonably with others.

There must come a point, though, when you have to decide to suspend the gathering of more information and to take action. It would be unwise to delay taking action once you have a reasonably sound background of information, as there will be further opportunities to gain relevant information as you proceed and continue to monitor the programme.

3. Examining the Resources, Support and Time Available

It would be of little use to plan a very detailed and beautifully designed programme of action if you were to find subsequently that you had neither the resources nor the time available to implement it. The action that you take must be based on a realistic assessment of your own situation.

(i) Resources
By 'resources' we mean all the available materials, activities and services that your nursery group has to offer. Thus, you should be sure that you have suitable toys, games and materials with

which to implement a programme of play
activities or take steps to obtain these.

Again, the amount of space and
availability of additional rooms can be
considered as a resource. In some open-
plan nurseries it may prove difficult to
find a quiet corner into which to take a
child so that he can receive some individual
attention and be afforded the opportunity
to concentrate on a task. It may be
possible to screen off part of the nursery
or use another room for this purpose. Try
to anticipate any difficulties and think of
ways of overcoming them; nursery teachers
and playgroup leaders, in our experience,
have proved to be very ingenious with very
limited resources.

(ii) <u>Support in the group</u>
A very important consideration will be the
number of adults that you have to help you.
In some cases you may have only limited
support but you should consider carefully
what is the best use of the resources
available to you.

(iii) <u>Time</u>
The time available to you will, of course,
depend to some extent on the support which
you have, but it might be useful for you
to look more closely at how you actually
spend your time, to see if you can save a
few minutes here and there that can then
be used to deal with a difficult child.
As we have said previously, a few minutes
each day may be all that is needed to begin
to change a problem behaviour, and this may
lead to your saving time that would otherwise be spent admonishing or trying to
control the child in question.

Of central importance is the question
of how much time you should spend each day
or every week on a special programme and
how long the whole programme should last.
Unfortunately, it is impossible to give
very precise answers to these questions as
they depend on many considerations such as
the type and severity of a problem, the
child's co-operativeness and ability to
learn, and the type or number of approaches
that you adopt. Some approaches, such as

play or language activities, can readily
be fitted into the ongoing routine of the
nursery, whilst others, like some behaviour
modification techniques, require specialised
procedures for which extra time must be
found. The best advice that we can offer
is that you try out the procedures that
you would like to use, and time these.
You can then decide whether or not it will
be feasible to start a programme using
those techniques or whether you will have
to cut them down in some way. As you
become more skilled in their use, of
course, you will reduce considerably the
amount of time spent in initiating and
carrying through those procedures, which
is why trying pilot runs will prove useful,
as we shall see a little later on.

4. Drawing up the Plan
To draw up a plan of action you will need to:

(a) note the most worrying aspects of the
    child's behaviour in the order of
    priority in which they will be tackled;

(b) write down the changes you hope to achieve;

(c) detail the approaches you intend to use,
    together with how and when they are to be
    implemented.

Section II of the record book provides space
for a summary of these details, but you will probably
need to have a fuller and more detailed account,
written down separately, that will serve as a guide
to direct your actions in implementing the programme.

(a) List the Difficulties in Order of Priority
You should now review thoroughly again all the
information from the assessment schedules and elsewhere that relate to the child, and then write down
a full list of the child's problems giving details,
where appropriate, of how often they occur, how long
they last, what seems to trigger them off and in
what situations they occur.
     Looking at the schedules and notes relating to
Brian (whom we met at the beginning of Section IV)
we might draw up a preliminary list of difficulties
somewhat as follows:

(i) Brian seems to lack adequate stimulation at home - he is rarely given interesting or attractive activities to indulge in and his parents do not seem to take a great deal of interest in him;

(ii) his behaviour at home is similar to his behaviour at school, but he seems to have more temper tantrums at home where his parents fail to understand his requests;

(iii) he plays rather aimlessly on his own for long periods;

(iv) Brian's language is very poor and has not progressed much beyond the one-word stage - he frequently uses gestures and grunts to communicate his needs;

(v) his scores on the initial behaviour check-list reveal 2 'c's:
Item 9 - "Has seldom been known to talk to anyone at all"
Item 10- "Frequently 'clings' to adult for assurance and does not attempt to attend to his own needs"
On the Behaviour Assessment Schedule he obtained a 'c' on item H - "Plays mainly alongside other children rarely with them";

(vi) new situations or changes in routine prompt him to seek adult help - explanations and instructions have to be simplified to help him;

(vii) a sample of observations of Brian's behaviour in the nursery group :

Outside Play (10 a.m.)

Brian and three boys are outside on tri-cycles. Brian follows Peter around and gently crashes into him. He smiles all the time but there is no verbal communic-ation. Stops crashing immediately when reprimanded by an adult. Continues to cycle aimlessly but happily.

Jigsaw Table (10.30 a.m.)
Brian and Julie. He is attempting to do a jigsaw - still with his outside coat on

as he cannot remove it and has not asked
an adult to do so.   Julie is being very
'bossy' and domineering about Brian's
choice of puzzles - he is totally acquies-
cent.

Car Table (11 a.m.)

Brian and four other boys.   Brian lies
prone alongside the car table moving a
car along a road mat.   Is oblivious of
the other children and makes no sounds or
attempts to communicate.

Number Corner (11.30 a.m.)

Brian and small group and teacher.   Brian
sits on his own, matching Lotto cards
slowly and silently.

Centre of Nursery (1.30 p.m.)

Brian and four boys.   Brian is wearing a
Batman cape and running around behind
the other boys, who are shouting "Pow!"
"Batman!"   "Zap!" etc.   Brian struggles
with "Ba!" but is making an attempt to
copy the others.

(viii) **Outside Agencies**
Because it has been suspected that Brian
might be deaf, a number of outside agencies
have been contacted, including the local
clinic, Brian's family doctor and health
visitor.   Finally he has been referred to
the Hearing Clinic at the nearby hospital
as tests done locally proved inconclusive,
but no report is available from them as
yet.

(ix) **Health problems prior to nursery enrolment**
Brian had no real health problems prior
to nursery enrolment apart from chronic
nasal congestion.   He was picked up at
the Child Welfare Clinic during routine
examinations, as he failed to score on the
language section of the Denver Test.   He
was tested by an educational psychologist
in January 1980 who recommended placement
in a nursery school.   His progress is to
be reviewed at regular intervals.

It is clear from this preliminary list that Brian's problems are numerous and varied, but we now have to try to summarise these difficulties and arrange them in order of importance. So, ask yourself the question, 'Is there any one problem that occurs more _frequently_ than others, or appears to be the cause of some of the other difficulties?' Looking again at the list it seems pretty clear that poor language development is a major problem because it is mentioned frequently, is a major area of development where he lags behind, and seems to underlie many of the other difficulties. Thus Brian is unable to follow instructions and cannot play cooperatively with other children largely because he cannot communicate with them. You will note that he does not shrink from contact with other children and plays happily alongside them, but he is unable to interact socially with the other children by word and deed. It would appear then that poor speech development and an inability to indulge in social play or learning situations are two major areas of concern.

In addition to these difficulties, however, Brian seems to lack the ability to concentrate or follow through any constructive activity, is subject to temper tantrums when frustrated and lacks some fundamental self-help skills such as being able to dress and undress himself properly.

The list of difficulties in order of priority might now be:

1.   poor speech development;
2.   poor social interaction;
3.   lack of concentration and persistence;
4.   tendency to have temper tantrums;
5.   lack of self-help skills.

Having drawn up this list you should check back through the information on Brian once more to satisfy yourself that you have assessed the difficulties properly.

As well as noting a child's difficulties, you should always try to pinpoint the positive aspects of his or her behaviour, however few and far between these may be. It is highly unlikely that you will come across a child who has no good points, and once these good points have been noticed you will probably have a much more balanced picture of the behaviour as a whole.

Looking again at the observations of Brian's behaviour, we might list the following as being his good points or assets:

1. he is often cheerful and happy, and enjoys
   rumbustious activity;
2. he is prepared to ask for help when he does
   not understand something;
3. he does attempt to do things that he finds
   difficult, e.g. doing a jigsaw, and
   copying the other boys when they are
   playing at Batman.

   When these assets are noted down separately they
seem to highlight the fact that Brian's case is far
from being a hopeless one.   He does not descend
into sullen and uncooperative withdrawal but tries
his best and soldiers cheerfully on despite his
difficulties.   These are excellent qualities that
can be built upon, and your programme of activities
should make use of them whenever possible.

(b)   Changes it is Hoped to Achieve
At this point you should try to detail the changes
that you hope to bring about in the child's behaviour.
As suggested in the previous section, you might
decide to use a number of approaches simultaneously
to bring about improvements in several areas of
Brian's behaviour over the same period of time,
but it would, perhaps, be wiser to set yourself a
limited goal in the early stages.   Of course, if
a child exhibits several minor yet irritating
difficulties that can be tackled by methods requiring
little time or commitment, you might decide to try
and bring about several changes at once.   As a
general rule, though, you would be wise to concentrate
initially on one or maybe two major difficulties
and worry about the others later.
   So in Brian's case, you might decide that you
want to:

1. improve his use of language and try to
   improve his ability to comprehend instructions;
2. encourage him to play with and interact
   more meaningfully with other children.

   These aims are still couched in very general
terms, however, so the next step is to work out,
wherever possible, the details of what changes you
would like to achieve by a certain date or point in
the programme.   To do that, you will need to have

a clear grasp of the techniques or approach that you
will be using and the time that will be involved
in the different stages of applying that approach.
You should now, therefore, go through the techniques
that you are likely to use and try to assess which
are appropriate and feasible.

(c)   Choosing the Approach(es) and Working out
Details of the Programme
You have now decided to try to improve Brian's use
and comprehension of language and to encourage him
to play and interact more with other children, so it
seems logical that the next stage is to examine more
closely what you normally do in the nursery group
to stimulate these activities.   It would be advise-
able also for you to read the sections on Language
Activities (pp. 67-80) and Play Activities (pp. 92-
128).   You may recall, also, that we discussed
some basic techniques in the Behaviour Modification
section(pp.146-148)that might prove useful in improving
speech and social play, so you might decide to have
a closer look at the appropriate parts of that
section as well.
     Having read this material once more you should
have picked up at least some techniques that you
feel you could apply,so it is now a question of
working out a programme in more detail.   Before you
proceed to work out these details, though, it would
be useful for you to summarise the general points
that this programme should encompass.
     In Brian's case, these might be as follows:

          (i)   from your notes you recall that he has
                been assessed by an education psychologist,
                been referred for speech therapy and is
                currently receiving one therapy session
                a week.   So you may decide to contact
                the speech therapist with a view to having
                the number of sessions per week increased,
                if possible; discuss the feasibility of
                the speech therapist designing a home-
                based programme (e.g. selected parts of
                the Portage Scheme) for the parents to use
                with Brian; and discuss with the speech
                therapist your own intended methods of
                encouraging language development, especially
                any new technique that you would like to
                try out;

          (ii) your own programme might aim to:

    (a) improve speech production and
        pronunciation initially by the
        use of simple programmes incorp-
        orating the techniques of shaping
        and positive reinforcement (pp.145-146);

    (b) widen Brian's vocabulary and develop
        his ability to use sentences of
        increasing complexity by direct
        instruction, using selected parts of
        a structured language programme such
        as G.O.A.L. (p.75);

    (c) increase Brian's involvement with
        other children by arranging situations
        so that he finds it difficult to avoid
        contact, and by using positive re-
        inforcement to strengthen this contact.
        Also, introduce role playing games
        such as 'Who am I?' to improve Brian's
        social skills;

    (d) develop social play further by the
        introduction of more structured group
        games such as 'Acting out Stories'
        (pp. 118-119).

Your choice of techniques will depend on
several factors, such as:

1. you feel confident that you have understood the method and feel able to carry
   it out;
2. you have sufficient backing from others
   to carry the programme out properly;
3. you have sufficient help from other
   staff where this is essential;
4. you feel confident the technique will
   work;
5. the technique is appropriate to deal with
   the difficulty being tackled.

Your final choice of techniques, then, depends
on your judgement of what is suitable for the particular situation you have to deal with and your
personal preference for one method rather than another. Remember, also, that problem behaviour can
often be tackled from several angles,so that if one
method proves unsuitable in your case you might
try another in its place.

5. Writing Down the Detailed Plans

You should write down a comprehensive plan of the action that you intend to take, giving details of how a particular technique will be applied, how much time you will spend on it each day and what situations you are most likely to find suitable to introduce it. Draw up a timetable to indicate when various stages should be reached.

It is not possible to give precise guidelines for you to follow, as individual programmes will vary considerably, depending on the type of approach adopted and the amount of time which that approach demands. However, you should aim to include as much detail as is necessary for the particular programme you have in mind. With an approach such as problem-solving, many of the stages are worked out for you in detail and you will not need to list each step in minute detail, and similarly many of the structured play activities have been clearly outlined already. However, individually designed activities or procedures will have to be worked out thoroughly.

Perhaps a good starting point would be to decide how long the total programme should last. In the case of certain behaviour modification techniques, for instance, you may decide that an initial period of twenty to twenty-five days will be long enough to try out the method on a specific problem - including both the baseline and intervention stages. However, no hard and fast rules apply here, and you should always aim to give a technique a fair chance of succeeding once you have made the decision to try it out.

Where you are attempting to deal with several problems at the same time or using techniques that require quite a long time to work out, or where changes in the behaviour may only emerge gradually, an extended programme may be necessary.

A fairly extensive programme would probably be required in the case of Brian, where improvements in the use of language and the level of social interaction may take some time to appear. His teacher might decide that the specialised programme of activities will take about three months to complete, and that she will spend one or two weeks on each of the various stages depending on how much material there is to cover in each. Of course, language difficulties and poor social skills are problems that are likely to require continuing help, and this might be offered as an ongoing feature of the nursery routine or by a further special

programme to be commenced at a later date.   However,
this first programme of intervention might be outlined as follows:

Stage 1.   Improving Speech Production by Shaping and Positive Reinforcement   (one week)

> Time: 20 minutes per day, Monday to Friday.
> Situation: Nursery teacher (or N.N.E.B.if
> appropriate) in one-to-one situation with Brian.
>
> N.T. to name objects laid out on table or in
> picture book;   asks Brian to repeat word after
> her;   N.T. will repeat words several times if
> necessary;   Brian's responses rewarded if good
> approximations to correct pronunciation
> (i.e. shaped).
> Repeat as necessary.
> Make out list of objects   e.g. cup, saucer,
> beaker, pencil, rubber, scissors etc.   Note
> down improvements, difficulties - any ideas of
> how to tackle these.
> Rewards to be used: simply praise and
> occasional hug e.g. 'good boy, you got it
> right that time' etc.   Specify any other re-
> wards.

Stage 2.   Improving Vocabulary and Comprehension (two weeks)

> Conditions: As in Stage 1 : 20 minutes per
> day: NT/NNEB
> Ensure that Brian can pronounce the words
> and then proceed to describe how the words
> are used.
>
> (i)   Naming Words (nouns):   words met in
>   stories;   naming classroom materials;
>   specialised materials or objects;
>   words denoting collection of things.
>
> (ii)   Words used to describe: colour, size,
>   shape and function of objects, e.g.
>   "a scissors is used to cut paper" etc.
>
> (iii)   Words denoting position: above, below,
>   under, first, last etc.   Arrange objects
>   and describe their positions etc.
>
> (iv)   Words used in questions: Who? Why? When?
>   How? etc.

Making a Plan of Action

Stage 3. Beginning of G.O.A.L. Programme (two weeks)

Conditions: As before.
Use of structured programmes

'What is my name?' (use of mirror)
'Where is my nose?' (parts of the body)
'What is this?' (pointing to hand etc.)

Specify further activities.

Stage 4. Extension of G.O.A.L. Programme (two weeks)

Conditions: As before.

(i) Use G.O.A.L. VOCABULARY CARDS - e.g.
'The Family'; 'Things we see around the
house'etc.

(ii) Use of more complex sentences.

Stage 5. Initiating Social Contact (one week
initially and then ongoing)

Time: Unspecified - as opportunities present
themselves (when Brian is near to other children, etc.). If little contact, try to form a
small group. This will be done at least
twice during the morning session; only two
or three in group initially.

Each time Brian approaches other children,
he will be rewarded - e.g. smile, word of
approval.
Any attempt at verbal contact will be specially
praised. If little contact, then call Brian
over to another child (someone he seems to
find acceptable, preferably) saying, 'Come and
see what David is doing, Brian' etc.
Attempt to keep Brian there and try to involve him
in an activity, e.g. helping David fill a
bucket with sand at the sand tray.
Specify other similar situations.
Try to create two or three such contacts in a
session (morning or afternoon).

Making a Plan of Action

Stage 6. Role-playing Games (two weeks)

Time: 20 minutes per day.
Situation: One-to-one initially, Brian and
N.T. (or N.N.E.B.). Later with group.

1. To improve Brian's chances of succeeding
   in a game and being accepted by a group,
   some of the following games will be played
   with him:

(a) Who am I?
    e.g. mime a policeman directing traffic;
    a postman delivering letters.
    Brian to imitate the teacher making sure
    he understands what is going on.

(b) What am I doing?
    e.g. mime eating, washing-up, driving a
    car.
    Brian to imitate the teacher.

(c) Bag of Hats
    Use (e.g.) nurse's hat and soldier's helmet.
    As above, get Brian to imitate and coach
    him as necessary.

2. Role-playing with a small group (e.g. three
   other children)

   Use (a) Who am I?

       (b) What am I doing?

       (c) Bag of Hats

   as before, only this time Brian is part of
   a group. If he gives the correct answer
   and offers to mime, encourage and praise
   him. If there is no response, ask him
   "Do you know, Brian; remember what we did
   before?" (i.e. try to coax him to respond
   in the group situation and mime for the
   other children).

Stage 7. More Structured Group Activities (two weeks)

Time: 20 minutes per day.
Situation: Group of children (not more than six)

Making a Plan of Action

1. Language games for group

   Use G.O.A.L. cards "Facial Expression"
   "Active Picture" etc., e.g. picture of
   child climbing.
   Get each member of the group to describe
   the picture in a sentence. Encourage
   and praise Brian especially (but not to
   the exclusion of other children).

2. Active group games

   (a) Nurse's hat : Brian to play role of nurse.
       One child pretends to be ill, nurse (Brian)
       has to look at his tongue, feel pulse,
       take temperature etc.

   (b) Fireman's hat
       Brian to play key role.
       Allow other children the key role as well,
       but try to involve Brian more - though as
       unobtrusively as possible.

   (c) Acting out stories
       E.g. 'The Three Billy Goats Gruff' and
       'The Three Bears' etc.

Home-based Programme
To avoid over-taxing Brian with too much activity
of the same type, it should be arranged that the
parents will begin a home-based language programme
once the school programme has progressed to dealing
with social interaction in the nursery group.

Note: Brian's parents and the teachers to meet
       to discuss what is to be done before the
       programme is started, and dates for
       further meetings to be fixed to liaise
       on Brian's progress in the nursery and
       in the home.

Planned Observations and Assessment of Progress

   (i) General observation will be continued
       as before on a day-to-day basis or as
       convenient during the whole of the
       programme.

   (ii) Some simple tests of vocabulary and use
        of sentences will be devised.

(iii) A full re-assessment using Schedules 1 to 5 will be made two weeks after the programme has ended.

(iv) A decision will be taken after this re-assessment whether to carry out a further specialised programme with Brian.

(v) A final full re-assessment will be made ten weeks after the first re-assessment.

In your plan, you can include as many details as you wish; for instance, make little notes or highlight key words to prompt you at a later date when you come to utilize the programme. The important thing is that <u>the plan should be down on paper</u> and not just in your head, and it should help to order your thoughts and guide you through the successive stages that you have mapped out.

6. <u>Trying Some Pilot Runs</u>

You will be familiar with some of the activities that you wish to use in your programme but you may need to practise some of the less familiar procedures. Though you may grasp what is involved fairly easily it would be wise to run through the procedure to see how it operates in practice. Thus you might go through the various stages involved in 'sit and watch' using a different child from the one that you will be aiming to help, just to get familiar with the practical steps involved.

Again, certain approaches such as problem-solving require some rehearsal before you will be able to run through the whole programme smoothly.

Have a good look at your intended programme and try out some of the less familiar procedures that it involves. Make sure that any helpers fully understand their role and are able to carry out the procedures satisfactorily.

Trying out a pilot run will also highlight any problems that might be caused to the routine of the nursery or group, and it is better that you find out about these beforehand rather than when you have already started a programme of help.

7. <u>Implementing the Programme</u>

If you are satisfied that you are now ready to start the programme, you should go ahead and do so as soon as it is convenient. Try to avoid the programme

overlapping with long holidays, and check that the
behaviour achieved by a certain time is still being
maintained if a break in the programme has been
unavoidable due to illness or vacation.   If problem
behaviour has reappeared or improvement has not been
maintained at the level it reached just before a
break then try to regain that level either by
introducing a crash revision course (i.e. going
quickly through the previous stages again) or by
modifying the remainder of the programme to incorporate some of the earlier procedures and allowing for more time to complete all the stages involved.

8.   Monitoring Progress
You should monitor the progress of the programme for
the whole period of the intervention.

   (i)   With a behaviour modification programme,
         you should continue to repeat the special-
         ised observations that you used during
         the baseline phase, but wherever possible
         these should be backed up by more general-
         ised observations of the child at work
         on some task or at play.   These broad
         observations might indicate changes in
         behaviour that might not be apparent from
         the more specific observations being made
         concurrently.

  (ii)   Where there is no specialised observation
         involved, continue to make sample observ-
         ations of the child's behaviour as you
         did in Section II of the Behaviour
         Assessment Schedule (Schedule 2).

 (iii)   Where appropriate, devise some simple tests
         to try to assess whether any improvement
         is being shown.   For example, in Brian's
         case you might draw up some simple tests
         of vocabulary or use of sentences to try
         to give some indication of the progress
         achieved.

  (iv)   Discuss your plan of action with other
         members of the staff from time to time,
         and especially those who come into contact
         with the child.   An improvement might
         show itself in a change in attitude or
         generally more positive approach to life
         which may become evident in the child's

behaviour in the playground, at dinner-
time or at home.

(v) Keep the parents in touch with what you
are doing and ask them to note any changes
in the child's behaviour which become
evident during and following the programme.

(vi) Rearrange the programme on the basis of
your experience. Though you should not
depart too much from the original timetable,
you might decide to balance out the
different activities involved to meet some
contingency. Thus, if Brian becomes very
tired of some of the language procedures
you might consider alternating these with
some group play activity or give him a rest
from the specialised attention that he has
been receiving. Follow your plan as much
as possible, but be prepared to be flexible
in handling certain difficulties as these
arise.

9.   Deciding when to Stop the Programme or Take Further Action

As we have said previously, you should give the
programme a fair chance of succeeding by persevering
with it, even if it has to be modified slightly to
suit the nursery routine or a change in the behaviour
of the child. If you find that the programme is
taking much more time or requires a greater commitment than at first thought you should modify it to
meet these needs, though without changing its
essential character. Again, a child might begin
to exhibit difficult behaviour that the programme
is not designed to meet, so you might have to adjust
it temporarily to cope with such a change.

Having said this, however, you should be certain
in your own mind that the programme does need to be
changed in the short-term and that you are not
merely being discouraged by the fact that it is a
little more difficult to carry through than you
had originally thought. As time goes on you will
find that you will become much more skilled in using
the various techniques and will carry out a programme
smoothly to its completion.

Assuming that you have carried out the original
programme as planned, you will then have to decide
whether to take more action or not. You should
look closely at the assessments and observations that

you have carried out during and immediately after the intervention and base your decision on these. Thus, if a child has improved markedly you may decide to suspend further action for the time being, to review behaviour in a few weeks time, and then to re-introduce the same or a slightly modified programme to boost this improvement if that is necessary.

Again, you may be satisfied that the difficult-ies that the programme was designed to help have largely disappeared but that there are other problems that need attention. You should design a further programme to tackle these. If you were Brian's teacher you might find, after completion of the programme, that his language skills and social behaviour were much improved and that the improve ment could be maintained by ensuring his continuing involvement in the nursery routine. So, you decide now to tackle some of his other problems and, specifically, his lack of self-help skills and proneness to temper tantrums. You might decide to plan a programme involving Task Analysis to help to train him to be able to dress and undress himself properly and use a behaviour modification routine to tackle his temper tantrums. It is a question of priorities, and if your original programme has led to a change in the priority of the difficulties, you will want to design a fresh programme to meet this change.

APPENDIX TO CHAPTER 6 : CASE STUDIES

We will describe three case studies carried out by the staffs of different nursery groups, using a pilot version of the present handbook.   The information given is taken almost verbatim from the record books kept by the nursery staff and the studies concern actual children, but the names of all children and staff have been changed to preserve confidentiality.   Each case report is followed by some of our own comments on the study.
It should be made clear at the outset that these studies were carried out over two school terms, apart from a few weeks during which the nursery staff read and familiarised themselves with the material.   For many of the nursery staff involved, the handbook contained much that was new and required them to use methods with which they had had no previous contact.   It is a tribute to all concerned that they were able to achieve so much in a comparatively short time, and encouraging to those who intend to use the handbook in the future.

CASE STUDY 1

JANE (aged 4) an example of a withdrawn, dependent child.

Behaviour Checklist Ratings

2(b) Will cooperate with other children in some situations (e.g. adult directed activities) but not others (e.g. where turn taking is involved).
4(b) Occasionally can be a disturbing influence in a group.
5(b) May complete an activity once started but is not immune to distractions.
6(b) Has looked tense or upset on occasions.
7(c) Wanders around aimlessly or stares into space.
8(c) Watches others play but makes no attempt to join in. Will not be coaxed to take part in group activities.
9(b) Rarely initiates a conversation with an adult, but will respond appropriately and will talk to other children.

10(c) Frequently 'clings' to adult for assurance and does not attempt to attend to his/her own needs.

Behaviour Observation

1. Avoids contact and play with other children - this behaviour occurs in many settings.
2. Jane displays withdrawn, dreamy behaviour which prevents her making good use of materials, toys and apparatus provided.

Behaviour Assessment

2(d) Concentration - rarely makes use of materials in an appropriate way.

6(c) Social withdrawal - withdrawn and dreamy - difficult to make contact with.

7(d) Reaction to strangers - shrinks back even before approach is made.

8(d) Participation in play - no interest in play with other children.

9(c) Physical contact - withdraws from physical contact, reluctant to take hand, sit on knee, be lifted or helped physically.

Emotional Adjustment

(c) Over-anxious, timid, fearful
(d) Fussy, complaining, whining
(i) Listless, finds everything a great effort.

General Assessment - Her Behaviour at School

Areas where the child functions well
Jane has good mobility and hand-eye co-ordination, and is adequately self-sufficient for her age. Her expressive language is good in that she has clear speech and good vocabulary. Her receptive language is also good, although she is slow to respond to instructions, more out of lethargy rather than poor understanding.

Areas where child under-functioning
Jane displays poor quality of play, i.e. lack of concentration and imagination. She is

under-functioning in her response to learning
and displays a slow response to new materials,
approaches, requests, changes in routine, etc.

Family Background
Jane belongs to a loving, caring family and is used
to a great deal of adult attention.   She is particularly attached to mother, who being partially
sighted has tended to keep Jane close to her both
for Jane's safety and to be mother's eyes as she
became more self-sufficient.   She is her father's
only child and spoilt by him and the half brothers
and sisters who are so much older.   The only other
child she had regular contact with before coming
to nursery is her mother's oldest grandchild, of
whom she shows marked jealousy.

Her Behaviour at Home
Jane displays behaviour quite normal for her age at
home, where she appears to be happy and outgoing.
Mother describes her as being a "bit dreamy" but
she is healthy, physically active and self-sufficient
for her age.   Her speech and vocabularly are good
and she is an incessant talker both with the family
and other adults who are known to her.   The only
behaviour her mother objects to is her unwillingness
to share material possessions and adult attention
with visiting children - particulary the grandchild -
who is the most frequent child visitor.

Her mother does also show a slight concern for
the fact that Jane does not - indeed never has -
slept on her own.   She always sleeps with mother
and will not go to bed until mother does.

Teacher's Conclusions
Jane presents a picture of a healthy, happy little
girl at home, but she resents attending nursery
since it means parting from "Mum".   Apart from a
few tears the first week, she has shown no outward
emotional signs of this, but her reaction has taken
the form of avoidance behaviour in that she avoids
any contact with the other children and physical
contact with adults, though she does offer conversation frequently to adults and her apparent
aimless wandering around the nursery does take her
in the direction of an adult, e.g. she frequently
follows me at a distance but if I notice her, will
turn away.

This behaviour is not disruptive at all to
the other children or to the calm, happy atmosphere
I encourage in the nursery, but it has a marked

effect on Jane since she is obtaining absolutely no
benefit from the nursery environment.   Her avoidance
of contact with other children means that she is not
concentrating long enough in any one setting to
finish a task or game (other than painting which can
be done without contact), or to obtain any enjoyment
from the materials provided.

Action to be taken

(a) I would hope to change Jane's behaviour
with regard to the other children. I
would like her to begin by tolerating
the presence of other children near her,
so that she is in a situation of "playing
alongside" another child. I hope that,
following on from this, she will progress
to participating in play and interacting
with another child in play situations.
This hopefully will progress still further
into co-operation with other children
in the use of space, furniture, toys,
apparatus and materials and to the
development of an attitude of sharing and
an understanding that the facilities in
the nursery are for the use and enjoyment
of all the children.
    I also hope to increase Jane's powers
of concentration and encourage perseverance
with regard to the use of puzzles,
instructional toys, modelling materials
etc. I hope to instil enough confidence
and sense of security in Jane that she
will be able to accept adult visitors in
the nursery.

(b) I intend to use a Behaviour Modification
approach, firstly to encourage Jane to
accept and tolerate the presence of other
children alongside her, secondly, to
encourage social interaction.
    I will begin with a time-sample
recording with observation periods of 30
minutes between 1.15 - 1.45 p.m. each day.
(Thus allowing children to settle into
afternoon session and allowing time for
latecomers - not allowing children to get
tired or interference from time-tabled
activities, i.e. use of hall and T.V.)
    I will continue time-sample recording
for a period of six days - data to be
graphed.

(c) I intend to use simple contingent re-
    inforcement procedures. Firstly, by means
    of intervention encourage Jane to remain
    at an activity when another child approaches
    and becomes involved. Every time Jane
    remains to play alongside a child she will
    be rewarded with a smile and verbal praise
    - "Good girl Jane, you are playing with the
    children." Every time Jane approaches
    another child she will be rewarded with
    this reinforcement plus the reward of
    giving the hamster a nut (Jane is very
    fond of animals) with the other child.
    This will be varied with holding Hammy,
    finding him dandelion leaves in the
    garden, cleaning his cage, changing his
    water etc. As soon as Jane begins to
    approach play situations and join in by
    self-motivation, prompts will be gradually
    faded out. This method will be implement-
    ed throughout the nursery session when
    necessary. Should this prove successful
    when the child is re-assessed at Easter,
    I will introduce a programme of play to
    encourage social interaction using suggest-
    ions from the section on 'Play Activities'
    (pp.123-127).

Time-Sample Recording 23.2.81. : Base-Line Period
Recording Social Interaction - defined as remaining
at an activity when another child approaches,
talking to or playing with another child.

        Time of day - 1.15 - 1.45 p.m. daily
                      5 minute intervals.

	5	10	15	20	25	30
23.2.81	-	-	-	+	-	+
24.2.81	+	-	-	+	-	-
25.2.81	-	-	-	-	-	-
26.2.81	-	-	-	+	+	-
2.3.81	-	+	+	-	-	+
3.3.81	-	+	+	-	-	-

4.3.81 Intervention programme begun. Every time
    Jane remained at an activity when another child
    approached she was rewarded with verbal praise
    varied with tasks related to hamster (see
    above). There has been very little initiation
    of desired behaviour by Jane during the first
    two days, so prompts to be introduced - Jane

to be led to a child, group or activity by
staff and encouraged to participate with
staff remaining with her.

Programme has been continued for next
ten days - there was a noticeable improvement
in Jane's behaviour after four days and prompts
were gradually dropped.

4.3.81. Time-Sample Recordings (Time as previously
recorded) Intervention Period.

	5	10	15	20	25	30
5.3.81	−	+	+	−	+	+
6.3.81	−	+	+	−	−	+
9.3.81	−	−	+	+	−	−
10.3.81	+	+	+	−	+	−
11.3.81	+	−	+	+	+	+
12.3.81	−	+	−	+	+	+
13.3.81	+	−	+	−	+	+
16.3.81	+	−	+	+	+	+
17.3.81	+	+	+	+	−	+
18.3.81	Child absent					

FIGURE 6.1 FREQUENCY OF JANE'S ISOLATED BEHAVIOUR
(FIRST INTERVENTION)

Making a Plan of Action : Case Studies

Continuing Record

<u>7.4.81</u>   Jane has been absent from school since
       27.3.81. She has a virus infection. I have
       completed first re-assessment.

<u>27.4.81</u> Returned to school after Easter break -
       Jane extremely withdrawn - not participating at
       all in activities.

<u>28.4.81</u> Jane again displaying isolated behaviour
       and resisted attempts to encourage any play or
       interaction with children.

<u>29.4.81</u> Jane absent from school - mother came to
       tell me she has measles after just recovering
       from a virus infection which persisted over
       the Easter holidays. Mother also informed
       me that Grandpa had died a few days earlier
       and that Jane was extremly upset because the
       family dog (aged 15 years) had died. All this
       can explain the child's behaviour on returning
       to school. I have informed mother that, when
       Jane is better, she will be joining the
       morning session with the older children, as
       she will be attending the reception class in
       September.

<u>11.5.81</u>   Jane returned to school.

<u>12.5.81</u>   Jane distressed on returning to school and
       for the first time was crying not to stay. She
       was difficult to pacify since she showed no
       interest in toys or materials. She exhibited
       extreme isolated behaviour but stayed fairly
       close to me although resisting my attempts
       to involve her in conversation or in any
       activity.

<u>13.5.81</u>   Jane did not cry today but was very with-
       drawn. She did ask to paint but chose the
       painting easel on its own away from the others
       and would not be persuaded to join the other
       children. At squash time she carried her own
       chair but carefully placed it about a metre
       away from the other children. Jimmy put his
       chair next to hers - she pushed him off his
       chair and said, "You're not sitting by me."
       This behaviour was unusual - Jane does not
       normally display aggressive behaviour but is
       rather timid of any physical contact. When I

sat by her at the table she moved her chair
away slightly but did not go.   The following
conversation ensued:

Mrs. T.	"Can you find me the red lego bricks, Jane?"
Jane	"My Mammy will buy me these for my house."
Mrs. T.	"You can sort them for Mummy then, Jane."
Jane	"My Mammy is going to buy me all these toys."
Mrs. T.	"You will have a lot to play with, Jane."
Jane	"My Mammy is going to buy me a whole nursery all to myself."
Mrs. T.	"We all enjoy sharing this nursery don't we, Jane?"
Jane	"My Mammy will buy me a Mrs. T. all for myself."

15.5.81   In view of this regression in Jane's
behaviour I decided to begin again with another
Time-Sample Recording - Time of day 9.30 -
10.00 a.m. daily 5 minute intervals for a
period of eight days beginning 18.5.81.
Nursery nurse to record Jane's behaviour.
      Intervention was begun 1.6.81. and
continued for a further eight days.(See Graph
6.2).

10.6.81   Jane has been slower to respond to this
intervention - prompts were not begun to be
faded out until the sixth day after the
intervention, so Jane was monitored for a
further two days.   Jane's isolated behaviour
decreased from around 70% at time of intervention to under 20% after ten days.

15.6.81   Contingent reinforcement procedures are no
longer necessary.   I intend now to encourage
Jane to interact with a larger group of children to cooperate in group games and activities
and encourage confidence when involved in
activities with the infants school.   I intend
to do this by using the following:

1. Jane to participate in group art work rather than her own which she likes to take home.
2. Use of snap games, lotto, matching and pairing games.
3. Cooperation in physical activities - throwing and catching in groups - using see-saw and wheeled toys which need two or more children to help each other - climbing tasks involving cooperation of a group of children.
4. Jane to do "errands" to infant school and headmistress.
5. Jane to be "helper" in nursery along with other children - a rota for a day helper. Helper to wear badge and feed animals - give children squash, take register etc. Two children at a time.
6. Introduce for 5 - 10 minutes daily dancing and singing games which involve all 25 children, e.g. Looby Loo, Farmer in his Den, On the Mountain, Duke of York, etc.

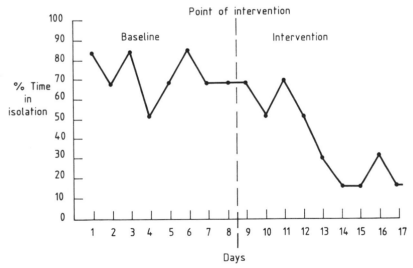

FIGURE 6.2   FREQUENCY OF JANE'S ISOLATED BEHAVIOUR (SECOND INTERVENTION)

Making a Plan of Action : Case Studies

First Behaviour Observation

1. Jane still tends to be listless and dreamy which impairs her use of toys and activities, e.g. will sit and day dream at puzzle table if not constantly encouraged.
2. Jane still withdraws from contact with strangers or even other adults she knows from the infants school.

Behaviour Re-assessment

6(c) Social withdrawal - still tends to be with-withdrawn and dreamy.
7(d) Reaction to strangers - child shrinks from contact with visitors.

Jane now has only two "c" and "d" scores - she has improved greatly in ability to concentrate and particularly in her interaction with other children.

Emotional Adjustment

(d) Fussy, complaining, whining.
(i) Listless - finds everything an effort.

Jane has shown some improvement. She can no longer be described as over-anxious, timid or fearful but appears generally more relaxed in the nursery.

First General Re-assesment

Areas where the child functions well

Jane is demonstrating a greater degree of self-sufficiency than before and her mobility and coordination are good. Her expressive language has also improved in that she offers conversation much more readily although this is almost always chat about her home and family. She is still slower than most to respond to instruction, but has improved in this respect.

Areas where child under-functioning

Her quality of play is much improved in that she will concentrate and persevere at an activity for longer but her imagination is poor, and she still does not like to participate in imaginative play. She does show a more enthusiastic approach to new materials and more interest in activities generally.

Second Behaviour Observation

1. Jane is still lethargic and dreamy and will sit doing nothing for long periods unless constantly encouraged.
2. Jane still withdraws from contact with strangers, indeed, she moves quickly as far from the door as possible when a visitor enters.

Behaviour Re-assessment

6(c) Social withdrawal - tends to be withdrawn and dreamy still.
7(d) Reaction to strangers - shrinks back even before an approach is made.
8(c) Play activities - mainly plays alongside children.

Emotional Adjustment

Jane still tends to be fussy, complaining and whining, and is listless, finding everything an effort and needs constant encouragement to participate in activities.

Second General Re-assessment

Areas where child functions well

Jane's mobility and coordination are good and hearing and eyesight normal. She has mastered a good degree of self-help skills and has good receptive and expressive language.

Areas where child is under-functioning

Jane is still under-functioning in play which is still moderate to poor in quality and has shown very little improvement in her response to learning and adaptability.

Progress Report

The graph of the first intervention which demonstrates the frequency of Jane's isolated behaviour shows a marked decrease in this behaviour from 70%

233

until the point of intervention to 20% after 9 days of the simple contingent reinforcement procedure. Time-sample recordings were discontinued and contingent reinforcement procedures gradually became no longer necessary. Jane appears to be more relaxed generally and happier than she has been in the past. I feel that my personal relationship with her has improved a great deal, and she no longer avoids physical contact but will approach me for comfort and reassurance. She is now seeking the company of two little girls, particularly that of another shy, quiet little girl who is new to nursery, and although she is not eager to partake in group activities, she does show more willingness. I am very pleased with these improvements to date and would tentatively assume they show some degree of success with the approaches used so far. Should this success continue when we return to school after the Easter break, I intend to introduce play activities to encourage greater participation in group activities and more social interaction with a greater number of children. I will also introduce activities which encompass the infant school to over-come Jane's apprehension of older children and adults she does not know well.

After the Easter break Jane's behaviour has regressed and the incidence of isolated behaviour was again around 70% of the time that Jane was observed. Time-sample recordings were again taken (this time by the nursery nurse) following the same criteria. Jane's isolated behaviour again de-creased after intervention to 20% although she was a little slower to respond to contingent reinforce-ment procedures. These are now no longer necessary and Jane is interacting well with the other children. She is happier and more relaxed than when returning from the Easter break and is making good use of materials and toys available. She does need encouragement still, since she is generally a lethargic child; this probably has much to do with the fact that she still sleeps with her mother and does not go to bed until mother does. Jane still lacks enthusiasm even for activities I know she enjoys, but I feel this must be accepted as part of her character. She offers conversation frequently to adults but is more reticent with children. Her conversation continues to be mostly about her home and family. I will continue to encourage greater social interaction with the introduction of more group activities.

<u>1.7.81</u>   Jane has made little progress in interact-
ion with other children since the above comments,
but despite this I feel some measure of success
has been achieved.   Jane will be in a
reception class in September and I feel this
might suit her better since she will be required to work alone to a great extent and will
be guided more rigidly in activities with the
introduction of more formal "work".

<u>Comments</u>
The nursery teacher, Mrs. T., achieved considerable
success with Jane in a comparatively short period
of time using a simple contingent reinforcement
procedure.   There was quite a dramatic drop in the
amount of time that Jane spent in isolated activity
following intervention on both occasions.
    It is a pity that Jane's illness and the Easter
break disrupted the ongoing programme, and likely
that a more permanent change in behaviour would have
been achieved if the contingent reinforcement
procedure had been backed up immediately by an
extensive series of play activities.   Such an
extended programme might well have built on the
progress already attained and established a solid
foundation for Jane's social behaviour, but
unfortunately it was not to be.
    Jane's behaviour in the nursery group reverted
after the break to being withdrawn and isolated,
and the decision to re-introduce the contingent
reinforcement programme was a perfectly correct
and appropriate one, and once more achieved its
purpose.   The follow-up programme of play activities
meant to encourage social interaction achieved only
partial success, though, in Mrs. T's estimation.
    It became clear that only limited success could
be achieved by the help given in the nursery school.
Jane was still very tied to home and to her mother.
It would have been useful to approach the mother
with a view to weakening the over-dependence
exhibited by both mother and child.   Of course,
this is a very delicate matter and would require
a considerable amount of time in order to build up
the mother's trust and confidence, and was not
feasible in the present study because of the limited
time-scale.   It is to be hoped that, as Jane is
required to spend more time in formal schooling,
the problem will gradually diminish and that a more
balanced relationship will develop between her and
her mother.

CASE STUDY 2

ERIC (aged 4), an example of an aggressive,
disobedient child, who is subject to temper
tantrums.

Behaviour Checklist

    1(b) Can be destructive and has to be watched
         more carefully than some children.
    2(c) Demands his own way in all situations
         and cannot 'take turns'. Often takes
         toys from children whilst refusing to
         share his own.
    3(c) Screams, bangs objects, has a tantrum
         whenever provoked; inhibited or frustrated,
         however minor the incident.
    4(b) Occasionally can be a disturbing influence
         in a group.
    5(b) May complete an activity once started
         but is not immune to distractions.
    6(b) Has looked tense or upset on occasions.
    8(b) Usually found in the company of one or
         two particular children. Takes part
         reluctantly in group activities.

Behaviour Assessment

    4(c) Aggressive behaviour - frequently rude,
         offers verbal aggression if thwarted or
         frustrated.
    5(c) Demanding behaviour - demands own way
         frequently and over-reacts (crying
         tantrums) if demands not met.
    9(c) Physical contact - tends to withdraw from
         physical contact; reluctant to take hand,
         sit on knee, be lifted or helped physic-
         ally.

Emotional Adjustment

    (b) Over-excitable.
    (e) Prone to temper tantrums.
    (f) Disobedient.
    (g) Seeks to be the centre of attention.
    (h) Tearful - when having a tantrum.

Making a Plan of Action : Case Studies

General Assessment - His Behaviour at School

Areas where child functions well
1. Good mobility.
2. Good co-ordination.
3. Vision apparently normal.
4. Good hearing.
5. Good self-help skills.
6. Good expressive language.
7. Good receptive language.
8. Good response to learning.

Areas where child under-functioning
8. Moderate quality of play - hampered by anti-social behaviour - unable to share toys - results in tantrums.

Family Background
Eric now finds himself the middle child -- he has an older brother (6 years old) and a new baby sister. This could result in aggravating his already obvious behaviour problem. He lives in the same street as his maternal grandmother and his aunts, of whom some are still of school age. They all play an active part in disciplining him - an unavoidable problem for him, I should say. I believe his father is unemployed - this more often than not creates tension in the home - this again is un-avoidable.

His Behaviour at Home
Mother has admitted giving in to his tantrums for "peace" as she said. She also said he listens better to his 'Gran'. I did mention to her that it is causing problems in school for him and that I cannot "give in" to his demands - it is bound to impair his learning - I suggested that she might have a word with him.

Help from Others

Nature of Problem	Agencies contacted	Information received/action taken
Possibility of child not having enough sleep	School nurse and Health Visitor	Not yet received

Teacher's Conclusions

It would be interesting to know when, during Eric's pre-school years, did he realise that by having a tantrum he could succeed in getting what he wanted - this habit had become quite a strong part of his behaviour before he came to school.

I feel it will take quite a while to break' him of it in school - he may still be allowed to have his tantrums at home - thereby making my task even harder.

His redeeming qualities are such that his tantrums do not last for very long and he can be eventually brought out of them by his observing an activity which interests him.

But I have failed to get his immediate interest in another activity - he still decides himself when he feels like picking himself up and joining in - as if nothing unsociable has occurred. I do not show too much concern for his tantrums. This I feel is the right attitude in that the more I take notice of them, the more demanding he will get. The other children are obviously aware of his unacceptable behaviour and do not bother him when he has his tantrum.

Action to be Taken

(a) For Eric to become more sociable - for him eventually to realise that my N.N.E.B. and I will see to it that he does have his share of the toys which attract him, just by waiting for his turn - he will be emphatically praised for his successful achievements and encouraged to help other less able children. He will be encouraged to lead "play" in an imaginative game - so becoming so pre-occupied with the activity that he might refrain from having a tantrum.

(b) Approaches I intend using with the help of my N.N.E.B.
1. Social Play: The first simple dice game I teach them involving four children - THE FLOWER GAME - a coloured die is used and petal shapes are given out to the children when their colour comes up on the dice. The first to complete a flower is the winner.

2. Rocking Boats: Having to co-operate with another child to "rock" successfully.

3. Steps and Slide: Having to wait one's turn to have a go - emphasising the danger of accidents if one does not wait.

4. Play People: Plastic Road Mat; Collection of Vehicles : A group activity - encourage children to speak for one particular "play" person.

5. A large piece of paper - a group of children will draw a picture of a farm, for example.

6. Faces: I'll use a collection of cardboard figures of the Seven Dwarfs. We'll discuss their names and their facial expressions - I shall encourage children to try making similar faces.

7. The Mouse and Clock - Dice Game: 4 or 2 players.

8. Flying Ball: throwing a ball between 2/3 players.

9. Puppets and "Guess Who I Am" games (see pp.117-119).

(c) These games will be implemented during the "Activities Session" - 9.30 a.m. - 10.15 a.m. Eric's reactions to them will be observed and noted.

Observations during Particular Activities

Dressing-Up Games: He was very difficult - he still wanted what others had. Could not be pacified. There was a selection of different shaped "guns" - I have decided to remove them and replace them with some wooden ones - all the same shape.

Climbing Frame: He did co-operate for about 5 minutes then cheated his turn - when told to wait he refused to continue to play.

Flower Game: He did not want to be leader and give out the 'petal' shapes - he became disinterested before the end of the game on the first occasion he played it, but stayed to the end during the second time.

Boats: He was happy to be with his cousin, Tom, but refused to go with another child. On another occasion when Tom was purposely given a task to do, he did consent to going with another child, Peter, who also lives near him.

Construction Toys: Fit-links, large lego and building blocks - he shows good powers of concentration to create things.

16.3.81 A Monday morning - he had a bad morning - he seems obviously tired, irritable, nothing was right for him. Baby sister has arrived.

17.3.81 Dressing-up game - an unpleasant incident - he hit another child. He had a little accident - tore his finger nail. He let me nurse him - he has refused before. Formal work - behaviour very good and painting, sticking pictures, sand and water play - no incidents. Mother brought his new baby sister for us to see - mother very rarely comes for him. It is usually another child's parent who takes Eric home for his mother.

23.3.81 One incident - when he was in the yard for a P.E. lesson - he would not allow another child to play with him and Tom - when I said that Peter was to play he immediately refused to join in the game and grizzled.

1.4.81 Still refuses to play unless Tom is in the group. Social play is improving, we have had a few days with no incidents! N.N.E.B. has observed that in the playground situation he continues to be aggressive and irritable if Tom does not always want his company. He needs to make other friendships.

2.4.81 We visited the Rural Studies Department in the Senior School to see the chickens, rabbits and bees etc., yesterday. Eric's comments while counting and colouring his chickens in his work book - "I'll stick a pin in the chicken." When I asked him, "Wouldn't it hurt the chicken?" he said, "No." But I explained that pins were sharp - he said, "Mammy sticks them in Gaynor's napkin."

6.4.81 He started off the morning session by crying for a cushion - not the same one as before. I told him to stop crying as he had not hurt himself - only babies cry for nothing.

He soon stopped.   This comment I may use
again to reduce the length of his tantrum.

<u>7.4.81</u>   He observed Tom (his cousin) having a see-
saw game with another child.   He started
grizzling.   We ignored his behaviour.   When
the time came for Tom to get off we asked Eric
if he would like to help Peter to make the
see-saw go.   He accepted and appeared to
enjoy the activity.   He is improving.

<u>8.4.81</u>   Our Annual Easter Parade through the
village - girls in home-made Easter bonnets -
boys dress up in whatever outfit they have
or can borrow from our collection.   Eric
refused to dress up and did not seem bothered.
He walked quite happily and had his photograph
taken without any trouble.
    His favourite colour is black - whatever
the picture is about his choice is invariably
black.   Can this be related to his mood?
His particular "off" days are Monday, I have
noticed, he appears more tired and irritable -
quite a number of children are not as receptive
to teaching on a Monday as they are on the
other days of the week, I have found.   They
are also noisier and more irritable - could
this be due to there being less restriction
on volume of sound they make and hours of
sleep are not quite the same as on week days?

<u>9.4.81</u>   He continues to create an incident over
which cushion he is going to sit on - I have
decided to remove boys from cushioned storage
boxes to chairs and let the nursery girls sit
on the cushions - their turn to have them.
This will stop Eric's performance.   These
cushioned storage boxes make up the nursery
'train'.
    He seemed to be more tired than normal
today.   He lay down in the T.V. room and
objected to anyone talking or touching him.   He
could be sickening for something.   He refused
to go with the N.N.E.B. and the nursery class
for toileting - I insisted that he went and
observed the school "pets" en route.   He has to
respond to teacher's instructions - other
children could begin to copy him, if I continually
provide an alternative course for him.   We are
continually over-compensating with praise for
good work and good behaviour.

Next term we hope to be more out of doors with large toys - cars, tricycles etc. - it will be interesting to observe whether Eric's behaviour problems will be more or less. He did seem to be happier on the few occasions when we have been out in the playground for P.E. during the past few months - having more space to move about in might suit him better.

Behaviour Assessment Checklist

4(c)Aggressive behaviour - less frequent lately.
5(c)Demanding behaviour - again less frequent.
9(c)Physical contact - refuses any physical contact other than being helped with shoe lacing or having plasters on cuts.

Emotional Adjustment

(b) Still quite excitable at times.
(e) Fewer temper tantrums than the original assessment.
(f) Disobedient - at times - according to his mood at the time.
(g) Still likes to seek to be centre of attention at times.
(h) Still tearful when having a tantrum.
(i) Sometimes shows signs of listlessness - these are times when I feel that he is obviously not 100% fit and he should not be in school.

First Re-assessment - General Assessment

Areas where child functions well

1. Mobility - good.
2. Good coordination.
3. Vision - apparently normal.
4. Hearing - apparently normal.
5. Good self-help skills.
6. Good expressive language.
7. Good response to learning.

Areas where child under-functioning

8. Moderate quality of play - tantrums are becoming less frequent in group games.

12.5.81 Eric has been absent for a few days - returned today - very fractious from the time he came in. He became more and more difficult

and obviously upset as the morning went on.
His older brother has chicken pox - perhaps
he could be sickening for it?   When mother
was told of his behaviour she replied that
that is how he was at home - not very
sympathetic towards him.   This may be the
reason why he will not respond to affection
from my N.N.E.B. or me when we try to console
him.   He has become so used to having tantrums
and having to get over them in his own time -
a very sad situation for a child so young.

8.6.81   Eric has returned after being off for two
weeks with chicken pox.   He appears to be
happy to be back - no tantrums today.

9.6.81   He came into school at 9.25 accompanied
by his aunt who is 11 years old.   He was
obviously in a tantrum over how he was to
spend his lunch money.   He had been to a local
shop and had not had his own way.   I ignored
his crying and went on to discuss our hymn
about holidays by the sea - not an easy task
but it succeeded - he stopped crying and then
joined in the activities for the rest of the
morning without an incident.

10.6.81   No incident today.   Eric took the lead in
a group activity - he was the "engine" driver.

11.6.81   Again he joined in amicably in a group
game - "The Flower Game" as previously described.

12.6.81   Eric is enjoying out of door activities -
use of large toys - tricycles,cars, barrows
etc.   I explained that they would have turns
on everything - he is accepting my word and
there are no tantrums - so far!

Behaviour Observation
The home situation remains the same for him - father
unemployed, mother has even less time for him with
another child to see to.   He still lives in the
same street as his grandparents and young aunties,
who are too young to take charge of him or to show
responsible control of his demands or needs.   Full-
time education from September should result in a
more stable and amenable environment for him but his
programme of activities must still be especially
chosen to help him with his problems.

Second Re-assessment - Behaviour Assessment Checklist

4(c) Aggressive Behaviour - offers verbal aggression if he has a tantrum, though tantrums are now less frequent.

5(c) Demanding Behaviour - less frequent than previous assessment but will still over-react if demands not met on some occasions.

9(d) Physical Contact - still tends to withdraw from physical contact; cannot be comforted when he over-reacts and becomes distressed - my guess is that he is not used to being comforted at home.

Emotional Adjustment

(a) His behaviour is noticeably better when he appears to be physically fit.

(b) He is obviously excitable. This is shown when he is chatting about his experiences.

(e) Less prone to tantrums now.

(f) Disobedient - can be when in a tantrum.

(g) This is shown especially in news chats.

(h) Tearful - when in distress.

(i) Listless - at times - I have queried this with the health visitor, have not yet heard her report on a home visit.

Second Re-assessment - General Assessment

Areas where child functions well

1. Good mobility - he enjoys being out of doors with large toys and P.E. equipment. He needs space around him but with no hall and our annual average rainfall at 100" approx., this is not possible for most of the year.

2. Hand-eye coordination good.

3. Vision - good.

4. Hearing - normal.

5. Good self-help skills.

6. Expressive language - good.

7. Receptive language - good.

8. Play - is beginning to obviously enjoy play in a group and has recently taken the lead.

9. Response to learning - good.

Areas where child is under-functioning

8. Tantrums are becoming less frequent and he is beginning to make new friendships as he is getting more involved with social play.

I trust this will continue so that wanting
to be involved will deter his reaction
to unsociable behaviour should he disagree
with other children's ideas.

Progress Report

By taking particular notice of things which can
create problems for Eric, e.g. cushions with a
variety of appliqued pictures on them; a collection
of various types of toy guns; it has proved successful to remove these things from his use for the time
being in order to help him behave more socially.   I
am hoping that as he makes friendships with other
children and gets to enjoy social 'play' activities
he might eventually take less notice of the 'props'
and more of the verbal response of other children.
        I shall, as a matter of interest, present him
(later on this term) with these things, which have
proved to arouse unsociable behaviour.
        I believe he is responding to our praise -
emphasising what a big boy he is - in helping to
carry apparatus and being able to do things babies
cannot do.   I have already mentioned that by saying
that "only babies cry for nothing" stopped Eric
crying.   He obviously wants to be considered as
a "big" boy not a baby.   Having an older brother
is a reason for this perhaps.   My N.N.E.B. and I
have to consciously try to give him as much attention
as possible because he obviously needs it, being
the middle child.
        He obviously likes talking and I often purposely
call upon him to tell us something about a topic we
are discussing - this obviously gives him pleasure
by the expression on his face - this I feel will help
him to gain self-confidence and it involves his co-
operation.   He comes into school quite cheerful and
usually has something to tell me or to show me -
this is a sign that our relationship is good.   He
comes willingly to me for more formal tuition and
his progress is average for his age.

Comments

This study reveals a picture of a child who is
aggressive and prone to temper tantrums when frustrated and who is quite often disobedient.   These
difficulties are gradually reduced by the efforts
of the nursery teacher and assistant, who praise
his achievements, play down the temper tantrums
and seek to involve him much more in play situations
involving cooperation with other children.   There

is no sudden or dramatic change but rather a gradual and general improvement in his behaviour.

It is not entirely clear whether the nursery staff had previously tried to control Eric's temper tantrums by means other than ignoring them, and whether the approach described would be a fundamental departure from what was commonly done. Again, it is not stated categorically that each and every temper tantrum was ignored, so how consistently this was done is a little uncertain. Perhaps it would have been better to make these points clear and to draw up the plan accordingly at the outset.

Further, though it is obviously desirable that Eric's social interaction be encouraged, and though the use of play activities is appropriate, it might have been advantageous to have included a procedure designed specifically to reduce the incidence of temper tantrums. This might have been the intro-duction of a consistent regime of ignoring such outbursts, and reinforcing behaviour that made them less likely to occur. The programme carried out by Mrs. T. contained elements of these procedures - but perhaps an initial period involving a more specific focus on temper tantrums would have been useful.

The nursery staff are to be admired for their persistence in giving Eric the special attention that he needed. His difficulties seemed to disappear for a while only to re-emerge again at a later date, either because of stress at home or some other reason not known to the nursery staff.

The situation in the home would appear to be far from satisfactory. Eric seemed to be largely ignored by his mother and he often seemed tired in the nursery,perhaps because of lack of adequate routine and rest at home. Though Mrs. T. approached the mother about this she had little success, seemingly, in bringing about any change in attitude that would benefit Eric. Again, the school nurse and health visitor would appear to have been rather slow in providing information and guidance to the nursery staff. This is not necessarily meant as a criticism of the individuals involved, since there are often very complex reasons why information is slow in coming, but it does highlight the need for information to be exchanged fairly quickly if suit-able action is to be taken in the home to coincide with the ongoing programme in the nursery group.

CASE STUDY 3

NICOLA (aged 4)   an example of a child who is restless, lacks concentration and can
be destructive.

Behaviour Checklist

1(c) Deliberately destroys her own and other
children's property.
2(b) Will cooperate in some situations but
not others.
4(b) Occasionally can be a disturbing influence
in a group.
5(c) Is unable to sit still, runs about, jumps
up and down and is easily distracted.
10(b) Needs adult support when tackling something
new.

Behaviour Observation

Lacks concentration and is overactive and restless.
This leads her into all kinds of difficulties.
Set out below are a few examples of Nicola's
behaviour taken from observations:

20.1.81   Free play - 10.45 a.m.
Nicola was outside playing and threw her scarf
down on the ground.   She was asked to pick
it up by Mrs. S.   Nicola ran inside, took off
her scarf and coat, dropped them where she
stood and two minutes later was back outdoors.

11.15 a.m.
Within the space of a few minutes she went
from pushing the pram to the sand tray, back
to the pram, into the music corner, then the
home corner where she finally settled.

26.1.81   Chalk board 1.45 p.m.
A new chalk board was brought out.   Whilst
the other children used it properly, Nicola
broke the chalk, spat on the board and managed
to cover most of the front of herself with
multi-coloured chalk dust.

Behaviour Assessment

1(c) Nearly always on the move, boisterous
active play, very wearing to others.
2(d) Constantly 'flits' from activity to

activity; rarely making use of materials
in an appropriate way.
3(c) Has no understanding of need to be careful
with breakables, tends to suck and chew
toys baby fashion.
8(c) Plays mainly alongside other children,
rarely with them.

Emotional Adjustment
Normal happy relaxed child.

General Assessment - her behaviour at school

Areas where child functions well

Mobility is good.   Shows this in her
enjoyment of outside activities.   Her span
of concentration improves during these sessions.

Areas where child under-functioning

Tends to make more mess than most children
when using paint, water etc.   Cannot concentrate and sit still for any length of time.

Family Background
Nicola is youngest of a second family, and both
families are closely knit, although the eldest
daughter has left the home to live with her natural
father because of a discipline problem with mother.
This elder sister has a big influence on Nicola and
she does miss her.   Mother seems a strong person
and is ready to seek advice from agencies outside
the home.   Since the departure of her eldest sister
Nicola has directed most of her affection towards
her brother, who is 15 years old.   She sometimes
sleeps with him.

Her Behaviour at Home
Nicola has been difficult about her mother working.
She cries when it is time for her to go to work,
although father and others are at hand.   Mother
works three evenings per week.   She generally has
to be kept occupied and can be strongwilled about
things she wants to do.   Nicola often takes part
in verbal quarrels with mother but shows remorse
later.   Sometimes when disciplined she is sent
to bed.

Help from Others
It is felt that because behaviour problem is not an
extreme case no outside agency will be involved.

248

Making a Plan of Action : Case Studies

Teacher's Conclusions

Generally, Nicola is a happy, carefree child, but we feel that she shows signs of insecurity, i.e. still tends to put things into her mouth and sometimes has a dummy; she also enjoys covering herself with bed-clothes and layers herself with dressing-up garments. Mother works part-time which takes her out part of the night and Nicola will demand to sleep with another member of the family during this time, again this shows her insecurity

Nicola seems to enjoy being in a mess. She is well dressed and seems to have a variety of fashionable clothes, but within a few minutes she is covered in paint, milk, water or clay.

Action to be Taken

Play activity approaches will be used because they will most easily fit into our nursery routine and we hope they will help Nicola apply herself in various situations and to prolong her periods of concentration. Two sessions of 15 minutes each day will be carried out. The group will consist of 6 children taken in rotation from the nursery class register. The two teachers concerned will take the group on alternate days. The work will take place in the Story Room, which can be closed off from the main body of the nursery. Morning session at 11.00 a.m. Afternoon session at 1.45 p.m.

Plan of Activities

A typical week's plan of activities, as follows:

Monday a.m.

Large toys will be used to promote cooperative and imaginative play. Children will be encouraged to use these to go on a journey to the shops and supermarket. Bags and other props will be provided. A group discussion together with large pictures will help to encourage their ideas.

Monday p.m

Bead threading, large jigsaws and sorting trays to be provided - again to encourage cooperative play. Two children will be assigned to each activity and it will be pointed out to them that they are helping each other in their work. A record will be kept of each child's activity and they will be encouraged to change their activity the next time they attend.

<u>Tuesday a.m.</u>

Large drawings to be provided for each pair of children for them to fill in with coloured felt pens.

<u>Tuesday p.m.</u>

Imaginative play - a trip to the seaside. Using large pictures to stimulate discussion beforehand, the children will be encouraged to play out a trip on a bus, building sand castles, paddling, having a picnic etc.

<u>Wednesday a.m.</u>

Action songs and rhymes. The children will be encouraged to participate as fully as possible in singing and carrying out the actions of these songs.

<u>Wednesday p.m.</u>

Games with rules. Each child to be given a card for a simple racing game using a die and counters, e.g. spiders up drainpipes, cars along a race track etc.

<u>Thursday a.m.</u>

Each pair of children to be given a set of picture dominoes and taught how to play, with encouragement to help each other to complete each game.

<u>Thursday p.m.</u>

Role play to be encouraged by providing a bag of hats and a bag of animal masks (made by the children themselves) for the children to assume a new identity, e.g. nurse, king, postman, cat, dog, mouse etc. Each child to pick out a hat or mask and act out a situation involving his chosen character and the other children. Help and encouragement from teacher.

<u>Friday a.m.</u>

Imaginative/dramatic play - acting out familiar nursery rhymes and simple stories. Each rhyme or story to be recited/told beforehand and the actions discussed.

<u>Friday p.m.</u>

'Planting the Flower' game. This is a simple

game which involves no competition between children but is dependent on the children helping one another.

We plan to repeat this weekly programme with variations, throughout the Easter Term.

Week ending 13th March

Nicola has not shown any change at all. She has been away from School for 2 days this week; therefore, has not had enough work done with her. It must be emphasised though, that during the sessions she has concentrated for short periods and has cooperated well.

Week ending 20th March

Nicola is beginning to show some signs of improvement. She has been seen to sit quietly for several minutes with a table top activity and does not seem to be quite so accident prone.

Week ending 3rd April

There has been a slight improvement in skills but she still tends to put toys and materials into her mouth.

Week ending 1st May

Nicola absent all week.

Behaviour Observation

Still lacks concentration, but we feel there is slight improvement in as much as she will sit at a table and concentrate for short periods.

Behaviour Assessment

2(c) Concentration: rarely perseveres long enough to make the most of a chosen activity.

Emotional Adjustment

Usually a happy relaxed child but has been sometimes tearful on arrival; we feel that because she does not attend regularly, she finds it difficult to re-adjust to the school routine.

First Re-Assessment - 1.5.81

Areas where child functions well

Nicola functions well during role play situations. Still favours outside activities. Has become most attentive during story periods.

Areas where child under-functioning

She is unable to conform to a more restricted pattern of activities throughout the day. She still enjoys the more 'free play' situation because she still tends to flit from activity to activity. Has become less messy when using paint, clay etc.

Progress Report

In the small group sessions we feel that she can now concentrate more fully and start and finish a task. Nicola enjoys all drama sessions but because she has been absent frequently this term there appears to have been little improvement in her general behaviour.

Week ending 8th May

Again absent.

Monday, 11th May

Nicola returned to school today. Her mother and father have separated,hence her two week absence.

Week ending 22nd May

Mother informs us that Nicola has become unruly at home. On one occasion she threw £15 into the fire and on another tipped over a tin of paint in a shop. If mother corrects her she tends to retaliate by saying that she is going to tell her teacher. I feel that she is missing her father and the split has obviously affected her, although her mother denies this.

Nicola does not, however show this kind of behaviour at school and in fact, she has been very attentive during group sessions (i.e. story time discussion etc.)

During a tape recording session, she showed signs of obvious embarrassment when hearing her own voice, but on another occasion she went off singing alone making up the words as she went along, demonstrating her vivid imagination.

Week ending 12th June

Nicola is beginning to show signs of unruly behaviour at school. She has to be corrected repeatedly and will pretend that she has not heard an instruction. Since introduction of more structured work in preparation for entry to infant school in September she has to be brought in from outside continually throughout the day. She does not seem to be able to cope with this more directed approach to the nursery day.

Week ending 26th June

Again this week Nicola has shown that she cannot conform to a more restricted situation, she has to be continually brought in from outside. She does not listen when asked to do, or not to do something.

Week ending 3rd July

General improvement in behaviour. During a dominoes matching session she concentrated sufficiently to complete the game.

Behaviour Observation

No remaining problems other than above.

Behaviour Assessment

2(c) Concentration:rarely perseveres long enough to make the most of a chosen activity.

Emotional Adjustment

Usually happy relaxed child but can be dis-obedient, not always responding to instructions. This has been more noticeable since the split-up of her parents.

Second Re-Assessment -17.7.81.

Areas where child functions well

As first re-assessment.
No improvement.

Areas where child is under-functioning

Still unable to concentrate. Her attendance is irregular, she often arrives late and this seems to put her on a bad footing for the rest of the day.

Comments

The staff of this nursery worked out a comprehensive programme of play activities both to help Nicola and another child who was experiencing difficulties. Initially it was felt that Nicola was making some progress, for instance, her attention during story time improved greatly. But a series of absences interrupted the continuity of the daily activities and hoped for improvements in other areas of her behaviour failed to materialise.

Nicola was included in the special activities whenever she attended nursery, although she continued to show signs of insecurity and her 'flitting' remained a problem. The programme had been in effect for a term when a major setback occurred; Nicola's parents separated and naturally this had an unsettling effect upon her. At around the same time the nursery introduced a more structured timetable to prepare the children for the kind of day they would shortly be experiencing on entry to Infant Schol. This added to Nicola's disorientation, as within a short space of time she had lost her regular routine both at home and school. The staff realised she was not finding it easy to cope with these new situations and maintained a firm but warm approach when dealing with her more exasperating behaviour.

An additional complicating factor arising during the course of the year was the series of staff changes this nursery suffered, and it is to the staff's credit that they managed to plan, maintain and monitor the programme for two terms. Although the staff felt they had only achieved partial success with Nicola, it is probably true to say that the events of the year could have had a much more adverse effect upon her had it not been for the extra attention she received whilst participating in the programme.

APPENDICES

A. The Schedules

    (1)   Behaviour Checklist
    (2)   Behaviour Assessment
    (3)   General Assessment
    (4)   Talking to Parents
    (5)   Help from Others

B. Record Booklet

C. Explanatory Notes

D. Guide to Case Studies

APPENDIX A:

SWANSEA   ASSESSMENT   SCHEDULES

SCHEDULE 1

SWANSEA BEHAVIOUR CHECKLIST

Child's name ....

Sex ....   D.O.B. ....

Name of school/Group ....

Date completed ....

Completed by ....

Schedule 1

Read all the descriptions carefully. Put a tick alongside the description (either a, b or c) which most closely approximates to the child's current behaviour. Do not omit any of the ten categories and check that you have exactly ten ticks when you have finished.

1. (a) Takes care of his/her belongings and those of the nursery, although like most children is occasionally destructive.

    (b) Can be destructive and has to be watched more carefully than some children.

    (c) Deliberately destroys his/her own and other children's property.

2. (a) Will play co-operatively in group situations and is prepared to share and 'take turns'.

    (b) Will cooperate with other children in some situations (e.g. adult-directed activities) but not others (e.g. where turn taking is involved).

    (c) Demands his/her own way in <u>all</u> situations and cannot 'take turns'. Often takes toys from children whilst refusing to share his/her own.

3. (a) Temper rarely seen at all, remains self composed unless the provocation is very great.

    (b) May become irritable or show temper under considerable provocation but can be steadied by adult.

    (c) Screams, bangs objects, has a tantrum <u>whenever</u> provoked; inhibited or frustrated, however minor the incident.

4. (a) Plays amicably and shows consideration of other children's needs.

    (b) Occasionally can be a disturbing influence in a group.

    (c) Disruptive, tends to annoy and may attack other children.

5. (a) Is able to work towards a definite goal and is usually capable of ignoring distractions to achieve it.

(b) May complete an activity once started but is not immune to distractions.

(c) Is unable to sit still, runs about, jumps up and down and is easily distracted from anything he/she is doing.

6. (a) Never looks bothered by things, a happy child.

(b) Has looked tense or upset on occasions.

(c) Appears miserable, unhappy or tearful <u>most of the time.</u>

7. (a) Makes enthusiastic use of the range of activities offered by the nursery. Is rarely unoccupied.

(b) May need help in choosing an activity but sometimes manages on his/her own.

(c) Wanders around aimlessly or stares into space.

8. (a) Joins in happily with other children and enjoys group activities.

(b) Usually found in the company of one or two particular children. Takes part reluctantly in group activities.

(c) Watches others play but makes no attempt to join in. Will not be coaxed or take part in group activities.

9. (a) Often initiates and can conduct extended conversations with adults and children.

(b) Rarely initiates a conversation with an adult, but will respond appropriately and will talk to other children.

(c) Has seldom been known to talk to anyone at all.

10. (a) Faces new tasks and experiences with confidence. Is self-sufficient in meeting his/her ordinary needs.

(b) Needs adult support when tackling something new.

(c) Frequently 'clings' to adult for assurance and does not attempt to attend to his/her own needs.

Appendices : Schedule

Behaviour Profile
Put a cross in the appropriate box, a, b or c,
according to how the child was scored for each of
the ten categories

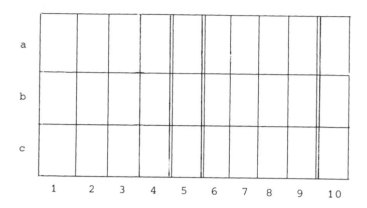

Key   'b' and 'c' scores indicate a degree of
      difficulty in the following categories:

    1, 2, 3, 4 - aggressive behaviour

         5   - overactivity

    6, 7, 8, 9 - withdrawn behaviour

        10   - 'clinging' dependent behaviour

Please answer these two questions briefly (continue
on separate sheet if necessary).

1. Does the child exhibit any other problem
    behaviour not covered by this checklist?

2. What is the child good at?

Next Step
If the child has scored 2 or more 'c's or 6 or more
'b's, go on to the next stage, ASSESSMENT.
    Consider also whether there are any other
children who might require further assessment, e.g.
those who score 4 'b's in the aggressive or withdrawn categories.
    Bear in mind the child's age.

SWANSEA   ASSESSMENT   SCHEDULES

SCHEDULE 2

BEHAVIOUR   ASSESSMENT

This schedule is in two parts:

PART I   consists of a series of recording sheets
             on which to note down your observations
             of the child's behaviour over a period
             of time.

PART II   is a checklist which describes in more
             detail the kind of problem behaviour
             which may be shown by a particular child.

Please read the instructions accompanying each part
before you begin.

             Child's name ....

             Sex .................D.O.B. ....

             Name of school/group ....

             Date(s) completed ....

             Completed by ....

PART I

Behaviour Recording Sheets
In order to assess the degree of a child's difficulty and the extent of the problem for both
yourself and the child, you will need to gather as
much information about the child's behaviour as
possible. To do this you will need to:

1.   observe the child systematically for at least
      a week using these recording sheets, which
      allow for ten observations daily (five in the
      morning and five in the afternoon);

2.   note down the time and date of each observat-
      ion as well as the setting (e.g. play house,
      sand tray) and the names of other adults and
      children in the vicinity;

3.   describe the behaviour as exactly as you can.
      It is important to be accurate, saying, for
      example, "Sid snatched a spade from Bert and
      hit him over the head with it" rather than
      "Sid was aggressive at the sand tray";

4.   include examples of the child's positive
      behaviour as you will need to know what he/
      she is good at and what interests him/her
      when you are planning a programme for him/her
      later on;

5.   observe the child in a variety of different
      settings and on several occasions in each
      setting.

BEHAVIOUR RECORDING SHEET

NAME: DATE: MONDAY A.M.

TIME	SETTING	ADULTS/ CHILDREN PRESENT	DESCRIPTION OF BEHAVIOUR
			MONDAY P.M.

PART II

Behaviour Assessment Checklist
Read the descriptions (a-d) in each of the
categories 1-12. Tick the description (either a, b,
c or d) which most closely resembles the child's
current behaviour.

1. Restlessness

    (a) Normally active child

    (b) Often does not settle down in any one place
        for long.

    (c) Nearly always on the move; engages in
        boisterous active play, very wearing to
        others.

    (d) Very highly over-active child; never stops
        for a moment.

2. Concentration

    (a) Capable of total absorption in one activity
        for a reasonably long period.

    (b) Can concentrate quite intently on one or
        two favourite activities (such as sand or
        water play).

    (c) Rarely perseveres long enough to make the
        most of a chosen activity.

    (d) Constantly 'flits' from activity to
        activity; rarely making use of materials
        in an appropriate way.

3. Destructive Behaviour

    (a) Careful with toys and possessions.

    (b) Can be careless with toys; sometimes
        breaks things; tears books etc.

    (c) Has no understanding of need to be careful
        with breakables or the need to preserve
        material objects; tends to suck and chew
        toys baby-fashion.

    (d) Extremely destructive child; dismantles and
        damages everything encountered.

4. Aggressive Behaviour

    (a) No more aggressive than most children
        of his age.

(b) Bossy; attempts to control other children forcefully.

(c) Frequently rude; offers verbal aggression if thwarted or frustrated.

(d) Predominantly aggressive style of play; frequently offers physical aggression to others (including adults).

5. Demanding Behaviour

(a) Makes no more demands than most children.

(b) Demands own way more often than others of same age but responds reasonably well to firm handling.

(c) Demands own way frequently and over-reacts, (tantrums)if demands not met.

(d) Very demanding in nearly all situations. Often persists despite adult intervention; defiantly refuses to accept situation and becomes very worked up.

6. Social Withdrawal

(a) Outgoing and relates well to all others.

(b) Shy; speaks in a low voice; averts eyes, even with people he/she knows well.

(c) Tends to be withdrawn and dreamy; occasionally difficult to make contact with.

(d) Extremely withdrawn; lives in own world; deliberately avoids or shuns contact with other adults and children.

7. Reaction to Strangers/Visitors

(a) Child carries on normally when visitors present.

(b) Tends to over-react - rushes up to visitor; acts in a silly or giddy way.

(c) Definitely disturbed by visitors; suspicious and wary; very excitable.

(d) Child will in some way withdraw or shrink back even before an approach is made.

8. Participation in Play Activities

(a) Participates actively in play in a group of children.

(b) Plays mainly with one or two particular friends.

(c) Plays mainly alongside other children rarely with them.

(d) No interest in play with other children; prefers solitary pursuits; wanders about aimlessly.

9. Physical Contact

(a) Readily accepts physical demonstrations of friendliness from staff and children.

(b) Accepts such contact when appropriate (e.g. comforting after a fall).

(c) Tends to withdraw from physical contact; reluctant to take hand, sit on knee, be lifted or helped physically.

(d) Shrinks away from physical contact, stiffens, refuses, cries.

10. Attitude to Nursery

(a) Always likes coming to nursery.

(b) Sometimes does not want to come to nursery/ school and makes a fuss on arrival; usually settles in after 15 - 30 minutes.

(c) Always makes a fuss on arrival; takes a very long time to settle in, often tearful.

(d) Does not like nursery/school at all (cries, screams etc.); constantly asked to go home; tried to escape from buildings or play- ground.

11. Dependent Behaviour

(a) Fairly independent in group situations; can stand up for self.

(b) Gives in unnecessarily to other children; looks for adult support if things go wrong in play with other children.

(c) Tends to be more clinging then most and/or not very happy about being left by mother for any length of time.

(d) Great difficulty in separating from mother; will not leave the side of a familiar adult.

12. Popularity

    (a) Popular; generally well regarded; often chosen by others to join in their activities.

    (b) Has one or two particular friends who seek him/her out.

    (c) Tries unsuccessfully to latch on to the most popular children of the group.

    (d) Unpopular, generally shunned and disliked by others.

Additional information:-

    Emotional Adjustment (Tick any of the following which apply to the child. More than one item may be ticked).

    (a) Over-excitable.

    (b) Over-anxious, timid, fearful.

    (c) Fussy, complaining, whining.

    (d) Prone to temper tantrums.

    (e) Disobedient.

    (f) Seeks to be the centre of attention.

    (g) Tearful.

    (h) Listless, finds everything a great effort.

    (i) Habits, tics, obsessional behaviour.

Please note any further information not covered by the above.

SWANSEA   ASSESSMENT   SCHEDULES

SCHEDULE 3

GENERAL   ASSESSMENT

This checklist is designed to give you an overall
impression of a child's general level of development.
Before you begin please read the accompanying
instructions with care.

Child's name ....

Sex .... D.O.B. ....

Name of school/group ....

Date completed ....

Completed by ....

Read all the descriptions in categories 1 - 9.
Based on your observations of the child over the
past few weeks <u>underline</u> any of the descriptions
within each of the categories which best fit his/her
functioning at the moment.

1.   MOBILITY

A.   Good Mobility
     Hops on one foot / jumps forward with both
     feet / walks up and downstairs with alternating
     feet / climbs up and slides down a slide /
     pedals a tricycle / runs easily / kicks a large
     ball when rolled to him/her.

B.   Moderate Mobility
     Walks without difficulty but runs unsteadily;
     awkwardly / bumps into things / cannot use a
     climbing frame; slide without assistance / falls
     down more than most children.

C.   Poor Mobility
     Walks a little unsteadily / has difficulty with
     stairs / has difficulty going up or down or
     two steps / finds slopes; slippery surfaces a
     problem / cannot step over objects / balance
     poor.

2.   HAND EYE COORDINATION

A.   Good Coordination
     Uses both hands singly or together as appro-
     priate / manipulates small objects easily /
     uses pencil or crayon purposefully / can catch
     a ball with both hands / uses scissors fairly
     accurately / can build a tower with 10 or more
     bricks / can thread large wooden beads / turns
     pages of a book one by one / unscrews lids /
     folds paper / shows a preference for one hand.

B.   Moderate Coordination
     Is slightly clumsy with hands / often drops
     things / manipulates small objects with some
     difficulty / holds pencil correctly but poor
     control / has begun to paint / tries to
     unscrew lids.

C.   Poor Coordination
     Holds pencil or crayon in fist / has definite

difficulty in using hands / has poor grip /
uncontrolled jerky movements / lack of
coordination of two hands / very poor at form
boards ; building with toy bricks; modelling
sand or clay.

3. VISION (If the child has a visual defect which
    is corrected by the use of glasses then please
    tick the most appropriate statement when
    glasses are worn.)

A. Good Eyesight
    Vision apparently normal / adequately corrected
    by glasses.

B. Moderate Eyesight
    Has no real problem in moving around but has
    some difficulty in judging distances / has
    difficulty in seeing small objects, pictures at
    a distance / seems to have difficulty with a
    'lazy eye' or squint.

C. Poor Eyesight
    Poor visual recognition of a person more than
    10 feet away / has poor orientation to objects
    more than 10 feet away / has occasional coll-
    isions with furniture / often 'loses' objects
    close to hand / poor vision is definitely
    hampering movement.

4. HEARING (If child has hearing aid please tick
    the most appropriate statement when aid is
    being worn.)

A. Good Hearing
    Hearing apparently normal / adequately correct-
    ed by hearing aid.

B. Moderate Hearing
    Does not hear quite as well as normal /
    statements often have to be repeated / some-
    times does not hear speech unless directly
    facing the speaker / speech has to be louder
    than normal for adequate comprehension.

C. Poor Hearing
    Speech must be much louder than normal even
    when child facing the speaker / perception of
    speech presents difficulties in all circumstances

/ does not always respond to loud voices or noises.

5. SELF-HELP SKILLS

A. Good Self-Help Skills
Beginning to use knife and fork well / attends to toilet needs without assistance / washes and dries hands and face / dresses without help except for shoe laces and difficult fastenings / copes well with taps; switches; drawers; lids; door handles etc. / avoids common dangers such as broken glass.

B. Moderate Self-Help Skills
Uses spoon instead of knife and fork / usually indicates need to use toilet / attends to toilet needs with some assistance / has occasional accidents / needs help in getting on coats and pullovers / finds dressing a struggle / has to be assisted with taps; switches; drawers etc / avoids hazards such as sharp furniture corners; open stairs.

C. Poor Self-Help Skills
Uses fingers in preference for spoon / sometimes indicates wet and/or dirty / does not indicate need to use the toilet / has to be toileted at regular intervals if to remain clean and dry / assists with dressing by holding out hands and feet in anticipation / has to be dressed entirely / no co-operation at all when being dressed / cannot cope with taps; drawers; door handles etc. / very little sense of danger / covers self and clothes with paint; mud; water etc. much more than most children.

6. EXPRESSIVE LANGUAGE

A. Good Expressive Language
Speaks clearly / vocabulary well developed for age / uses complex sentences ('I didn't come to school yesterday because I was poorly') / describes past events in a fairly well organised manner.

B. Moderate Expressive Language
Speech a little unclear but no specific defect / has a slight stammer / has mild speech defect

(not stammer and not baby speech) / knows names of most objects / language and vocabulary rather poor for age / uses simple sentences / uses 'babyisms' ('me want dat').

C.   Poor Expressive Language
Speech very unclear but no specific defect / bad stammer / moderate to severe speech defect (not stammer and not baby speech) / language and vocabulary very poorly developed for age / unable to describe / sentences usually incomplete / uses mainly nouns / tends to use gesture to obtain needs.

7.   RECEPTIVE LANGUAGE

A.   Good Receptive Language
Understanding entirely normal for age / can follow a series of three instructions well / is attentive to quite long stories / is able to recall the sequence of events in a story / will answer questions about a story correctly / responds to humour.

B.   Moderate Receptive Language.
Understands most of what is directly said to him but is less able than most to understand conversations when not directly involved / follows simple instructions only if given slowly with repetition / will follow a short story if encouraged / tends to jumble sequence of story.

C.   Poor Receptive Language
Understanding of what people say is very limited / has great difficulty in following a simple instruction / does not seem to understand questions put in the normal course of day / rarely listens to stories / listens only for a short period of time / shows no interest in stories at all / has no concept of what a story is.

8.   PLAY

A.   Good Quality of Play
Very good at making things with plasticine; sand; clay; wooden or plastic constructional toys / plays a lot with toys and creates very

realistic games using cars or dolls etc. / inventive and realistic in playing other roles (e.g. in play house) / uses props to maximum advantage / paints and draws often and produces imaginative or realistic pictures / normally agile and energetic in active games both inside and outside / enjoys group games and can relate his/her actions to others.

B. Moderate Quality of Play
Constructions; models never look much like the object they are supposed to represent / plays with toys and creates fairly realistic situations and games / does take on other roles in play but limited repertoire and imagination / likes to paint and draw but often loses direction and ends up with scribble or coloured mess / occasionally plays active games but not very keen on them / not physically agile / will join a group game but is often with the group but not part of it.

C. Poor Quality of Play
Likes to handle plasticene; sand; clay; constructional toys but never achieves an end product / manipulates toys but little idea of how to use them realistically / never adopts another role is always himself/herself / rarely paints or draws and only produces unrecognisable scribble or daubs / seldom takes part in active games / physically very awkward / unable or unwilling to take part in any group game.

9. RESPONSE TO LEARNING/ADAPTABILITY

A. Good Response
Is quick at doing things / responds quickly to new materials; teaching approaches; requests; changes in routine / seeks and enjoys most new experiences provided they are not frightening.

B. Moderate Response
Tends to be rather slower than most / often has to be hurried up / always last or behind / slow to respond to new materials; teaching approaches; requests; changes in routine etc. / tends to prefer familiar routine and is a little disturbed by change / over reacts to new experiences.

274

C.   Poor Response
Extremely slow in every way / never seems to
complete anything / takes a very long time to
do even the simplest task / functioning appears
at 'half speed' or slower / adheres to routine
whenever possible / rigid adherence to routine
regardless of what is going on in environment.

Any Additional Information you Care to Record

Note
The individual items in each section are organised
in such a way that the first item in each section
denotes a higher developmental level than the last.
You must remember, however, that individual children
may vary markedly in the order in which they achieve
certain skills and the stages presented in the
schedules should be regarded merely as guidelines.
    If the majority of your underlinings fall in
the first section of any of the categories 1-9.e.g.

    2.   Hand-eye Coordination
    A.   Good Coordination

         Uses both hands singly or together as
         appropriate / manipulates small objects
         easily / uses pencil or crayon purpose-
         fully / can catch a ball with both hands/
         uses scissors fairly accurately / can
         build a tower with 10 or more bricks / can
         thread large wooden beads / turns pages of
         a book one by one / unscrews lids / folds
         paper / shows a preference for one hand.

this will give you an indication of what the child
is particularly good at.   Now that you are aware of
the child's strong points it may be possible to use
them as a basis for tackling his/her problem behaviours.   You should always bear a child's positive
qualities in mind when devising strategies to overcome his/her difficulties.   Also, take into consideration that a marked weakness in a particular
area may be due to an additional handicap, e.g.
deafness could be affecting both expressive and
receptive language.   The schedule may in such cases
indicate areas where the child may require extra
help.

What to do Next
When you have completed this schedule transfer the
information to the relevant section of the Record
Book (pp.290-302) where you should be building up
a clearer picture of the child's strengths and
weaknesses across a broad front.
    Having come so far in your assessment of a
child and his/her difficulties you may feel that now
is the time to approach his/her parents, with a view
to gathering information about home background
factors and possibly enlisting their support in your
plan of action to help the child.   See the chapter
'Talking to Parents' (pp.39-49) and associated
schedule.

SWANSEA   ASSESSMENT   SCHEDULES

SCHEDULE 4

TALKING   TO   PARENTS

Child's name ....

Sex .... D.O.B. ....

Name of school/group ....

Date completed ....

Completed by ....

The Swansea Assessment Schedule No. 4 : Talking to Parents (or other caretakers)

Introduction
This schedule is in three parts, I, II and III; it has been drawn up to help you obtain relevant information from parents about the child's family background and behaviour in the home.

PART I consists of some general areas and a list of items of a reasonably routine nature that you may feel free to approach the parents with directly,i.e. ask a direct question about the child's behaviour.   Note that this is a list of items, and that the way you ask the questions has been left to you.   Take into consideration what has been said(pp.42-47) about how to phrase a question so as to avoid biasing the answer.

PART II consists of items of a more personal and delicate nature which will have to be broached very carefully.   Here, the onus is very much on you as the interviewer and practitioner to probe these.   These Part II items are merely 'starters' to guide you into talking with the parents.   Many other items or areas of significance will occur to you and should be entered and reported as attached inform-ation to Part II.

PART III is simply a series of blank pages on which you are required to give a description of the child's family background.   It may repeat much of the information already given in Parts I and II, but this does not matter.   It will be very useful to have a brief total picture of the family, and this may, of course, contain some information obtained from sources other than the parents.   Whenever possible try to quote the source of your information, and state how reliable you feel this is.

Recording
In this particular situation when you are talking confidentially with the parents (and it is emphasised that you should ease the parents' minds on the confidential nature of your discussions), you will wish to keep them relaxed and create an easy at-

mosphere, so it would be very unwise to make notes
or tick off items on a sheet whilst asking the
questions.
        What we suggest as the best course is to
tick off the items and make notes in Part I and II
as soon as possible after talking to the parents.
By doing this you will ensure that you have the
most accurate recall of the information possible.
A considerable amount of evidence exists that recall,
even after a matter of hours,is subject to wide
distortion and you would wish to avoid this source
of error.
        Do not feel bound to the format of Parts I
and II; they are merely some suggested items that
you may want to know about.   You will almost
certainly think of more questions to ask and have
to make notes at your convenience; do this and
worry about collating the information later.
        Again, a number of items, in both Schedules,
may be covered by a single general question (e.g.
What is X like at home?   Is there anything that
you would like to tell me about the family?   Is X
in good health?),but if you feel that the information
given is incomplete or inaccurate pursue the matter
with more specific questions.

PART I

Direct Items of Information from Parents
Listed below are some general areas of the child's
behaviour in the home with examples of specific
items that you may feel free to ask the parents
about directly.   You might open the conversation by
asking a general question and then go on to ask
about individual items one by one.   Ensure that
you have asked about the individual items listed
and any others that might occur to you (note these
down).   Try to give a description or example of
the behaviour in question and remember that this is
information about how children behave at home and
should not be coloured by your knowledge of how they
behave in the nursery group.
        You may wish to ask about:

1.   The family background

        (a) How many children in the family?
        (b) Position in the family (1st, 2nd, 3rd
            etc., child)?
        (c) The other children's ages?

(d) The sex of the other children?

2. <u>General activity and self-help in the house</u>

Does he/she
(a) help mother and father and join in activities in the home?
(b) show interest in his/her surroundings and is normally active rather than lethargic?
(c) have any special interests or abilities?
(d) dress and feed himself/herself?

3. <u>Physical attributes and health</u>

Does he/she
(a) have normal vision and hearing?
(b) eat and sleep well?
(c) have any special physical defect or attribute?
(d) see a doctor and dentist regularly?
(e) have any health problem for which he/she is currently receiving treatment or which has required specialised help in the past?

4. <u>Intellectual and lingusitic performance in the home</u>

Does he/she
(a) recognise and name familiar objects or sounds?
(b) respond to simple instructions?
(c) have a good memory and show curiosity about his/her surroundings?
(d) talk freely to other children and adults?
(e) express himself/herself clearly?
(f) like listening to stories?
(g) ask questions and listen to the answers?
(h) repeat words not normally heard in the home?

5. <u>Emotional characteristics of the child</u> at home

Is he/she
(a) well-adjusted to (i) adults?
                       (ii) children?
(b) well-adjusted emotionally (i) as an individual?
                               (ii) in a group?
(c) shy or timid when in someone else's house?
(d) subject to temper tantrums when corrected or frustrated?

      (e) happy and contented in general?
      (f) very variable in mood during the day?
      (g) stable in temperament on the whole?
      (h) upset by anything in particular?
      (i) especially happy with anything in
          particular?

6.   Play, co-operativeness and social functioning

Does he/she
(a) regularly become absorbed in play
    situations of all kinds?
(b) have many friends?
(c) have a lot of children of his/her own
    age range in the immediate vicinity?
(d) have a favourite pastime?
(e) have a pet hate - something he/she
    dislikes doing intensely?
(f) prefer outdoors to indoors or vice-versa?
(g) take his/her turn with other children?
(h) take good care of things he/she uses?
(i) which of the following best describe
    him/her

    (i) is fairly obedient on the whole;
   (ii) will eventually listen to appeals
       before sterner measures have to be
       invoked;
  (iii) often has to be restrained physically
       in order to achieve the desired
       behaviour.

PART II

Indirect Items of Information from Parents
The format here is 'open-ended'; thus more space
is provided for your written comments and observations.

1.   The Child

    (a) Lives with his/her natural parents.

    (b) Both parents are alive and living
        together.

    (c) Is adopted/fostered.

    (d) Has another adult (e.g. grandparent, relation or friend of the family) who exerts a particular influence on him/her.

    (e) Is from a single-parent home.

    (f) Has a family background which is not typical.

    (g) Anything special to note about any other member of the family?

2. **The Family**

    (a) Tend to do things together (are closely knit).

    (b) Individual members tend to go their own way (loosely knit).

    (c) Father has a particular problem/worry.

    (d) Mother has a particular problem/worry.

    (e) Family as a whole has a particular problem/worry.

(f) Father/mother/other is head of and
    strongest influence in family.

(g) Child pays most attention to...

PART III

Write a brief description of the child's family
background; include information that may have been
obtained from sources other than the parents.
Give more details about those aspects of the family
that you feel are particularly relevant to the
child's difficulties.   Do not worry if you repeat
information given elsewhere.

SWANSEA   ASSESSMENT   SCHEDULES

SCHEDULE 5

HELP   FROM   OTHERS

Child's name ....

Sex ....   D.O.B. ....

Name of school/group ....

Date completed ....

Completed by ....

Place a tick in the appropriate box. If no action
has been taken yet, you should consider whether it
would be useful to contact someone knowing what you
do about the child.   If in doubt, it is better to
make contact and be safe rather than sorry. Discuss
the matter with your Headteacher/Principal.

	Agency already in-volved	Contact pending HT has asked for help	No action taken yet
A. School based behaviour problem			
Advisory teacher			
School doctor			
Peripatetic specialist teacher (e.g. of the deaf)			
Educational/school psychologist			
Child psychiatrist			
Social worker			
School nurse/health visitor			
Educational home visitor			
Other			
B. Speech problem			
Speech therapist Peripatetic specialist (e.g. of the deaf)			
School Doctor			
Educational school psychologist			
Child psychiatrist			
School nurse/health visitor			
Educational home visitor			
Other			

	Agency already in- volved	Contact pending HT has asked for help	No action taken yet
C. Home-based behaviour problem Advisory teacher			
Educational home visitor			
Educational/school psychologist			
School doctor			
Social worker			
School nurse/health visitor			
Other			
Local community organisation			
Appropriate voluntary organisation (e.g. Association for all Speech Impaired Children; Dyslexia Institute; Toy Libraries Association)			

N.B. With some children it may be necessary to complete more than one section.

If the child has been seen by anyone, summarise any
information received;

Has the child already been seen or is he or she
currently being seen by any specialist in either a
hospital or a clinic? If so, indicate for what
purpose, how often, and, if possible, the name of
the person(s) concerned.   Is there to be any follow
up?

If the child has been referred to anyone, what
action has been taken following that referral?

Underline as necessary

school visited and head/principal seen by

....

school visited and teacher seen by ......

....

arrangements made for child to attend

clinic (specify which) ....

....

arrangements made for child to be seen in

school by ....

home visited by ....

case conference called by ....

....

school has received a report from ....

....

school has been asked to submit a report to

....

regular review advised by ....

on-going treatment being undertaken (specify)

....

....

....

....

no action as far as known (follow-up required)

any other action taken (specify) ....

any other action contemplated (specify) ...

RECORD   BOOKLET

Child's name ....

Sex .... D.O.B. ....

Name of school/group ....

RECORD BOOK

(see pages 29-31)

The record book is in four sections:

Section I   -   a summary of information from the assessment schedules

Section II   -   a detailed plan of the approaches to be used

Section III   -   a weekly progress report

Section IV   -   a record of termly re-assessments using schedules 1 and 2

Appendices : Record Book

SECTION I

Summary of Information from the Assessment Schedules

(a) Behaviour Checklist   Date completed ....
Note down in the appropriate category any 'b' and
'c' scores the child obtained.

aggressive
behaviour

| 1 | | 2 | | 3 | | 4 | |

over-
activity

| 5 | |

withdrawn
behaviour

| 6 | | 7 | | 8 | | 9 | |

dependent
behaviour

| 10 | |

(b) <u>Behaviour Assessment Part II</u>

   <u>Date completed</u> ....

   Make a note of any of the 'c' or 'd' behaviour
   descriptions which were ticked for the child.

   e.g. 1. <u>Restlessness</u> (d) Very high overactive
           child, never stops for a moment.

   Note also any descriptions ticked under the
   heading <u>Emotional Adjustment</u>.

(c) <u>General Assessment</u>   <u>Date completed</u> ....

Make a note below of any categories in which
the child functions well.

e.g. 1.A Good Mobility. 5.A. Good self help
                                skills etc.

Make a note below of any categories where the
child is experiencing difficulty, e.g. 6.C
Poor expressive language.   7.C Poor receptive
language etc.

Note any particular difficulties related to
<u>VISION</u> or <u>HEARING</u>

Appendices : Record Book

(d) <u>Talking with Parents</u>   <u>Date completed</u> . . . .

    Please summarise below any information
    concerning <u>Family Background</u>:

    also the <u>Child's Behaviour at Home.</u>

(e) <u>Help from Others</u>   <u>Date completed</u> ....

Summary of child's health problems prior to a nursery enrolment and treatment received.

Summary of treatment/therapy child is currently receiving, if any.

<u>Nature of current difficulty</u>

<u>Agencies contacted</u>

<u>Information received/action taken</u>

Appendices : Record Book

Write down your conclusions about the child and his/her difficulties based on the knowledge you have gained so far.

SECTION II

Planning your Approach
(see pages 203-222)

(a) Note the most worrying aspects of the child's behaviour in the order of priority in which they will be tackled.

(b) Write down the changes you hope to achieve.

(c) Detail the approaches you intend to use together with how and when they are to be implemented.

SECTION II

Planning your Approach (cont'd)

SECTION III

Weekly Progress Report
At the end of every week note down how the approach
is working in practice, how it is being received
and what effect it is having upon the child etc.
If you decide to modify your original plan in any
way please record the changes you make.

SECTION IV

Re-Assessments

At the end of each term, re-assess the child using
Part II of the Behaviour Assessment Schedule
(Schedule 2) and the General Assessment Schedule
(Schedule 3).   On each occasion mark the schedules
with different coloured pens so that you can see
at a glance any improvements that have been made
by the child.   Record your findings in the appropriate spaces below.   Finally, write down your
comments about the progress made during the term.

First Re-assessment

(a) Behaviour Assessment Part II

   Date completed ....

   Make a note of any 'c' or 'd' behaviour
   descriptions ticked for the child.

Emotional Adjustment

(b) <u>General Assessment</u>   <u>Date completed</u> ....

Make a note of any categories showing
improvement. e.g. 5. Self-help skills.

Any categories showing deterioration?

<u>Termly Progress Report</u>

Carry out the 2nd and 3rd re-assessments in the
same way as you have done for the first.

Appendices : Explanatory Notes

APPENDIX C

EXPLANATORY NOTES

The Handbook was devised in the United Kingdom and
tried out in pre-school facilities there.   It,
therefore, reflects current practice in nursery
schools and playgroups in that country, practice
which may show differences from that in other
countries.   It is felt, however, that the basic
principles in the Handbook have universal application
and that the approaches advocated can inform and
extend methods of working with young children
wherever they may be.

There are, however, references to people or
procedures which are typically British.   The
following notes may help to explain these as it was
felt that it would not be appropriate either to
remove the references or pause to explain them in
the text itself.

Advisory teachers.   Advisory teachers have special
responsibility for various aspects of education.
As well as an advisory teacher for children in
early education, there is usually in each district
an advisory teacher whose concern is special
education and who has working with him/her a number
of organising teachers, for example, for the deaf
or partially hearing, the visually impaired or the
physically handicapped.

Court Report.   This was drawn up in the U.K. in
1976 by the Committee on Child Health Services under
the title of 'Fit for the Future'.   It recommended
among other things that there should be general
practitioners with a special interest in young
children.   This, however, has not been supported
by the medical profession who prefer to increase the
paediatric component in the doctor's general training.
The report also urged the setting up of 'handicap

teams' of various professionals to discuss children
with special needs.

Education Welfare Officers. It is envisaged that
education welfare officers will have a role not
unlike that of social workers. They have close
links with specific schools and are well placed
to be the main point of referral for teachers and
head teachers concerned about a child's development
or progress. How far they can take up the social
worker role depends on their training and on local
policy, but it has been shown that it is to them
that headteachers are most likely to turn. Although
not attached to pre-school provision, they can often
provide valuable information if contacted through
the local primary school as their work with families
extends beyond problems of non-attendance.

Educational psychologists. Educational psychologists
have a contribution to make to the comprehensive
assessment of young children in each district
although, in recent years, the emphasis on formal
testing for placement has declined in importance.
Educational psychologists, who in the U.K. normally
have had teaching experience, are now more concerned
with programme planning, discussion and monitoring
of children's progress and development. They have,
in fact, the responsibility for dealing with any
child from the age of two years, although some
psychologists with a special interest in young
children will be involved with them from birth.

Health Visitors. Since 1956, health visitors have
been seen as being primarily concerned with health
education and social advice. As part of this
function, they visit all homes in which there is a
new baby and should continue to give advice and
guidance at least until the child is five years of
age. The number of visits made is left to their
discretion so that they can accommodate to differences and fluctuations in need. The health
visitor, therefore, is unique among other professionals in having access to every home with a young
child in it, whether or not that child or home has
a problem. The health visitor will be qualified
in nursing and have taken a subsequent course in
health visiting. On her routine visits, the health
visitor normally carries out a series of screening
tests as well as her usual advisory commitments,
and these tests are especially important in picking
out children with problems of vision, hearing or

speech.   Any child suspected of having difficulties, particularly in these aspects, is referred for further investigation and treatment.

Medical examination.   All pupils should have a routine medical examination on entry to school carried out by the school doctor.   Subsequent examinations are made when the need arises.   These may be carried out by the doctor, the school nurse or nursing auxiliaries depending on the nature of the inspection.   If difficulties arise, children can be examined medically at times other than those normal for their age group on the special request of the headteacher.

Nursery classes/schools.   A nursery class is attached to a school for older children and children move from it into that school.   A nursery school usually consists of several classes and is in a separate building which may or may not be near the school the children will go on to.   Children, usually aged 3-5 years, attend part-time (morning or afternoon sessions) or, in special circumstances, full-time.   No payment is made for this provision.

Nursery nurses.   These are non-teaching assistants who receive a two-year training in the care and and stimulation of young children.   They are examined by the N.N.E.B. (Nursery Nurses Examination Board) and are sometimes referred to by these initials.

Playgroups.   Playgroups, which have flourished in the U.K. since the 1960s, are registered with and supervised by the Social Services Departments if they run for more than two hours a day.   Premises must be suitable for young children and there are restrictions on the number who can attend in relation to the number of adult staff available. A small payment is made by parents unless they are financially unable to do so.
      In a number of areas, courses aimed at training playgroup leaders and helpers are run and those who are trained supervise the mothers who have vol- unteered to help.   Playgroups have done invaluable service in offering nursery-type experience to young children in areas of the country where such experience would otherwise be unavailable.   There is also considerable interest in setting up 'mother and toddler' groups for children below the age of three years.

School Nurses.   It is desirable but not necessary for school nurses to have had additional health visitor training.   Some school nurses may be without such a training but, if this is so, they will work closely with qualified health visitors and have access to their expertise.   The health visitor/school nurse is the key person for advice on health problems in young children.

School Psychological Service.   Educational/school psychologists staff this service along with other professionals such as social workers and remedial teachers.   The extent of the service obviously varies with the size of the area covered, so that large urban centres will have several psychologists and perhaps separate special and remedial education organisations.   Some rural areas may have a single psychologist who directs other services and may operate from a school psychological centre situated in a convenient place.   The service usually offers help and guidance to schools, sees individual children and their family and organises workshops, lectures or other training session for teachers.

Speech Therapists.   Before 1974, speech therapists might work under either the health or the education authorities.   Since 1974, however, they have moved over completely to the District Health Authority where they are organised under a District Speech Therapist.   It has been estimated that there ought to be 6 speech therapists for every 100,000 of the total population but many areas do not have their full complement.   In addition, many speech therapists are part-time, which may give rise to problems of continuity.

The Warnock Report.   The full title of this report, drawn up in 1978 for the Department of Education and Science, is 'Children with Special Needs'.   It suggests that schools should tackle the question of how much help a child needs through a series of discussion with various personnel, the parents also being actively involved.   It provided the basis for consultation leading to the drawing up of the 1981 Education Act with reference to special education.

CHILD STUDIES INDEX

* denotes imaginery child

311